FORGETTING FROLIC

Wedding party making its way through the churchyard in Youghal, Co. Cork, *c.* 1835. The women in the foreground are waiting for money to be handed out according to custom by the bridegroom. Mr and Mrs S. C. Hall, *Ireland, its Scenery, Character etc.* (London, 1845).

FORGETTING FROLIC
Marriage Traditions in Ireland

Linda May Ballard

Then, forgetting frolic, they settled down to their ordinary occupations.
Lageniensis, *Irish Folklore* (1870)

The Institute of Irish Studies, the Queen's University of Belfast
in association with the Folklore Society

First published 1998
The Institute of Irish Studies,
The Queen's University, Belfast in association with The Folklore Society,
University College London, Gower Street, London, WC1E 6BT

Editors: Margaret McNulty, The Institute of Irish Studies
Jennifer Chandler, The Folklore Society

This book has received support from the Cultural Diversity Programme of the Community Relations Council which aims to encourage understanding and acceptance of cultural diversity in Northern Ireland.

British Library Cataloguing-in-Publication Data.
A catalogue record for this book is available from the British Library

ISBN 0 95389 666 6

Set in Times Ten

Printed by W. & G. Baird Ltd, Antrim

Contents

In loving memory of my father, Maurice H. Smith.

Acknowledgements

I should like to thank Dr Jonathan Bell, Acting Director, and the Trustees of the Ulster Folk and Transport Museum for their support of this project, which began as background research for an exhibition at Cultra early in the 1990s. I am also very grateful to Professor Brian Walker and Margaret McNulty of the Institute of Irish Studies, to Dr Myrtle Hill of Queen's University and to Jennifer Chandler of the Folklore Society for their help and encouragement.

For her typical generosity, my thanks go to Mairead Dunlevy and I am also grateful to Dr W. H. Crawford, Mr R. Dixon, Mr and Mrs A. Griffith, Dr C. Harvey, Mrs R. Lavery, Ms C. McCullough, Mr P. S. McWilliams. Mrs S. Peile, Colonel Percival Price, Mrs S. Skilling, Ms L. Simpson, Dr E. Steiner-Scott, Dr G. B. Thompson, Dr F. Williams, and to the late J. R. R. Adams, a great scholar and a good friend. I should also like to thank the museum's photographers T. K. Anderson, Mr A. McCartney and Mr G. Wright. Many other people helped in various ways, including providing information (and hospitality) to me during fieldwork sessions, and some are named in the text. To all those, named and unnamed, I am very grateful, as I am to Ronnie and Eimear.

I owe a great debt of gratitude to Mrs Maureen Paige for all her work in wrestling with my handwriting and preparing the manuscript, and another to Mrs Frances Weir for proof-reading the manuscript.

I am grateful to the Deputy Keeper of the Public Record Office of Northern Ireland for permission to quote from original sources held there. The quotation from *Kathleen's Field* is reproduced with the kind agreement of the author, William Trevor.

List of Illustrations

Front cover illustration: A Donaghadee farmer and his bride, 1890s. Ulster Folk and Transport Museum photographic archive, L3992/4. Background, detail of Carrickmacross lace wedding veil of similar date, UFTM, TR227/1.

The illustrations are reproduced by kind permission of the following people and institutions: front cover, Mrs Rea; pp. ii, 7, 44, 136, The Ulster Folk and Transport Museum; p. 15, Miss H. Bruce; p. 37, Mrs Diamond; p. 52, Mr and Mrs N. L. Green; p. 62, Mrs Cathcart; p. 63, Mr and Mrs Wallace; p. 79, the Pritchard family; p. 82, private collection; p. 85, Mrs Hesbrook and Mrs Cummings; p. 88, Mrs J. Evans; p. 89, Mr and Mrs I. Gourley; p. 95, the Order of Poor Clare; and p. 117, Mrs Hesbrook.

Introduction

This study, while it may claim to be historical in so far as it deals with the past, employs a priori the discipline of the folklorist rather than that of the historian. Folklorists in general, and perhaps lady folklorists in particular, have been seen as something of a scourge to historians, for folklorists have appeared to consider the past through a lens which has not been ground to the historian's specification. Over at least the last two decades, this distinction has become a little less clear, and the methods of the folklorist have gained in use, relevance and respect. Social historians have increasingly utilized the concept of oral history as an acceptable one, and have gathered useful data through the means of the oral, generally tape recorded interview, drawing on the techniques and expertise of the folklorist in the process. The value of these techniques has also been viewed with greater sympathy in the field of Social Science, as the therapeutic aspect of reminiscence has increasingly been recognized.

The focus of the folklorist on the folk, the fact that the discipline of the folklorist is centred on people, on the individual in as well as the individual and society, rather on the document as a reliable indicator of the past, is now better understood and accepted as a useful and valid discipline in its own right. Indeed, this has been well understood in many European countries, including Ireland, for at least one hundred years, and in parts of Scandinavia for much longer. Folklore is also a respected academic discipline which is taught in universities in many of the United States.

The fact that folklore reflects the individual in society may be very frustrating to the historian, who may dislike the impression of generalizing from the particular rather than the provision of statistical data and the like. The most widely held concept of folklore is that it deals with oral material: folk-tales, stories of the experience of the individual, accounts of local happenings, for example. A given folk-tale may have been passed to an individual storyteller via a long and hallowed oral path, and be in that sense traditional, but the version told by that individual will by virtue of particular characteristics and nuances of performance be distinctive. It is in this way that ecotypes of very widely known tales are formulated.[1]

The tale speaks both for the person who gives it voice and for the society by whom it is heard. The tale itself in the telling is effectively a contract between hearers and teller. It must communicate and articulate an understood and shared set of values, otherwise it will be meaningless, disregarded and without respect. It is in this way that certain types of folklore become lost as they lose relevance for a social group. For example, a storyteller may be very reluctant to tell stories of the fairies if he thinks he will be scorned for doing so, thus exposing his rusticity, superstition, failure to move with the times, downright simple-mindedness or whatever. Tales of the fairies may reveal a great deal about attitudes to the natural and spiritual environment, and in order to collect them and hope to reach an understanding of them, the folklorist must forge a new contract with the tale teller. He or she must also generalize from the particular of the story and its teller to the audiences for which the tale was originally intended. This is not the accepted wisdom of the historian, but it is none the less a valid method of raising a curtain on the past.

In dealing with custom and belief, the folklorist also seeks for evidence of the persistence of a given attitude through time. This may also be frustrating and irritating to the historian, who may suspect that underlying this trait is a failure to understand that the past is a complex and constantly changing place, and to view it as monolithic and unchanging. This is not the case. The folklorist may well trace and interpret change, sometimes very subtle change through time, but may also detect consistency of attitude in the face of historical change. Perhaps it is for this reason that the techniques of the folklorist are increasingly appreciated by social scientists?

In addition to those branches of folklore which are sometimes termed *non-material culture* (folk-tales, ballads and the like), folklorists are increasingly concerned with *material culture*, artefacts which may reveal much about life and attitudes in the past. Most historians appreciate the value of museum exhibitions in revealing aspects of the actuality of the past by confronting viewers with real survivals from that past. This, too, is a case of generalizing from the particular. A particular dress of the 1870s becomes greater than itself, standing for *all* garments made and worn in that decade, just as a specific lunula gives us the clearest of glimpses of many aspects of an ancient and otherwise unarticulated social order. Folklorists interpret material culture as vital evidence of many aspects of the actualities of life, generally of simple and often otherwise unrecorded everyday life, in both the distant and the recent past. This study relies heavily on the interpretation of folkloric data, both material and non-material, in the light of relevant historical background information.

A study of marriage from an historical perspective leads in a certain set of directions and an excellent volume of essays on exactly this subject, illustrating a huge variety of perspectives, was published a decade or so ago.[2] Included in that volume is a paper on folklore and marriage which shows clearly that, at the very least, folklore helps to humanize the historical record, and assists in individualizing the experience of the past. Study the folklore of marriage by reference only to traditional oral materials and it is hard to avoid developing an image of a 'typical' wedding, particularly a rural wedding of the past. This resource therefore complements historical records in a valid and exciting way. Encounter the artefacts left by the inhabitants of that past, and another dimension begins to emerge. The gowns worn by Ulster brides of the past help to bear out certain comments by travellers in the countryside, particularly the preference of Ulsterwomen for owning or aspiring to fashionable gowns of silk. Juxtapose these with oral accounts of past wedding traditions, attempt to resolve some of the questions raised by such a juxtaposition, and once again one comes face to face with the complex and microcosmic nature of the subject.

When the author moved from responsibility for the Ulster Folk & Transport Museum's archival collections of oral narrative and lore and became Curator of Textiles, it was the need to understand and to interpret just such a collection of dresses which led to this study. The composition of the collection determined that the associated research was rooted in the culture of Ireland and the northern counties of Ireland in particular. and, therefore, of present-day Northern Ireland. Certainly, to an extent the dresses were self-selecting and are not a complete record of all dresses worn by all past brides, but this does not invalidate them as a record. They are a direct, intensely personal and individual touchstone to the past, capable of contributing depth and richness to our understanding of that past. The nature of the study is diverse and many faceted, but it is to be hoped that it also has cohesion. Marriage is a subject which is at once universal and individual, a diverse and complex issue. Society in Northern Ireland is itself at once cohesive and diverse, run through with issues of economics, politics, religion, continuity and change. The experience of the individual is acted out against this backdrop, and by drawing on elements of local oral and material culture I have set out to understand the diverse experience of individuals in relation to marriage in local society during the past.

In considering the historical dimensions to these issues and questions, we might begin, like Robert Benchley, with some pertinent questions, such as 'What is marriage?' and 'Where (and exactly what) is Northern Ireland?'[3] In answer to the first, some hint of the complications involved may be understood by reference to the late John Barkley, who comments on the history of marriage among Irish Presbyterians: 'The Presbytery of

Laggan, Co. Donegal, as early as 1673, complained that marriages conducted by its ministers were regarded as fornication.'[4] It was to be almost two centuries before this problem was completely ironed out, and many other complications besides. Until the passage of 7th and 8th Victoriae C81, *An Act for Marriages in Ireland, and for registering such Marriages*, which came into effect in April 1845, the question 'When is a marriage not a marriage?' was a vexed one in the case of many Irish partnerships, quite apart from the difficulties posed by common law and other more casual liaisons. Church and State strove to regularize matters pertaining to marriage, and slowly the problems were resolved. The fluidity of attitudes to marriage in early Ireland was succeeded by a complex range of issues generated by social, cultural and religious diversities, often accommodated by compromise uneasily reached. Although during the nineteenth century many of the legal problems were resolved, in part the legacy of these complexities still affects marriage in Ireland today, particularly if partners belong to differing religious denominations.

The answer to where and what is Northern Ireland is also less straightforward than it seems. Laggan, Co. Donegal, for example, is situated in the north of Ireland, but not in Northern Ireland. The six counties which constitute the political unit of Northern Ireland are Antrim, Armagh, Down, Fermanagh, Londonderry/Derry and Tyrone. Together with three other counties, Cavan, Donegal and Monaghan, this area is usually perceived to have constituted the ancient province of Ulaidh or Ulster. Since partition in the early twentieth century, the last three counties have formed part of the Irish Free State, later the Irish Republic, often referred to colloquially as 'the South'. Consequently, the most northerly part of Ireland, the Inishowen peninsula, might be said to be in the South. The six counties form part of the United Kingdom, governed from London. The parliament of the Irish Republic is Dáil Eireann, sitting in Dublin. In the nineteenth century, partition had not occurred, and the extent to which Northern Ireland was a distinctive region was a cultural matter, albeit with the potential for political consequences, rather than a matter of officially recognized demarcation.

There is much debate on the question of exactly how culturally distinctive Ulster is from other parts of Ireland. The ancient epic the *Táin Bó Cuailgne*, in which the demigod Cú Chulainn single-handedly defends Ulster against the incursions of Meadhbh of Connacht, is sometimes understood as an expression of a lengthy sense of separation (although Cú Chulainn had to take the job on independently as an indiscretion meant that the men of Ulster were visited by tremendous debility when under attack). Certainly, there is a degree of regional and local diversity even within individual counties, and there are ancient and strong links with Scotland. Where researches led beyond the museum's collections to other sources the distinctions were often subtle rather than dramatic. Whilst much has been said about cultural differences within Northern Ireland itself, some writers have sought to stress similarities between communities which might lead to greater social cohesiveness. Even as a geographical issue, partition was not a simple matter. As an example of one of the problems, consider a point made by John Cunningham, who, writing about events in 1922, when the Boundary Commission determined exactly where partition should happen, illustrates the particular difficulties experienced over territory on the boundary between counties Fermanagh and Donegal:

> The Pettigo area was almost 60% Loyalist – and intensely loyalist – and wanted to be in Northern Ireland. The Belleek area was over 90% Free State inclined and fully expected to be included in the ambit of the Dublin government. Both expectations were doomed to disappointment.[5]

Similar questions of regionality and identity have led to all too familiar consequences in the course of the twentieth century.

In recent years, much thought and debate has been devoted to questions of social and cultural identity within Northern Ireland. Issues such as the 'Irishness' of Belfast-born rector's son and poet Louis McNeice are of endless interest, while the recently formed Ulster-Scots Language Society declares that its aim is 'to promote the status of Ulster-Scots as a language and to establish its dignity as a language with an important part to play in our cultural heritage',[6] fervently hoping that Ullans will formally be recognized as a 'European Lesser-Used Language'. Irish Gaelic, which already enjoys this status, is spoken in some areas of Belfast and elsewhere, though most native speakers live in peripheral regions of the Irish Republic. Gaelic is a compulsory subject of study in schools in the Republic, and, for many years of this century, to fail in Irish in a public examination meant failure in all subjects. Gaelic is currently, if discreetly, being promoted on local BBC radio by means of imaginative teaching programmes and in other ways.

It is impossible to focus on the history and traditions associated with a subject like marriage without bringing issues of this sort into play. The complexities surrounding the question of marriage in Ireland make it an effective microcosm of the forces and tensions which operate and have operated throughout Irish society. It would have been impossible to write about the history and traditions of marriage in Northern Ireland without reference to the rest of the island, but the writer is a native of Belfast, and her study is the direct consequence of an attempt to understand and to interpret something very specific. The Ulster Folk and Transport Museum's textile collection includes a superb collection of wedding gowns, most of which were worn by Ulster brides in the course of the past two hundred years. This study was sparked by an urge to investigate the circumstances and meanings which these dresses imply. A similar study undertaken solely from the perspective perhaps of Co. Kerry might reflect another set of nuances entirely. The folklorist draws on the methods and data provided by scholars in other fields, most particularly on the work of geographers, historians and anthropologists, whilst working in a distinct discipline which is not the same as any of these. Like the historian, the folklorist may refer to literary descriptions, both oral and written, for information and for sources of comparison. Above all, while the folklorist is of course concerned with the Big or at least the Bigger Picture, it is the individual in society, space and time which engages the folklorist, and with whom he or she is concerned.

1 Preparations for Marriage

Many nineteenth-century travellers in Ireland have commented on the fact that Irish people married early, although they may have exaggerated the ages at which marriage occurred. While their conclusions may have been rather impressionistic, recent research has tended to confirm some of the claims made by these earlier observers. There is widespread agreement that, in pre-Famine Ireland, women especially were inclined to marry young. It has long been understood that this was the situation in eighteenth-century Ireland, and more recent studies have found evidence that, in the seventeenth century, Irish women, except for those in service, tended to marry earlier than their contemporaries in other parts of Europe.[1]

Until 1972, when a Marriage Act in the Irish Republic established that it was illegal for either men or women to wed until they reached the age of sixteen, Irish girls could legally marry at the age of twelve, males at fourteen.[2] However, there is evidence that women were likely to marry when in their early twenties.[3] In the seventeenth century, both Catholic and Protestant women might marry early, as Dickson has established:

> Irish Quaker women were consistently marrying earlier than their English co-religionists and ... their behaviour was very similar to ... their Catholic neighbours ... [T]he common pattern of Catholic and Irish Quaker marriage is an indicator that explanations for the distinctiveness of population behaviour in the seventeenth century must be ecological rather than cultural, related to the volatile but expanding economy with its colonial and frontier characteristics, not to the archaic primitiveness of the indigenous population.[4]

During the nineteenth century, major changes were to take place in Irish attitudes to marriage and, by the mid twentieth century, the rate of marriage in Ireland was the lowest in Europe. During the 1960s, marriage again became more popular and once again people began to marry at earlier ages.[5] Not surprisingly, the Potato Famine of the 1840s marked a

1

watershed in this and in many other aspects of life in Ireland, but historians have traced aspects of the pattern typical of the post-Famine period
to the early nineteenth century. It has been noted that the preference for
postponing marriage, generally considered a characteristic of post-
Famine Ireland, was registered among larger landowners even in the
early nineteenth century.[6] This suggests that concern with the passage of
land from generation to generation, which became a major preoccupation after the Great Famine, was already an issue for many families in the
earlier period. As we shall see, negotiations about land and inheritance
were often the major issue in brokering a contract between prospective
marriage partners. The issues of legitimacy and inheritance had an impact
on events which led to the passing of the Marriage Act in the 1840s. It has
also been argued that, in the early nineteenth century, women were an
important economic force, but that in the post-Famine era their economic
status, and with it their prospects of marriage, fell into decline.[7]

Whether or not it was actually achieved, marriage was the goal to
which young women were encouraged to aspire. Formal education available in the National Schools by the second half of the nineteenth century
emphasized the importance of domestic skills. While at school, girls were
trained in various types of plain sewing and in garment making, with a
view to improving their standard of living and that of their families.[8] By
the turn of the present century, cookery was also taught to young girls at
National Schools, and their mothers became the target of a widespread
campaign to educate women in cookery and in nutrition.[9] There was substantial official concern to raise standards of living by providing relevant
education for women.

Formal education in needle skills often reinforced training which girls
received at home. Some were introduced to sewing as a means of helping
their mothers to supplement the family income through decorative
embroidery.[10] Others received early instruction at quilting parties, where
they could expect to graduate gently from threading needles to participating in actual sewing. As the needlework samplers produced by young
schoolgirls during the course of the nineteenth century illustrate, girls
were expected to be reasonably proficient in needlework before they
reached the age of ten.[11] Needle skills were essential to a young girl in
accumulating the contents of her 'bottom drawer', also known as her
'hope chest' or 'dower chest'. This contained household items, particularly linens, which would be useful when the time came for her to set up
home. It could also serve another purpose, by helping her to advertise her
industry, thrift and competence. Assembling a bottom drawer was a fea-

ture of the lives of young girls in many parts of Britain and beyond. One gathered together by a girl who married in the west of Scotland in August 1846 included 'a Dookin' gown' or christening robe, and a 'cutty sark', or nightgown suitable to be worn in childbirth.[12] Death might also be anticipated in the contents of a bottom drawer, which could be expected to contain a winding sheet in which to wrap a corpse,[13] or a set of good, white bedroom linen, intended to be kept for best use, which often meant for laying out the dead. Quantities of patchwork quilts might be worked and stored in the bottom drawer. These provided opportunities for creative expression, and were often important decorative items. The patchwork, or fabric piecing, was often done by the girl herself, perhaps with help from sisters or mother. When the patchwork was complete, it was usually finished by being stitched to a backing fabric to which it would be quilted for reinforcement. Quilting was often a communal activity. The bedcover was stretched on a frame, and friends and neighbours were invited to come and help with the work. A quilting party was a very sociable event, and the work of sewing might be repaid by supper and perhaps by a dance, which in turn gave an opportunity for courtship. While working, there was a chance for the women to chat, and children could play under the canopy of the quilt while young girls were gradually initiated into this important aspect of social and domestic life. Many women continued to make quilts throughout their lives, whether married or not, so quilting parties were not exclusively associated with the production of items for a bottom drawer. However, young girls often made many quilts in anticipation of setting up home, thus generating plenty of opportunities for practical parties. The quilting party also meant that a girl's work was subject to the close scrutiny of her seniors and her peers, and thus could help to enforce a high standard of needlework. Quilting parties may also have helped to curb youthful impulses to experiment with patterns, and to enforce conservatism in aesthetic sensibility.

The bottom drawer fulfilled an important practical purpose, and assembling one also allowed girls to exhibit their skills, so most young women would prepare at least a proportion of the necessary items for themselves. Those who could afford to could augment their bottom drawers by buying items, and some retailers advertised complete packages of household linens. Harrods were among those who supplied such items by mail order. In 1895, a house of seven rooms could be completely stocked for £10 5s. 2½d. For a house of twelve rooms, the cost varied from £25 9s. 8½d. to more than three times that, at £90 5s. 11d., depending on the quality of the items chosen.[14] Of course, it was possible to continue acquiring household linens after marriage, if resources were available. In October 1898, *Irish Society* advised young girls anxious on the subject:

> You can begin with a certain amount and then add to your store every year, for instance eight table cloths, one dozen breakfast napkins, one dozen dinner napkins, six pair sheets, three pair servants' sheets, and one dozen pillow covers with two dozen bath towels will be enough. One dozen kitchen rubbers, only give out six at a time, and one dozen glass cloths: I should think this would be enough to start on.[15]

Not all girls concerned with accumulating household linens might expect to have to administer servants. Obviously, many factors influenced the precise contents of an individual bottom drawer, and the accumulation of one implied the expectation of a reasonably permanent home. There were many for which such an aspiration was unrealistic. The accumulation of a bottom drawer continued to occupy many young women until well into the twentieth century.

As she acquired her linens, a girl was also expected to develop domestic skills. Like her needlework, these might provide her with a saleable commodity. Many young women made a living by going into domestic service.[16] As the nineteenth century progressed, girls' lives were increasingly shaped by the expectation of domesticity, and many embraced this willingly, taking pride in being assured of becoming 'a great wee housewife'. In Irish households of the Edwardian era, while boys were seldom expected to assist with domestic chores, girls had to shoulder much of the responsibility for the daily running of the home. Friday nights were often devoted to housework.[17] While young women worked, their brothers might become involved to the extent of helpfully pointing out where something had been missed, perhaps by lifting oilcloth from the floor with the toe of a boot, to expose hidden dust, assistance which no doubt was gratefully appreciated by their sisters. This pattern of behaviour persisted until well into the twentieth century, and its effects are still registered by many young women setting up home.

Girls often took responsibility for much of the rearing of younger siblings, thus leaving their mothers free to perform some of the more attractive domestic duties, shopping and the like, and to administer the household. There may have been reluctance to hand over responsibility for certain work, such as the preparation of food, which could involve control of the kitchen, and mothers, of course, would choose which chores they preferred to delegate. Valuable domestic experience must have been gained in this way, but some daughters must have drawn the conclusion that they would prefer to run their own households than to assist to run their mothers'. In the absence of a mother, the eldest daughter often took on full responsibility for running the home. One young woman, a member of the Irish Travelling community who for many years kept house for her widowed father and was responsible for rearing her younger brothers and sisters, reflected that her marriage freed her from a great deal of work, as at least for a time she had only two people to care for. Her previous responsibilities devolved upon the sister next in line.[18] Rearing of younger children by older sisters often established strong, lasting bonds of affection, and did not deter older sisters from wanting to become wives and mothers on their own account.

While for many women domesticity was an attractive goal to which to aspire, there were a few who were less than enthusiastic about this ideal. Concern about the emergence of feminist ideas was expressed in the popular media as fears of the assertive New Woman began to be registered. The *Girls' Own Paper* urged resistance to such notions and expressed in rhyme its views on behaviour inappropriate to women:

> Alas! for household ways
> Lost in these latter days!
> When each new-fangled craze
> Sets the 'new girl' ablaze
> And, wild for power and praise
> She makes not wifely ways
> Her truest dower.[19]

Although the New Woman was registering on the Irish literary and political scene, the march of female assertiveness has been slow to be persuasive or acceptable to many Irish women,[20] and issues related to Women's Rights are only slowly gaining ground.

A girl might begin very early to acquire the domestic skills and material possessions essential to her capacity to set up home. These activities, while they could act as a focus for aspirations to the married state, long predated any actual expectation to marry a specific individual. Once she became committed to marry, a young woman might turn her attentions from preparations for her household to preparations for herself. In the nineteenth century, the trousseau could be a matter of great importance. While this might be interpreted as including both household and personal items, the 'bottom drawer' was more usually devoted to the former, the trousseau to the latter. The period between agreeing to wed and actually marrying might provide a time to consolidate preparations for the household, but it was also an opportunity for a girl to devote attention to herself. After marriage, it might be some time before she had another chance to indulge herself in this way.

Like the bottom drawer, the contents of the trousseau would be influenced and determined by many factors, and, for those with money to spend, the trousseau could be very lavish. Many retailers, such as Robinson and Cleaver in Belfast, advertised themselves as specialist trousseau suppliers. Reports of society weddings often gave publicity to the trousseau and to those charged with the important matter of supplying it. In the last decades of the nineteenth century, *Irish Society* refers repeatedly to Lewers of Grafton Street, Dublin, as a purveyor of fine quality undergarments, while Mr Alfred Manning, also of Grafton Street, is described as 'that prince of Irish costumiers'.[21]

Magazines counselled against acquiring too many items for a trousseau, recommending quality above quantity, and suggesting 'half a dozen of each kind of underclothing' as optimal.[22] Trousseaus continued to be important in the first half of the twentieth century, and brides were still advised to favour quality over quantity. Some trousseaus, like that supplied by Mrs Sims of Grafton Street for Princess Louise, who married the Earl of Fife, were reported in great detail. Her selection included many beautiful gowns, among them one of 'crimson poplin' embellished with 'several very wide bands of Irish point lace'. Acquiring trousseaus must have given the wealthy many opportunities to support the 'buy Irish' campaign favoured by Lady Aberdeen, which helped to promote Irish home industries including lace and embroidery.[23] The reporter of Princess Louise's trousseau also noted that 'several of the evening dresses have two bodices, a most useful and sensible arrangement'.[24] Many less affluent brides were equally aware of the advantages of maximizing the wearability of their clothes. Wedding dresses of the late nineteenth century were often two-piece affairs, and no doubt more than one trousseau included blouses intended for wear with the skirt of the wedding ensemble.

Although a girl's preparations on her own account were an important aspect of the preliminaries to marriage, they have received less attention from historians than has the dowry, the financial or equivalent settlement which might be made on her behalf. Connell comments:

A settlement was the preliminary to marriage, and settlements in these years [of the late eighteenth century] were made readily available by a swing from pasture farming to arable, by the subdivision of holdings and by reclamation of waste land, and by a more general dependence upon the potato as a foodstuff.[25]

This willingness to subdivide land holdings was no less a characteristic of Irish rural society in the early nineteenth century.[26] While subdivision may have had some impact on provision for daughters, it was of more relevance to sons, who were thus supplied with a tract of land by means of which they could hope to support a wife and family.

The wife herself had also to make a contribution to the anticipated prosperity and well-being of the establishing family, and this reciprocity was the basis of the 'match', usually negotiated on behalf of a couple by their parents. While subdivision may have been made possible by a switch in emphasis from pastoral to arable farming, a girl's dowry often depended on the pastoral tradition, for since very early times until within living memory it was common to 'fortune' a girl with a cow.

ROBERTSON, LEDLIE, FERGUSON & CO., Ltd. 77

£10 Wedding Trousseau.

Item		£	s	d
6 Chemises, Trimmed Embroidery	3/6	£1	1	0
6 Pairs Knickerbockers, Trimmed Embroidery	2/9	0	16	6
6 Night Dresses, Trimmed Embroidery	5/6	1	13	0
4 High Bodices, Trimmed Embroidery	2/6	0	10	0
2 Low Camisoles, Fancy Fronts	3/6	0	7	0
1 Pair Corsets		0	10	6
1 Dozen Diaper Towels		0	11	6
1 Chamois Leather Band		0	1	0
2 Flannel Petticoats, Embroidered	6/9	0	13	6
2 White Petticoats, Trimmed Embroidery Flounce	7/6	0	15	0
1 White Petticoat, Trimmed Lace		0	12	6
1 Petticoat for Winter Wear		0	10	6
2 Cotton Petticoats for Summer Wear	4/6	0	9	0
1 Flannel Dressing Gown		1	1	0
1 Flannel Dressing Jacket		0	6	6
1 Pair Suspenders or Garters		0	1	6
		£10	0	0

List of a trousseau available from Robertson, Ledlie Ferguson and Co., 1903. The Belfast Branch was better known as the Bank Buildings. A box of breakfast cereal at the time cost about 6d., an embroidered nightgown eleven times as much. The trousseau was an important part of the bride's preparations for marriage and young women often used the opportunity to ensure that they set aside a store of items for their own use, as after marriage they might have less time to devote to themselves. *UFTM archive.*

This pastoral tradition is deeply rooted in Irish culture and is fundamental to the ancient *Tána*, epics on the theme of cattle raiding. One scholar goes so far as to suggest that daughters and cattle might stand as equivalents:

> [T]he young man's incursion is a raid and will be met with military strength. Because the daughter and the cattle are treated as a virtual equal in these stories, either explicitly so, as in the *Táin Bó Legamain* or else by attributing ownership of the cows to the daughters as in the other *Tána*, it is never entirely clear which the father is defending.[27]

From as early as the eighteenth century, scholars have been aware of the relevance of cattle to a bride's dowry. As early as 1788, one commented: 'The lawful price of a Queen's clothing, if she brought a royal dowry, is six cows.'[28] In order to endower a wealthy bride of early times, cattle might have been levied from the community to which she and her father belonged, and Anglo-Norman marriage arrangements also featured cattle.[29] Evidence of livestock levies made in order to acquire a dowry may be found in a presentment for 1537, which states that, 'when Ossory or Poer married a daughter, the former demanded a sheep from every flock, and the latter a sheep of every husbandman and a cow of every village'.[30] This levying of livestock has been interpreted as the background to the custom of 'mumping', reported by Thomas Dineley, who travelled in Ireland during the seventeenth century:

> MUMPING A SORT OF BEGGING — The very better sort of old Irish, that are under some cloud, or indeed in tolerable good condition, are wont upon the matching of a daughter, in order to it, to go up and down, and beg for a twelvemonth before hand, after this manner, to rayse her porcon:
>
> The person to be married, sometimes her mother, with her a sort of gentlewomen, a speaker, two to drive the cattle, and a waiting mayd, hard to be distinguished from the mistress with a draggled tayle, these all enter the house, sitt down on the stooles and benches, according to their distinctions, without uttering one word for above an hour or two. Then the attendant speaker riseth, and after a salute or honour made, he or she after a short introduction by the way of a speach desire a Coonagh Sprea, which being interpreted is an help for a porcon, viz something to bring about a marriage.
>
> So, lately, a person of quality, but not of condition, gott for her daughter seven or eight score collops (head of cattle so called), the vulgar are afrayd to deny, and give each a cow, or yearling, calf, sheep, or the like.

The scullogues or comon sort also mump, but not with the same formality, and procure sheep, lambs, piggs, geese, turkeys, etc. Yett with them a marriage is never compleated untill they have an iron pott, gridiron, hutch, an Irish chest so called, and a caddow or rugg or blankett.

The giving of ten shillings English answers a collop.[31]

It is generally agreed that in Ireland historically a marriage took place as the consequence of 'a carefully negotiated bargain'.[32] This was as true of the early twentieth century as it was of much earlier times, and the dowry was not invariably a feature of marriage negotiations. The ancient Brehon Laws refer to a 'bride price' payable to rather than by a girl's father,[33] and O'Clery comments that 'there seems no reason to doubt that in pagan times in Ireland no marriage was deemed legal unless the full bride price was paid'.[34] Like the dowry, the bride price might be paid in cattle.[35] Both dowry and bride price were factors of status. In ancient times, it was possible to marry without a dowry, but in its absence women of relatively low status were more likely to become concubines than wives if involved in relationships with men of higher social standing than themselves. Such concubinage continued to be a feature of life in Ireland until late in the medieval period. Full marital status was unlikely to be achieved unless a measure of material equality could be demonstrated between the partners.

While for centuries many marriage settlements were made up in part or entirely of cattle, they might also be made in cash or in goods. The following passage outlines a marriage settlement which was drawn up in medieval Drogheda:

In 1456, William Cashell, acting on behalf of his son Nicholas, and John Abell, acting for his daughter Matilda, drew up such an agreement in a notary's house in Drogheda. Under its terms, the future bride's father was to give 40/0d. and a brass pot, the future groom's father 40/0d. The money and the pot were to be kept by William Cashell until the couple came of age and set up house together. If either of the parties to the wedding arrangements died beforehand, the father of the deceased party would have his contribution restored to him.[36]

One traveller who visited Ireland in 1834 remarked that, in the Claddagh fishing region of Galway, 'The tocher [dowry] brought to a girl on her marriage is generally a share of a boat.'[37]

This oral account from Co. Tyrone gives a dowry payment as the reason for a change in the name of a townland:

The land in our area was confiscated, and it was given to Ogilvie of
Scotland. And as I said, Ogilvie of Scotland had plenty of estates
here, so he was what you call an absentee landlord. So, he sent his
agent over to look after the estate, and collect the rents, etc., and the
name of the agent was Buchanan, and he lived in a house to the east
of Tattysallagh school ... Well, he had a daughter, and the daughter
married a man called Rogers ... When Rogers married the daughter,
... she got half of the area, as her dowry (the collection of the rent).
So, today, part of Tattykeel is called Tattykeel Rogers, and the other
part of Tattykeel is Tattykeel Buchannan.[38]

Tattykeel is one of a number of townlands shown by the Ordnance
Survey map of 1834 to have been subdivided, but no other account of a
reason for the division is known. Of course, the story hints that the col-
lecting of rents would be a lucrative occupation.

Early twentieth-century evidence from the west of Ireland suggests
that the dowry was often paid to the groom or to his father, sometimes
even to the groom's siblings. Rather than directly protecting the material
welfare of the bride, who by means of it established a right to become
dependent for her maintenance on her husband and his family, the dowry
might be disposed by her husband's family in any way they pleased,
including, presumably, to provide a dowry for her sister-in-law. To 'fortune' a girl with a cow might be a more secure way of ensuring her material future, especially as women were responsible for dairying, so cash
could be realized through the sale of milk and butter.

Although some brides went entirely without dowries, for others payment could be substantial. It has been suggested that, if a bride married
into a substantial farm, an equivalent cash payment might be expected
and that at one time the average dowry payment was £3 an acre (4,047
sq.m.).[39] Some girls may have married into fairly substantial farms without bringing a dowry, but the process of land transference was not always
a straightforward one. In some cases, a bride's dowry might help to ensure
control of the farm. Arensberg and Kimball cite the example of one
'Mulveney' who ran off and married a servant girl, after which his
mother, who was to have left him the family farm, refused to acknowledge him, and instead sold the farm to the local publican.[40] It has been
shown that, in the early nineteenth century in Tipperary, daughters of
small farmers could expect a dowry of £25, while in Co. Kilkenny, farmers with holdings of between ten and thirty acres (4 -12 ha) might provide
between £50 and £100. A dowry for the daughter of a Cork man with a

large farm might be as much as £300. It has also been shown that such substantial sums helped to enforce parental control over their children's behaviour in relation to marriage.[41] Taking account of the cost both of the dowry and of the marriage celebrations, Fitzpatrick sets this in illuminating context: 'By 1880 ... a modest Connaught match had become ten times as expensive as a passage to America.'[42]

Not surprisingly, dowries could often be the cause of disputes, especially as provision was sometimes made to pay them by instalments. 'Brutal, venal and sometimes fatal' is Fitzpatrick's summing up of such disputes, and he cites a case which occurred in Leitrim in 1893, when an unfortunate bride was returned by her husband to collect an unpaid portion of her dowry. The ensuing fracas had fatal consequences for her sister-in-law.[43] This incident dramatically underlines the tensions inherent in preparations for marriage and in marriage itself, not only for the bride and groom, but to a greater or lesser extent for those around them. Plans to marry held important implications for the couple concerned, for their immediate families, and for the community to which they belonged.

When Lady Helen Stewart married the Earl of Ilchester in January 1902, the ladies of Belfast presented her with a robe of hand-made Carrickmacross lace acquired from the Bank Buildings, accompanying it with an illuminated address. At the time garments of hand-made Irish lace were the height of fashion, so this was quite a lavish gift and the Bank Buildings took the opportunity to advertise their involvement in supplying it. *UFTM archive.*

2 Marriage Divination

Property and the related degree of parental control were major issues governing marriage in Ireland at many social levels in the past. The general emphasis may have varied from era to era – subdivision of land in the pre-Famine era permitting more marriages to occur, consolidation in the later nineteenth century allowing for only a single heir, with provision perhaps being made for a dowry for one daughter – but the question of a balance in property between bride and groom retained its importance. Of marriages contracted primarily or solely with regard to property, Connell remarks that they were 'gratifying less to ... partners than to their fathers'.[1] Arrangements which take no account of mutual appeal and which appear to have little to do with any possible romantic interests of the couple, and everything to do with maintaining the integrity of the land or the balance of property, might serve to rule out any question of curiosity on the part of a young woman or man over whom she or he might eventually be called upon to marry.

Perhaps this is a surprising background to the widespread local popularity of customs of marriage divination, although there may be something in the argument that a society which allowed little choice of marriage partner might actually help to foster divination practices as a counter-measure to lack of personal control. Whatever the factors which mitigated in its favour, marriage divination was very popular with young unmarried people, a fact which shows that the possible identity of a future marriage partner was of great interest if not something of a preoccupation.

Marriage divination practices are most usually associated with, and have been documented most in relation to, young girls. Girls eagerly sought pieces of wedding cake which were put under pillows and slept on, to induce dreams of future husbands. This tradition, recently associated with fragments of elaborate iced wedding cake, is very ancient and once applied to crumbs from the wheaten bannock which served as 'bride's cake'. An elaboration observed by girls at a Dublin boarding-school in the 1960s was to place the crumbs of cake in an envelope and to write the initials of four prospective suitors, one set in each corner. At night, the envelope was put under the pillow. Each morning for three days, a corner would be torn off the envelope. It was essential that eyes were kept closed while this was done. The set of initials remaining on the fourth morning were those of the future husband. For added piquancy, a question mark might be used instead of one set of initials.[2] The same custom was well known in Co. Londonderry:

> An unmarried girl given a piece of wedding cake can put it under her pillow and dream of the man she will eventually marry. She can also put the cake in an envelope and write the names of three possible suitors on three of the corners, leaving one corner blank to represent 'Old Maid'. When she wakes for the next three mornings she slips her hand under her pillow, feels for a corner and pulls it off. The corner left ... will tell her her fate. [3]

In the 1960s, some adolescent schoolgirls also employed another method of marriage divination. If a girl was interested in a particular boy, the names would be written on the blackboard and the common letters cancelled. The remaining letters were counted across, with a sequence of or to the effect of 'Love, like, hate, adore, kiss, care, marry', to deduce the likely success of the relationship, thus:

JENNIFER STEVENSON   ADORE ⎫
JIMMY MCBRIDE   LIKE   ⎬ MARRY
                                                  ⎭

If the outcome was unsatisfactory, there were various methods of cheating. If an interest either in or on the part of a girl was suspected, her friends might write up the names concerned and count them out, leaving the result written up as a tease.

Many of these popular practices are closely paralleled by more ancient traditions, some of which involve the use of plants. Interesting in several respects is this account from Cadian, Co. Tyrone, of an attempt at marriage divination which backfired:

> It was aye a lucky place the forth. I myself was courting a wee girl and she was pulling flax. And what did she do but steal a ragweed off the ring, so that she could sleep on it and dream of the man she might be after marrying. But not a wink did she sleep that night at all, and as soon as daylight come she brought it back and left it on the fort again. And that finished her capers with Cadian. And it so fell out

that I married another and not her at all, and maybe that was best for both of us.[4]

The 'forth' or 'fort' is often regarded as a popular dwelling of the fairies, and ragweed is also often associated with them. The implication is that the girl was seeking their help, always a risky occupation, and the tenor of the story calls her character into question. Such suspicious behaviour would not be desirable in a wife. Consorting with the fairies, well known for their interference with the dairy, was inappropriate in the extreme, implying an interest in witchcraft (also often associated with women and the dairy) and in the supernatural.

Much marriage divination was seasonal, and while it was unacceptable to gather ragweed, especially from a forth, gathering yarrow, either on May Eve or on St John's Eve, was perfectly permissible. While pulling the plant, the following rhyme was to be repeated:

> Good morrow, good yarrow,
> Good morrow, good thrice to thee
> I hope before this time tomorrow
> My own true love I will see.[5]

After saying the rhyme, it was necessary for the speaker to keep silent till morning, when her reward would be to see her future husband. Sometimes, like wedding cake, the plant was slipped under a pillow so that, while 'she slept in azure-lidded sleep, in blanchèd linen, smooth, and lavender'd',[6] her future partner might appear to her – in a dream. At St John's Eve, or midsummer, bonfires were lit as part of the general celebrations, and many associated traditions involved the bringing of good fortune. Anyone about to undergo a journey, either literal or metaphorical, might jump the bonfire to ensure a safe passage, and so couples who were about to marry might jump the St John's Eve bonfire in order to ensure the success of the partnership.[7]

In Ireland, the most popular season for marriage divination was Hallowe'en. This has usually been understood in relation to the agricultural year. The long winter evenings, being relatively free from work, meant that more time was available for courtships. Weddings could then be timed so that the couple could be established and ready for a new working season. Fitzpatrick observes:

During the 1870s, the first quarter of the year accounted for nearly two-thirds of Clare marriages and forty years later the proportion still exceeded one half. Spring marriages, of course, were neither a

peculiarly nor a generally Irish preference:many peasant popula-
tions have tended to marry in spring, whereas Irish Protestants (perhaps less eager than their Catholic counterparts to embark upon
seven weeks abstinence straight after the wedding feast) were more
inclined to marry in the second half of the year.[8]

During the medieval period, the Church exercised considerable control
over the times when marriages could be solemnized. In Ireland, some
attempts were made to relax these regulations as a means of encouraging
people to marry in church,[9] and it seems that in very early times,
November may have been a popular month in which to marry.[10]

A wide choice of Hallowe'en divination practices was available to
those interested. Again, these primarily involve girls eager to find husbands, although some reveal a degree of anxiety on the part of men about
the possible identity of future wives, or at least about the potential success of a specific partnership. One method of investigating this was to
name a pair of nuts, often hazelnuts, for a given boy and girl, and to place
them in the fire. The likely outcome of the relationship could be deduced
from the way in which the nuts burned, as described in this mid nineteenth century account:

Harvest knots were exchanged between young men and women as symbols of a
romantic attachment. The autumn was the season most closely associated with
courtship, especially in rural communities, and Hallowe'en was particularly an
important time for marriage divination. *Sketch courtesy of H. Bruce.*

T'BURN NUTS ON A HOLL'EVE

First dry them well, and then let them burn on a hot griddle, or on a bar
i' the grate, iv its broad enough; or on the hearth stone. If they burn up
t' wan another, that's a sign the couple 'ill be marriet, but if they jump
away, the pigs 'll run through it. If they go out soon, they'll not be
longlivers; a' if wan o' them blazes over tother he'll be verry proud ov
her. If the big nut o' one pair burns up toarst the wee one ov another
pair, its leckly meeby that a widda man 'll marry a widda wumman.[11]

A second account describes very clearly another popular method of divination, 'the custom of placing three dishes in front of a blindfold person
who then puts his fingers in one of them':

The first might be empty, the second contain clean water, and the
third dirty water or earth; if the first was chosen, the person would
never marry, if the second, his partner would be a bachelor or maid,
and if the third, a widower or widow.[12]

Other methods of divining the identity of a future marriage partner
included deductions based on the shape or cleanliness of cabbages, on the
presence or absence of grain on a stalk of corn, or on who may be induced
to appear in a mirror or in a dream.[13]

One method of marriage divination which must have offered many
opportunities for the playing of pranks is described by a Tyrone woman
talking of her mother's youth about or slightly before the turn of the
twentieth century:

There was lime kilns in her young day, when she was about sixteen,
and they would have great nights, on Hallow Eve night. They would
throw the ball of wool down, (they'd have knitting you know) and
they would throw the ball of wool down into the lime kiln and they
would say a whole lot of words, like 'Is there anyone down there?
Who's down there? Answer me, is there anyone down there? Is there
anyone down there holding my wool?' And they would hold the
wool, whoever was down there would hold the wool, (told me this is
the truth) and she would hold the wool and maybe whoever was
down there would say, 'I'm Kevin,' or 'I'm Micky,' or 'I'm Johnny.'
And that's the name of the people they would marry. Oh, she said it
happened to her, ... she threw her ball down, and she said a few of the
things that they say. I forget what they were and whatever she said
anyway, 'Answer me,' she says, 'what do they call you?' He says, 'I'm
Micky,' and she married a man called Micky![14]

Another widely known method is described in this story from Co. Cavan:

You go to this point of the stream at three townlands (i.e. where three townlands meet) at twelve o'clock, and you take your chemise, or shirt, or whatever else, and you start washing it, and you say, every time you wash it,

> I wash my shirt of all this dirt
> in the name of Hannah MacDowell
> I wash my shirt of all this dirt
> in the name of Hannah MacDowell

And you do that three times, and you look up, and you'll see the intended husband, or the intended girl you're going to marry. By gob, I heard of a lassie done it, one time, she was very anxious, and she had no belief in it, but she went and done it, and this handsome lad was standing looking at her and he vanished like that in a minute or so ... And she went to America after, the same lassie, and she met this fellow, and got married. They got married, and this night, they were talking. You know, they were going to retire, and she was admiring him. She says, 'I seen you two years ago.' He was born in America, alright. And he says, 'You couldn't see me two years ago, for I never was out of this country and you were in Ireland.' 'I seen you,' she says. 'You couldn't have.' 'I'll tell you how I seen you.' She told him the thing. And he studied a while, and he walked out, and he got a double-barrelled shot-gun, and blew her brains out when he came in ... He remembered the same night at that time, about twelve o'clock, he got into a horrid sickness.[15]

'Hannah MacDowell' is probably an anglicization of the Gaelic words *in ainm an diabhail* ('in the name of the Devil'). If it was inadvisable to interfere with the fairies, to attempt to contact the Devil was even less wise, and likely to carry dire consequences.

The same method of ascertaining the identity of a future husband is described in 1812 by a traveller in the north of Ireland:

Two girls went out at the dark of the moon, and washed their shifts in south running water, in the devil's name. They hung them before the fire in the room where they lay, keeping awake and silent, as the charm requires. Towards morning two apparitions came in, and turned them. The one was that of a man with a rope about his neck, the other was that of a man in a coffin. Shortly afterwards the two girls were married to men bearing the forms in question. One of them was hanged for horse stealing, and the other died the day after his marriage. A comely servant maid of a neighbouring farmer, went out in a similar manner, to wash her shift in the devil's name. The apparition of her master passed. As she had left him asleep in bed, she was in terrible fright. She came in and told the circumstance to her mistress, who persuaded her to go out a second time, and to take with her a pair of scissors. The apparition once again slowly passed. She, unobserved, cut off a piece from the skirt of its coat, and returned with it to her mistress. 'Well!' said the good woman, 'what must be must; you will be his second wife, and be kind to my children, for I have but a short time to live.' The servant maid, however, forgot this injunction, and when married to her master, which she was about twelve months afterwards, proved a very step-mother.[16]

The clear message imparted in many of these stories is to leave well alone. While marriage divination may seem like an attractive idea, these stories with their implications of improper behaviour helped to bolster the right of parents to decide the matrimonial prospects of their children. Although Hallowe'en was also a time for more general divination, marriage was particularly highlighted at this season. While much of the divination was often light-hearted, and many of the practices actually referred to as 'games', these warnings against interfering with the supernatural and invoking the Devil provide a reminder that marriage is a rite of passage. Brides are one of the categories of people deemed to be at greatest risk of abduction by the fairies. In addition to supporting the rights of parents, it is well-known that folklore acknowledges and underscores the liminality of those associated with the change of state inherent in the act of marrying.

Although marriage divination, particularly at Hallowe'en, is most usually associated with rural areas and with an agrarian way of life, there is evidence that these practices were also known in urban districts. The following extract from a story entitled 'Hallowe'en' describes a party which might have been held in Belfast in the 1840s:

Supper was ended; and the revellers broke up into petty groups eager to spend the remainder of the festival in the most approved and ancient fashion. Some betook themselves to the nursery, where was arranged a long line of basins set apart, for 'clean water, dirty water, and no water at all' and, by stumbling upon one of the cabalistic vessels, the blind-folded and curious Miss was to learn her after fate. Others poured boiling lead through the ring of a huge key into cold water, and tried to learn the mystic signs which should unfold their destiny. Several burned nuts for the same laudable object, while many a romping girl tore the brilliants from her braided hair, and plunged her lovely tresses in an immense tub filled with the cooling element of an adjoining stream, that she might have the exquisite pleasure of 'ducking for apples'.[17]

Many of these traditions were widespread and well known in various parts of the British Isles.[18] The Belfast street song 'My Aunt Jane' includes the lines 'My aunt Jane, she's awful smart/She baked a ring in an apple tart', which alludes to the tradition of preparing special food for Hallowe'en. This often included tokens by which the future could be foreseen. Whoever received the portion with the ring would be the first to marry, or would marry within a year. Courtship was a popular theme in Ulster street songs, and is still well represented in children's skipping and clapping rhymes. One currently popular with Co. Down primary schoolchildren includes the lines:

> My boyfriend gave me apples
> My boyfriend gave me pears
> My boyfriend gave me (kiss, kiss, kiss)
> And he pushed me up the stairs
> I gave him back his apples
> I gave him back his pears
> I gave him back his underpants
> And I kicked him down the stairs

– a telling insight into the present attitudes of primary schoolchildren. The more apparently innocent practice of removing the petals of a daisy one by one while reciting 'He loves me, he loves me not' is also still popular among children.

The variety of marriage divination customs, together with their widespread distribution and their prolonged appeal, underlines the importance attached to finding a suitable marriage partner. Light-hearted or not, these customs provide an illuminating insight into the frame of mind of young people many of whom, whatever their own ideas, must have married in accordance with the wishes of their parents and in the interest of maintaining property and land.

3 Courtship and Made Marriages

In early Ireland, marriage was or could be a fairly fluid state, especially for those who were not members of the 'Mandarin class'.[1] A wide variety of types of marriage contract was available, as was divorce by mutual consent or, in certain circumstances, unilaterally.[2] Further colour is added to the picture by the idea that a recognized phenomenon in early Irish society was marriage by capture.[3] Although in the post-epic era various cultural influences were greatly to change many aspects of Irish society, it seems that kidnapping or abduction was long to remain an option available to a man anxious to marry a particular woman. Connolly comments, 'A man who could not match the expectations which a farmer entertained on behalf of his daughter could kidnap the girl', and cites an observation made in 1825 by a priest from Co. Clare which illustrates that 'kidnapping' could be done quite unobtrusively:

> The common practice was not to force them by night; but to meet them in the day-time, and turn them into a house, and there to keep them two or three hours, and such is the delicacy of the Irish people, that no man would marry her after, thus he was sure of her being his future wife.[4]

Abduction is occasionally found as a theme in Irish oral narrative, sometimes with the implication that it occurs as the consequence of witchcraft, although in these circumstances marriage is not always the outcome, as illustrated by this Co. Cavan narrative:

> There was one old fellow lived his lone up there in Cornakeagh, he was an old fellow they called Ramon [?] McCarty. By God he had some kind of a charm. He was as ugly as myself, you know. But he lived his lone, and he had some kind of a charm and any young lassies, he'd talk to they'd follow him and go home with him. And, oh damn it, there was people would be looking for them, and every damn thing, and they couldn't know the hell where they'd get her.

20

She was content and happy with Ramon McCarty. Living with him. And he had an old shack of a house was a terror. And he was this day in a fair to the Black [Blacklion], and this lassie came in on the Florencecourt Road, she was a minister's daughter. You know, a minister's daughter at Florencecourt. And she was a real flash lassie, and a real step with her. 'Oh Jesus, lads, look what's coming!' And them all stepped out to have a look at her, and oh now, she was a handsome beauty alright and she knew it.

'Aw wait,' says Ramon McCarty, 'till I get a look at her.' And he stepped out in front and smiled at her and asked her how she was and God, she melted down, 'Aw, come on,' he says, 'and have a bottle of lemonade.' Went to the pub, and away she went with Ramon to the pub. Her and him wasn't seen more, and by God she was looking for. People was looking for her and they'd searched everywhere, and Jesus, they were three or four days before someone directed them, she might be there. And she was away with Ramon McCarty in that house in Cornakeagh and he had that charm all along.

Oh Christ, the first one told me about him's an old woman, now she was dead, she's dead about fifty years ago anyway, and she was a very old woman and aw, Lord, she'd tell you stories about Ramon McCarty and oh God, the nice girls that used to go to his house and live with him for days. And nobody knew where they were, he had a way of looking at them, and putting them in some kind of a trance, you know? Oh, that was no codding, because I heard several people telling about him, you know, and I heard about him hypnotising that minister's daughter down there, at the fair in the Black.[5]

Other accounts suggest that more conventional forms of abduction were very common, at least in the regions of counties Tipperary, Limerick and Laois:

Here the young men are distinguished by a spirit of gallantry worthy of the ages of romance. They often meet in parties of a hundred, to carry off some female, either with or without her consent, and so prevalent is this practice, that few young women are married, that are not run away with in this manner.[6]

Some young women were abducted by fortune hunters, and Malcolmson comments: 'The abduction of heiresses, mostly small time heiresses, was a crime of common, though exaggerated occurrence in eighteenth century Ireland.'[7]

In addition to abductions, straightforward elopements occurred on occasion. Writing from Delville to her sister in reply to a letter which had evidently provided her with news of a scandal, Mrs Delany described two elopements which took place in 1747:

> One is of a young lady, youngest daughter to a Captain Johnston here, a very pretty girl just sixteen, who ran away on Friday night with Sir Robert King, a vile young rake of a considerable fortune in this country. They went off on Friday night: the father pursued and overtook them on Saturday morning, held a pistol at the knight's head, swore he would shoot him through the head if he did not instantly marry his daughter, which rather than die he consented to do. A parson was ready and called in, but Sir R. K.'s servants rushed in at the same time, gave him a pistol, and an opportunity of escaping, which he did, and left the forlorn damsel to return with her father. They all appeared at church in Dublin on Sunday morning, and the girl appears at all public places as unconcerned and brazen as if she had acted the most prudent part in the world.
>
> The other story is indeed much more notorious and shocking. You don't know any of the people, so I shall not name names, but a gentleman's daughter who has for several years borne an extremely good character, about twenty-six years of age, has managed her father's house with great prudence, and always shewn a great tenderness for him on all occasions, has gone off with the schoolmaster of the parish, a clergyman who has been married several years, and his wife a very good kind of woman! He *now says* he never was married to her, and accuses her with carrying on an intrigue with the lady's father and brother that has run away with him! These are sad strokes in a family! how much less is *the death* of a dear friend to be lamented than such wicked conduct! [8]

Evidently Mrs Delany's views on a fate worse than death were not universally shared. As we shall see, in eighteenth-century Ireland, the question of exactly what constituted a legal marriage was not as straightforward as it might at first appear. The gentleman concerned in the second case might have found various grounds by which to substantiate his claim in relation to his first marriage, even if a ceremony had been performed.

Elopements of this type were different in character from the 'runaway' marriage which appears to have been quite a common feature of Irish rural society in the past. It has been suggested that, early in the nineteenth century, this was an essential element of 'Irish' as opposed to 'Scottish' weddings, and that runaways were a feature of native rather than of planter culture. Many writers have been keen to suggest that this behaviour was considered the appropriate prelude to marriage: 'However suitable the match, it is but a tame exploit if the groom does not first run away with the bride.' [9] Some writers have seen in the runaway, and in certain other aspects of behaviour associated with marriage in Ireland, echoes of the ancient custom of marriage by abduction.

Oral sources usually account differently for the runaway, suggesting that it was a means of escaping a marriage arranged on behalf of a young woman by her parents, or of securing parental agreement for a match which would not otherwise be approved. A classic runaway of the late eighteenth century involving a minor heiress is described in *Saunder's Newsletter*:

> At Mullingar, Mr Christopher Hughes of Lissaryon, aged fourteen to Miss Jane Cadden, of Edgworthstown, Co Longford, aged thirteen, an amiable young lady with an affluent fortune; what renders this youthful junction the more singular, the lady was in the same night to be married to a man who might reasonably be her grandfather when our youthful adventurer timely advanced and prevented the unnatural union. [10]

Phil Dolan of Blacklion, Co. Cavan, described a less conventional runaway which happened in that area:

> He was a tailor, he was a cripple. He was a good tailor, you know. Of course, everybody had to go to a tailor, that time, to get a suit of clothes, because the bend of clothes you'd get in a shop, you couldn't wear them to a dog's funeral, there was neither shape nor make on them, the same as if they were put on you with a pitchfork. And doing a good trade, but damn it, he got friendly with this lassie, and he used to ride an ass all over the country, and him and her decided to run away … She knew she wouldn't get permission at home to marry him. By Gob, they came to [a certain house] and there was a few of them in. She came and tapped the door, and she said, 'It's a runaway, can we come in?' 'And why not?' or 'Come on.' 'Some of yous come out, now, and tie the ass,' she says, and she carried [the groom] in her arms off the ass, and put him up on a bench, and they had the runaway, sent out for whiskey, and had a bit of a hooley, and a dance, and then there was a wedding. It was a must, after the runaway, do you see? Well, they done alright. [11]

Such behaviour would be sufficient to compromise a girl, who by means of it would show herself to be headstrong and sexually aware, although stress is often laid on the fact that runaways did not involve any degree of sexual misconduct, an activity which convention dictates ought to be beyond the scope of young Irish men and women. Her parents' hands would usually be forced, because to refuse consent for a marriage subsequent to a runaway would be to leave a daughter with few future prospects of marriage.

For a young man to renege on such an arrangement was considered very unlucky, as the Fermanagh storyteller George Sheridan shows:

> [A man] ran away with a girl and he didn't marry her, and the girl prayed that if ever he had a son, that he'd be a country show or something, and that's how it worked out, you know. It was very unlucky to run away with a girl, and not marry her.[12]

For a girl to want to renege on such a bargain seems to have been beyond the range of popular imagination.

Oral accounts of runaways frequently present them as light-hearted events which provided opportunities for drinking, dancing and fun, and often support the idea of the young pair daring to defy their parents. A runaway was none the less a serious preliminary to marriage, and a closer examination reveals that this kind of conduct was not universally approved. By the late nineteenth century there was clerical opposition to runaways, and in some regions the priest might 'frequently admonish the young women from the pulpit upon the subject'.[13] It is difficult to judge whether the priests held the young women alone to be responsible for such misconduct, or if they felt a warning to girls might be less likely to fall on deaf ears, especially if it carried an implication of total disgrace. Such clerical opposition might be echoed by the wider community:

> They didn't like Fr Markey whenever he was talked about, nobody seemed to care for him. And he put down the runaways which made such a lot of fun for the people. And maybe they weren't such a good thing. My mother always favoured him, because she said he was right to put down the runaways.[14]

A further account, like the last one from Co. Armagh, gives additional insight into attitudes to runaways and the degree to which they were disapproved of. For a man to renege on a bargain might be looked upon with more than disapproval, especially from the family of the girl concerned, and evidently some men were susceptible to coercion:

There was a lot of cases where they didn't [marry after a runaway]. And they kicked up, and sometimes you would get a mean man and he wouldn't be getting enough money with the bride and then her character was spoiled, you see if she ran away with somebody and that he didn't marry her. That was a terrible affair and she would leave the country, go away to America or somewhere. That was one of the dangers of it. My Aunt Ellen would tell about a man who ran away with a girl and then he wouldn't marry her, whatever kicked up, he wouldn't marry her and the following Thursday he was coming up from Newry, walking with his hands round another one. That was a terrible crime. And I pictured he was going like this with the hand back and front of her. But an uncle then, of my father's, and of this aunt met him somewhere and said 'You ran away with a good girl and if you don't go and marry her, what will I do to you.' So he came that very night and asked her to come again, to go ahead. They used to say how he said till her. 'Now, or never.' And she says 'Well, now and forever.' But then when she died she wouldn't bury with him. She got buried with her parents. She was, so my aunt would always say. 'She went with him first, but she was buried with her parents.' [15]

Place of burial still has a powerful hold on the psyche of many Ulster people, and this gesture of reconciliation would strike many resonances in the long memories of the members of the local community, but it is hard not to speculate on the quality of life which might subsequently have been experienced by the bride concerned. The treatment of the body after death is itself a very emotive issue, and attitudes to burial are interlinked with beliefs about the resurrection. One such belief is that people who have been married twice will be judged at the Last Day with the first marriage partner.[16]

Whilst runaways met with disapproval, and financial sanctions might be applied to couples who behaved in this way,[17] on some occasions financial considerations might actually encourage a couple to stage a runaway for reasons quite other than escaping a contract arranged by parents. This account shows the tactics which might be brought into play:

I was a comfortable man, and had four cows and a heifer, till my daughter got married, and played me a trick that a good many girls have done before; she ran off with a young man, and after a week's sport, he sent her back without having married her; she never stopped at me, saying he wouldn't take her without a fortune, until I was forced to give her three of my cows, and money besides; moreover I had to pay the priest.[18]

A young couple might connive to run away together in order to encourage the prospective bride's father to be more generous with the provision of her dowry. Evidence given in the 1830s to the Poor Inquiry suggests that in some parts of the country it was common practice to stage a runaway in order to compel a higher settlement than would otherwise have been available,[19] although evidence already cited illustrates the risks such behaviour might entail. A couple had to be careful not to miscalculate and end up with nothing.

The business of matchmaking, which could help to ensure material compatibility between bride and groom, was often of great importance in Irish rural society. Despite the relevance of the girl's marriage portion and the degree to which her 'bottom drawer' might highlight her suitability to become a responsible housewife, oral accounts usually emphasize the male initiative in matchmaking, and often suggest that the man's material standing was an important issue. This, together with the fact that the girl's parents are usually represented as speaking on her behalf, increases the impression that the female takes a very passive part in the proceedings. Whatever may have been the facts of any specific situation, the perception of correct female behaviour is that a girl should acquiesce to whatever is decided for her. Sometimes a matchmaker was engaged as a go-between to act on behalf of a young man anxious to wed. The matchmaker might be unofficial, perhaps a friend, family member or a person of some standing who was well respected in the community. An unofficial matchmaker was sometimes known as a 'blackfoot'. If a recognized official matchmaker was engaged, he would expect to receive a fee,[20] and in 1908 a 'returned Yank' paid a matchmaker a fee of £5 plus expenses in order to be provided with a bride.[21] Go-betweens also helped to broker marriage treaties among the aristocracy.[22]

Other matrimonial agencies were also active in Ireland. The *Belfast Newsletter* of 1 April 1889 carried an advertisement for *The Matrimonial Herald and Fashionable Marriage Gazette* which boasted that it was 'the original and only recognised Medium for high class introductions' and claimed to be the 'largest and most successful Matrimonial Agency in the world'. Advertisements for computer dating services, marriage bureaux and 'Lonely Hearts' columns in various publications suggest that contacting a suitable partner is an enduring and often problematical preoccupation. Curtin remarks: 'That arranged marriages have not entirely disappeared is indicated by the seventeenth annual report of the Knock Marriage Bureau, which claims to have arranged to date 370 marriages and to have received 15,395 inquiries.'[23]

Matchmaking, official and otherwise, is a feature of the autumn gathering at Lisdoonvarna, where it is still possible to contract a broker to help arrange a marriage or at least an introduction, the intended outcome of which is well known to those involved. The socializing and dancing which are essential parts of the Lisdoonvarna celebrations are all strongly geared to allow couples to meet and establish courtships, and those seeking partners know that a visit to Lisdoonvarna in September will increase their chances of finding a suitable candidate.

Arranged marriages were characteristic of other European societies. For example, it has been stated of the area of Bearn in the Pyrenees: 'Those who wanted to marry against the wishes of their parents had no choice but to leave the house at the risk of being disinherited in favour of a brother or sister.' [24]

The mores and social convention associated with matchmaking in rural Ulster are described in this account from Co. Armagh, which illustrates an only but eventually successful attempt at matchmaking undertaken by a particular blackfoot:

My father made a match, the man had been left, I think his mother lived on pretty long, and he must have been in the forties when his mother died, and he said to my father that he wanted a good [?wife]. 'Do you know of a sensible one? It would be fool looking for the likes of me to go over the country looking for a woman, for they would all laugh at me. But if you knew of a good sensible woman that would be some use, and wouldn't be silly.' So my father said 'Would you not be as well and go and look a bit yourself?' 'Och, now, sure where would I go? I'd have nothing to say to them.' He was a bit bashful you see, because he'd had his nose to the grindstone and I suppose he was under his mother's thumb. So my father knew of a family a couple of miles away. 'Ach,' he said 'they are fine girls.' And he had a chat with the father and mother and they said 'Oh bring him over, to be sure.' So one of the girls had gone to a commercial school, but it wasn't such a common thing you know then, for of course people just hadn't the money to pay fees, to pay the train to go to the town. But the two girls were left and they were working very hard on the farm, but there were brothers there and they would seem to be looking to bring a woman in, but no one would like to go in where there were two girls and a mother and father. So my father arranged with this man to come over on a certain evening in springtime and they walked across the fields, and they didn't go the road and they didn't go in a trap or anything to draw attention to themselves. They went the fields, and that landed them out at a gate and they crossed the road and they got over at the next gate into another field and they went down to the house that way. So, of course, they were all dressed and all arrayed [?in] their bibs and tuckers and they went into the house and chatted and shaked hands all round. My father kept up a good lot of chat and all about the crops and all, but the other poor fellow hadn't much to say, I think he was a bit overawed. And they went out to have a look at the animals, the father said 'Come out now to see the cattle and the cows and all.' It was a good thing, to make a good impression, you see. So they went out and looked round and the prospective bridegroom didn't say very much. And coming in again my father fell behind a bit in the troup and a girl, the eldest one said 'He has nothing to say for himself, I don't think you need bring him back.' So he said, 'Alright, that's alright now.' So there was tea ready when they came in, you see, that gave the women a chance to have the tea ready, and they had apple tarts and they had ginger bread, and I don't know what. And then they were asked to go down into the parlour and there was a big fire there and they got into good chat and my father drew this man out to tell about some (I think it was Minorca) hens that he had, and slipped out then and went up to the kitchen to talk to the father and mother and there was right good crack going on in the room. So then my father says, 'Look at the time it is, it's getting near home time, are you coming Joe?' So they got up to come and my father was making on out through the door like, he wasn't going to let them think he was waiting for a second invitation. So the girl wagged the finger at him and she said 'Ach,' she says, 'maybe you should bring him back, he was a good way of cracking there at the last, he's livelier than you would think.' So he said. 'Alright now, whatever you like yourself, like.' So that was it, and they were married in about six months' time.[25]

'Good crack' or easy, entertaining conversation is an important aspect of local social life, and an attractive quality in a marriage partner. This account crystallizes many aspects of local family life. Only one daughter is provided with a career, and that was well beyond the prospects of many girls. The more sisters married and left the farm, the better the marriage prospects became for their brothers, but as the bridegroom's experience illustrates, these might also depend on the relationship between mother and son.

In most of its particulars, the Armagh account is in agreement with the general picture of the exchange by means of which a match was arranged. It provides an interesting example of the way in which the young woman concerned found means of making her own views known. Several accounts suggest that, while the parents at least of the prospective bride and sometimes also of the prospective groom were the parties directly involved in negotiations, the wishes of the young couple were often taken into account before any agreement was reached. However, there were some occasions when marriages were arranged without any consultation of the young people concerned, and it might happen that they did not even meet before the wedding. Peig Sayers had an experience of this kind: 'I never met my husband till the day I married him ... but it was a love match till the day he died. And why shouldn't it, for he was a fine big man.' [26]

Arranged marriages are still quite commonplace among the Irish travelling community, and even in cases where a couple is free to conduct a courtship their liberty is carefully curtailed and the bride's father will be approached for permission before they become engaged. Many travelling women, especially those now over the age of thirty-five, had their marriages arranged on their behalf, usually when they were in their mid to late teens, by fathers or brothers. Although they were consulted before a bargain was struck, some could expect to be cajoled if they were unenthusiastic about a prospective husband, and occasionally marriages in this age group were the result of a 'runaway', which behaviour is or was until very recently stigmatized among the Travellers.[27]

The fact that material concerns were often paramount when a match was being made did not escape unremarked in oral tradition. The first of these incidents tells of a blackfoot protecting the interests of his client; the second focuses on the family of the bride:

He wanted to make out that this prospective bridegroom was a bit bashful about what he owned, and he said, 'Like, whenever you tell the number of cows you have, like, I'll say "Blethers, he's not telling half enough".' So he said he had three cows, and the other says, 'He's double that.' And the father says, 'How many sows now would you have?' 'Och, I've three sows.' 'Och, blethers, indeed he has – he has double that.' And the mother says, 'I suppose you'd be over thirty?'

'Och, blethers' says he 'he's double that!' I think they'd had a wee drop out of the bottle first, you see, and the man forgot himself.

Then there was another time and the father wanted to impress the fellow who was coming and he borrowed some cattle from a neighbour, to have plenty of cattle. It was very important that the bride's people should be good doers you see, and have plenty of animals, and plenty of land and all that, and this man said, 'So and so's coming to see our Lizzie, and maybe you'll let me have a half dozen of them young cattle of yours, and we'll put them in with ours and they'll look plenty?' 'Oh, I will, to be sure.' So they drove them down and into the field that morning, and had their dinner and all went out to see, 'Oh come on out till you see my young cattle.' And the suitor looked at them and 'Oh, now' he said 'they're alright but they don't seem to be agreeing too well.' They were all fighting with the strange cattle.[28]

Obviously, each side in the arrangement was equally anxious to impress.

The obsession with property could be taken too far, however. In this tale, from Co. Tyrone, the bride is driven to the last resort to make her views known:

This I was told happened at the village of Cullohun below Bundoran. The girl's father owned a little black heifer together with some other animals, how many I do not know. A young man courted her and having gained her consent to be married proceeded to get all he could by way of dowry from her parents. Eventually her father promised him everything he had with the exception of one little black heifer which he said he had to pay the rent with. But no, the young man would not marry her unless he got the black heifer too. So that also was promised. The girl let the wedding arrangement go on, and went to the chapel on the appointed day. The service started, and when it came to the part where the groom was asked if he would have this woman for his wedded wife, the girl answered for him and said, 'Oh no! It's not me he wants, it's my father's black heifer.' Each time the priest asked the question, the girl answered saying it was her father's heifer he was marrying so the wedding could not go on and the contracting parties returned to their parents' houses.[29]

The Halls are among those who point out that the ensuring of material compatibility was a preoccupation, at least among parents with a degree of comfort and material well-being to protect when overseeing their children's marriages:

If two young people form an attachment for each other and have hardly enough between them to pay the priest his dues, the only parental observation is 'well sure! – we did the same thing ourselves.' But if a farmer can bestow a cow with his daughter, he will insist on a horse, or an equivalent in pigs, 'slips' or full-grown. We have known a match broken off without the question ever being asked whether the young people's affections were engaged or not, only because the girl's father would not bestow a feather-bed on the young couple as a set-off against the two-year-old heifer which the boy's parents proposed to give.[30]

While beauty, especially when coupled with talent and a pleasant disposition, might win admiration for a young woman, it was seldom that a girl at any social level could rely entirely on her face as her fortune. Mrs Delany, reflecting on the sad case of a Miss Letitia Bushe, who in 1731 suffered a very disfiguring attack of smallpox, helps to show how prosperity was the quality ultimately sought after in a bride:

I think I never saw a prettier creature than she was before that malicious distemper seized her, a gay, good humoured, innocent girl without the least conceit of her beauty; her father has been dead about six months, a worthless man that has left a very, uncertain fortune. She paints delightfully. All the men were dying whilst she was in danger, but notwithstanding their admiration of her, not one of them will be generous enough to marry her while the lawsuit is pending, now indeed even their adoration will cease, they will not acknowledge her for a divinity since she is divested of those charms that occasioned their devotion.[31]

Among the wealthy, as among the farming classes, while good looks and other attributes were appreciated, property was an important consideration for many people when planning to marry. A pretty face might attract attention, but a girl with neither looks nor means had few prospects of marriage.

Oral accounts show that a girl's aptitudes and capabilities might enhance her opportunity to marry and some illustrate that the role of the matchmaker might extend beyond simply acting as go-between – some were expected to be aware of the availability of potential brides:

Many a time men out at fairs and selling cattle and buying cattle, were in houses where there was a bit of chat and maybe a man would say, 'Do you know a likely looking girl, one that would be sensible,

and be able to make butter and a bit of bread, and all that?' That was
very important. [Then there was] the man [who] said that he would
like a girl that would be able to cook and make good bread, and have
good cold hands for butter making. [32]

There are echoes here of the story which circulates currently, telling of
the man who places an advertisement for a wife in a 'Lonely Hearts' col-
umn, specifying that she must have her own tractor (or boat) and finish-
ing 'please send picture of tractor' (or boat etc.).

Not all young women who married to please their parents did so hap-
pily. This sad account is of a wedding which took place during the 1890s:

> As monitress, I was allowed occasionally to take the senior girls into
> the church for the service and during my five years I witnessed a
> great many, and at one time I could have repeated the marriage ser-
> vice having heard it so often. Only three of the weddings stand out
> in my memory, one of them being a young woman who hadn't long
> left school who cried during the whole service and greatly embar-
> rassed the rector as she could scarcely answer the responses. It was
> an all white wedding and she was a lovely bride. We were all full of
> sympathy because we had heard that she was marrying a farmer
> twice her age (who had a home prepared for her) although she was
> in love with a young man her own age who had no prospects, and she
> was pleasing her parents. [33]

It is to be hoped that her marriage was happier than her wedding day, and
perhaps by making this such a special occasion, marking it out as a 'white
wedding', her parents hoped to compensate for her disappointment. The
'white wedding' in the 1890s was an important indicator of property and
conspicuous consumption.

Some folklore illustrates a general sense of unease in relation to inter-
lopers in a community, and this was among the reasons for approaching a
matchmaker. There were fears that a person who was not well known
might misrepresent his or her material standing. One popular folktale
deals with the quick-witted untidy son of an impoverished blacksmith
who talked his way into securing a wealthy bride for himself by being
generous, rather than economical, with the truth.[34] The following account,
in which both blackfoot and groom come from a distance, illustrates the
concerns felt by many who feared being caught in such a situation:

> [T]he negligent and thriftless young farmer of Duffrey or Bantry,
> being marked with an indifferent character in his own neighbour-

hood would, with his blackman, take the pass of Scollagh, or the village of Bunclody in his way, make a descent in the homestead of some farmer and through assumption of high breeding, great acquaintances and possession of a good farm, dazzle the young damsel and her parents, and bring her to a home much less comfortable than the one she had quitted.[35]

Oral tradition does not suggest that such trickery was confined to prospective bridegrooms. A south Armagh tale tells of a man who experiences difficulty in finding a bridegroom for his daughter, so he spreads a rumour that the girl is to be provided with a handsome dowry:

'And might I axe (*ask*),' says he, 'how much it is?'

'You might indeed axe,' says he, 'and I'll tell you, and not a word of lie: I'm giving her a hundred,' says he, 'and that man there,' says he, 'will be a witness.'

'And when will she get this hundred?' says the fellow, for he thought, do you see, that there might be a catch in it that way – awe, he was no gham (*fool*).

'She'll get the hundred the day she's marrad. I'll go to your house myself with it that night,' says he, 'and let this man here be there to see me hand it over to you on your own hearth stone.'

'That's word enough for me,' says the fellow. And he went away as plazed as a cat with two tails for he never expected more than five and twenty at the most.

Well, everything was settled and they were marrad and they were waiting in the house that night for him to come and the other man was there too, and wasn't there a rap on the door.

'That'll be him now, that'll be your father,' and he went and opened the door and the ould lad came in and hell'th o me sowl if he hadn't a bag on his back, and he dropped it on the hearth stone.

'There,' says he, 'There's your hundred, and damn the better hundred weight of priddies (*potatoes*) you'd find in the townland the year.'

Now wasn't he a fly ould codger that.[36]

While no one wanted to be the victim of trickery, there were those who were prepared to outwit their neighbours, given the chance.

In some areas, especially those in which girls were outnumbered by boys, young women might find pressure to court within their own group being exerted on them by their male peers. Competition for girls has been characterized as an element of English society,[37] but similar forces were registered among Ulster people, where this was sometimes a factor of the strong sense of place and of location found in various other forms of cultural expression:

> [A] small town like Larne comprised distinct districts, e.g. the so-called 'factory' area, centred around the former Brown's linen factory – a staunchly protestant/Orange area and a source of several international footballers. There was, too, the 'harbour' area. These were almost towns within the town and something akin to a clan system operated within them, and many couples married within the clan. By the same token a hopeful swain could risk some hostility from the local lads if he pursued a girl in a clan area to which he didn't belong! [38]

A system like this would, of course, help to foster conservatism in many matters. Few people of either sex could risk overstepping the boundaries of appropriate behaviour without being passed over in the marriage stakes. Provincial towns also had (and have) lively gossip networks, which helped reinforce this conservatism. It was not enough to keep a check on one's behaviour, care had to be taken not to feature in gossip either for apparently justified or for unjustified reasons.

Competition for girls could take more direct forms than coercion to court within a given social group. Mr and Mrs Hall record a contest which apparently occurred between rival suitors:

> A young man, a carpenter named Linchigan, applied to the father of a girl named Corrigan, for his daughter in marriage. A rival called Lavelle asked for her also, on the plea that as he was richer 'he wouldn't ask for so much with her' whereupon the factions of the swains were about to join issue and fight, when a peacemaker suggested that the boys should run for her. The race was run accordingly, a distance of some miles up and down a mountain; Linchigan won, and wedded the maiden. [39]

While this may represent a triumph of physical prowess over material concerns, it also emphasizes that the initiative in such matters could be expected to lie with the male. The girl's reaction to the entire event is unrecorded, as if the identity of her husband was a matter to which she might be completely indifferent.

Arthur Young's account of a similar competition which apparently took place in the region of Londonderry during the 1770s suggests that the woman's views were possibly the last to be taken into account:

> There is a very ancient custom here, for a number of country neigh-
> bours among the poor people, to fix upon some young woman that
> ought, as they think, to be married; they also agree upon a young fel-
> low as a proper husband for her; this determined, they send to the
> fair one's cabbin to inform her, that on the Sunday following she is
> to be horsed, that is carried on men's backs. She must then provide
> whisky and cyder for a treat, as all will pay her a visit after mass for
> a hurling match. As soon as she is horsed, the hurling begins, in which
> the young fellow appointed for her husband has the eyes of all the
> company fixed on him; if he comes off conqueror, he is certainly mar-
> ried to the girl, but if another is victorious, he has certainly lossed
> her, for she is the prize of the victor. These trials are not always fin-
> ished in one Sunday, they take sometimes two or three, and the com-
> mon expression when they are over is, that such a girl was seal'd.
> Sometimes one barony hurls against another but a marriageable girl
> is always the prize.[40]

Community involvement in the event of a wedding is more usually
expressed through disruptive behaviour in association with the actual
ceremony, but Young's account assigns a leading role to the community
in deciding when a match should be made. The local community might
also express disapproval of people who remained unmarried for a longer
time than was generally considered appropriate. In many parts of Ireland
the most usual time for couples to marry was very early in the spring,
before the beginning of Lent. In the south and west of Ireland, customs
such as those associated with 'going to the Sceilig' and 'Chalk Sunday'
were observed. The first of these made use of the idea that, as Easter was
reputedly observed later on Sceilig Michael than on mainland Ireland,
those who failed to be wed by Shrove Tuesday could still be married on
the island. This led to people being carried through the streets to the
accompanying jeers of their neighbours who teasingly pretended to be
taking them to the Sceilig. On Chalk Sunday, the first Sunday in Lent,
marriageable people who were still unwed might find the backs of their
clothes marked with chalk, a teasing sign that the community of their area
disapproved of their status.[41]

Some matchmaking traditions were reserved until after Lent. The following description is of the 'cake dance', a matchmaking custom remembered from Co. Sligo in the late nineteenth century:

> On Easter Sunday ... the young boys and girls of a particular village
> assembled at a certain house where a large soda cake ... was tied in a

white cloth and placed on top of the churn-dash outside the door of
the house. The young people were generally laughing and talking,
singing and dancing, lilting and flirting ... in a field near by, or on the
road opposite the house, or in the yard of the house.

Then a certain young man was given the cake which he presented
to his favourite *cailin* which she cut up and divided among those present ...

As a rule, the match or matrimonial contract between the young
man who presented the cake and the girl to whom he presented it
was made. So a wedding was the next to follow.[42]

The perceived seasonality of marriage patterns in Ireland is also to be
observed in the custom of exchanging 'harvest knots'. These love tokens
of plaited straw provide welcome evidence of mutual affection and
regard between men and women. As their name implies, they were made
in autumn, the traditional time in rural Ireland for establishing
courtships, and were usually the symbol of a committed relationship.[43]
They took various forms, and might be worn on a garment, or (by young
women) in the hair. Sometimes a harvest knot was worked for a girl with
the ears of corn still in place, as a symbol of fertility.

In the Newtownstewart area of Co. Tyrone and perhaps in other districts too, in the 1920s and 1930s, the harvest service itself offered the possibility of meetings between boys and girls. Girls could be relied upon to
attend these services, and, as the meetings drew to a close, boys on bicycles arrived in the churchyard, shining their lamps on the young women as
they came outdoors. One woman recalled: 'If you didn't "click" after harvest, that was you for another year', although she herself met her future
husband during celebrations for the 12th of July.[44] (The term 'click' has
largely been replaced by 'get off with someone' in popular speech.)
Church and other social gatherings provided chances for meetings, and
some girls attended their own church on a Sunday morning, but went to a
service of another denomination in the evening, one reason being to
assess the suitability of any boys in the congregation as potential partners.

As autumn was considered to be the appropriate season for courtship,
with love tokens exchanged at harvest and marriage divination a feature
of Hallowe'en festivities, it is not surprising that until fairly recently St
Valentine's Day does not seem to have been of great significance in the
Irish traditional calendar, although some people were aware of the tradition that birds chose their mates at this time of year.[45] With the establishment of a postal service, the increasing availability of commercially

Engagement photograph of Mary Wilson Corry who came originally from Donegal and Robert Laird Chambers, who met when they were both studying pharmacy and became engaged *c.* 1917. After their marriage Mr Chambers established a pharmacy business in Lisburn, but like most middle-class women of her generation, Mrs Chambers ceased to practise her profession when she married. *UFTM L3270/8.*

produced Valentine greeting cards, and increasing urbanization and shifts in traditional modes of living, St Valentine's Day has become more and more prominent.

During the period of transition from harvest and Hallowe'en to St Valentine's Day as the festival most appropriate for the exchange of messages and tokens of love, these activities sometimes centred on Christmas. To an extent this is reflected in the fact that commercially available printed cards carrying romantic motifs such as hearts, flowers and birds were considered appropriate for Christmas use as well as for sending as Valentines. Evidence of the popular custom of sending messages of affection at Christmas may be gleaned from postcards sent during the month of December in the early years of the present century. A particularly clear example was received by a young man from Keady, Co. Armagh, in December 1905 from a girl who signed herself 'Olive Oil'. The greeting carried by this card took the form of rhymes which have long been popular as Valentine verses:

> As sure as the vine grows round the stump you are my darling sugar lump.

> Albert Dear,
>   You'll be surprised at hearing from me, but round is the ring that has no end for on your love I will depend the ring is round the bed is square so you and me will make a pair.[46]

The subsequent turns taken by the relationship unfortunately go unrecorded, but the greeting is a clear example of the fusion of Christmas and Valentine customs.

Postcards are a fertile source of evidence of popular attitudes which may be deduced both from the printed greetings and from the handwritten messages they convey. Cards on the theme of Leap Year enjoyed some popularity early in the twentieth century. These played on the notion of anxiety on the part of young women over the problem of finding suitable marriage partners. In 1904, a number of these cards was received by a young Belfast woman, warning her against pursuing a certain young man.[47] The notion that women may propose marriage in Leap Year, and that if refused they may claim a forfeit, is still popular, and at one time certain countries enshrined this right in law. Traditionally, a girl could demand a silk gown if rejected, and in the mid twentieth century, before such an idea became opprobrious, a fur coat was considered to be suitable compensation.[48] A wide range of attitudes is revealed by postcards, including the romantic, the amorous and the downright cynical. Some illustrate the point that concern over finding a partner was registered by men as well as by women.

If a young woman resorted to taking a case of Breach of Promise, compensation was an important factor. Breach of Promise was established in common law, and by the mid eighteenth century was a matter of some social relevance.[49] In Northern Ireland, the right to take an action for Breach of Promise remained open until 1985,[50] although the system of arranged marriage which prevailed for many people into the twentieth century may have helped to ensure that few actions actually came before local courts. During the nineteenth century, cases taken in English courts were quite regularly reported in the local newspapers and no doubt gave rise to some *frisson*, providing considerable enjoyment for Ulster readers.[51]

Lengthy courtships were a feature of Irish society, and have often been the subject of humorous songs, poems and recitations. Some couples courted perhaps for decades without actually committing themselves to marriage, and it has been suggested that Breach of Promise might be threatened, a woman perhaps going so far as to issue a writ, in order to spur on a reluctant groom. Some cases were settled without ever coming to court.[52] Of the few cases of Breach of Promise reported as having been brought locally, one suggests that in comparatively recent times to take such an action must have been a last resort. In the case of Johnston v. Irvine, brought on 6 November 1931, the pregnant plaintiff was the daughter of a small farmer. She claimed that she had been seduced and then promised marriage, a set of circumstances which caused various complications, so the case was remitted to the Fermanagh County Court, where the plaintiff was awarded costs.[53] Her case, like that almost a century earlier of Sarah Morrow below, provides little evidence of the scheming which seems to have characterized many cases of Breach of Promise in England.[54]

The case of Sarah Morrow, brought before the Down Assizes in July 1846, illustrates the humiliation a plaintiff in such circumstances might expect to undergo. Sarah was introduced to a Scottish widower by the landlord from whom both her father and her suitor held farms, and was recommended as 'an excellent young woman, and one who could manage well his dairy and domestic concerns', although her dowry of £100 fell £50 short of her suitor's (a Mr Menzies') expectations. An agreement was reached between the bride's father, the landlord and the suitor, in front of another witness (not the bride), but Menzies, of whom it was alleged that he conducted courtships with several young women, married one whose fortune was reputed to be £600, leaving Sarah in the lurch. The writ found in Sarah's favour, but not before even her physical appearance was called into question, and it was suggested that 'she could have suffered nothing in her feelings, for her feelings were not concerned. She should pay the defendant for getting rid of him.' None the less, the circumstances were regarded by the court as being serious in nature, and the defendant's behaviour was condemned as sordid.[55]

The involvement of the landlord as matchmaker in this case is of interest, although the report illustrates the risks which might be run as a result of taking on this responsibility, for it was even suggested that he should be considered liable, having acted as 'mischiefmaker'. Landlords, including very high ranking ones, might be called upon to exert their influence in circumstances of this sort. The possibility that in the 1770s the Earl of Abercorn came to the aid of one Jane Caldwell may be inferred from her grateful letter to the earl:

> I can only say, my Lord, I have the highest sence (sic) of your Lordship's goodness, and to that also do I ascribe my present felicity, a felicity I must ever account it to be rid of the most disagreeable family I could ever meet with. My perjured swain met me at Ardstraw bridge, and my friends with me, and paid the money, but indeed, my Lord, it was with a very bad grace.[56]

It may have been concern to avoid either a case of Breach of Promise or an arranged marriage which motivated John Wilson, a hosier and Elizabeth Brady, both from Antrim town, to swear in February 1801 before a Justice of the Peace that they had promised to wed 'by mutual consent'.[57] Their contract was sufficiently unusual for it to be described as a 'curious form of betrothal', perhaps simply because they arranged it on their own behalf.

The landlord might also have used his influence to ensure that marriage took place in cases of prenuptial pregnancy. Robert Gage, landlord of Rathlin Island, which lies off the coast of Co. Antrim, records in his diary for 26 June 1880 that he went to speak to one of the islandmen 'about his son John marrying Rose McQuilken, as there is now a necessity for his so doing, and this afternoon here he has gone over [the channel to the Antrim coast] for the necessary licence'.[58] Morality was guarded as closely as possible by representatives both of Church and of State. Oral accounts tell of the objections of Catholic priests even to dancing, in case it gave rise to occasions of sin. The lengths to which

priests were reported to go in order to disrupt such activities are graphi-
cally described in this account from north Cavan:

> There was a priest over there, he was a very contrary, terrible Hitler,
> you know. He was a Father. He got word there was going to be a
> camp in Paddy Frank's. What they called a camp was, you know, them
> all used to grow flax at that time. And they'd have a crowd of women
> what they called 'scutching' the flax. You know, kind of yokes for
> pulling the tow out of it, stuff like wadding, you know? And there'd
> be a dance that night, they called it a 'camp'. So he went up to scat-
> ter the nest anyway, landed with a blackthorn stick and had his coat
> up and the old round collar hiding. And he met John James Irwin at
> the road. 'Were you up at the camp?' he says. 'I was.' 'And it's the big
> dance?' 'Oh God, it's a great dance.' says John. 'And there's girls at
> it, and great girls, and a couple of strange lassies there, and they're
> great lassies.' 'Are you going home?' 'No, I'm not going home, I just
> dodged down here to see was there any of our lads from the Bar
> coming.' 'Aw, come on back up,' he says, 'and we'll have a dance.'
> 'Alright.' So, he walked up with John and gave him the whole rates
> of the dance, and what fellow was going with such a lassie, and who
> was playing. And he walked in with Jonty into the dance, and he was
> the first man he hit with the blackthorn when he got in.[59]

The Presbyterian church also exercised great vigilance in relation to
morality. The session book of Templepatrick church details punishments
meted out for various transgressions:

> For immoral conduct, the punishment was generally 'To stand in the
> publique place of repentance before the pulpit, in the face of the
> congregation.' There the culprits had to take up their position,
> Sunday after Sunday, till the Session 'were satisfied with the signs of
> their repentance'. Besides it was enacted 'that all persons standing in
> the public place of repentance shall pay the church officer one groot'
> ... The crimes that most frequently came before the Session were for-
> nication, adultery and sabbath breaking.[60]

It is unclear if these transgressions are themselves listed in order of their
popularity.

There is some debate as to whether the custom of bundling or
'queesting' was ever countenanced in Ireland. Bundling was a courtship
custom which permitted a couple to enjoy the warmth and comfort of
being in bed, which must have been very welcome, especially during the

cold winters' nights when many courtships are likely to have been fur-
thered. Bundlers were not expected to indulge in sexual intercourse, but
even so, the idea that the practice might have been observed in Ireland
seems to run counter to the impression of morality and sexual repression
often associated with Irish life, particularly in the post-Famine period.
Evidence from folklore supported by other sources suggests at least that
some individuals may have been less repressed than others, even during
this period of apparently strict restraint. There is direct reference to
bundling in Co. Fermanagh in the late eighteenth century,[61] and Irish
labourers have been credited with introducing the custom in parts of the
English Fens, where apparently it was enthusiastically adopted.[62]

Local oral tradition also provides accounts of the use of love potions or
charms to attract the attentions of members of the opposite sex. One such
charm could be made by placing a biscuit in the armpit until it is impreg-
nated with sweat, while repeating 'certain incantations'. The following
account deals with the unforeseen consequences of using such a charm,
which was given by a young woman to a man who had caught her eye, and
who responded by teasing her:

> 'You're looking nice. Oh Lord, but it's we'd be happy if I'd my arms
> round you, and was married to you. I see the lassie I love.' And, you
> know, he was only codding her, you see. But anyway, he was going
> over the bog this evening, with a creel of turf on his back. You know
> what I mean by a creel? And he was smoking a pipe, and he met her
> coming from Dowra and, 'God,' he says to her, 'girl I never seen you
> looking as handsome. God I wish I was married to you, I'd be fierce
> happy.' And well, she talked, she says, 'I got you no sweets, but here's
> a nice biscuit for you.' And she gave him the biscuit, when he was
> smoking the pipe, you see? And he says, 'Thanks very much girl, I'll
> eat that when I'm done smoking.' So he put the biscuit in his pocket
> and went on home. Anyway he left the creel of turf at home, and he
> had a bit of foddering at cattle to do, and it came on a horrid, dirty
> wet evening, you know? And, you know, at that time, his clothes was
> all kind of wet. And he came in. He decided he'd go to Dowra and
> have a couple of pints. So, he took the pipe of tobacco and knife and
> matches out of his pocket and threw it on the table, and then he came
> at this biscuit, you know. It got wet, and crumbled in his pocket in
> wee bits. And he threw it out on the floor, do you see? And there
> came in a hen, and the hen picked up the biscuit, and ate it, and by
> God, the next thing, the hen lit up on his trousers and started to

'croo' up at him. And, oh Lord, he went to Dowra and the hen followed him. And he had to get a creel out of a house and put her
under it till he came back, and she followed him. He put her into the
house, he went to bed, and the window was open while he was sleep-
ing, and when he wakened in the morning, the hen came in, and she
was at his lug, lying up against him. You see, it was the charm! The
biscuit. The same lassie was hired after. But I heard about her, and I
asked her about the charm she worked. She told me she'd give it to
me, the charm, if I'd bring her twenty woodbine out of town. And she
did. And I got the charm off her. And I gave it to a couple of lasses.
I do charge them five pound for it.[63]

While those in authority sought to apply acceptable standards of
morality and of behaviour, there were individuals who defied these
efforts. Oral accounts are useful in that they hint at the diversity of individual attitudes which may actually have obtained in any given regime
and which must often have been at odds with the views of authority.
During the eighteenth and nineteenth centuries, marriage legislation was
increasingly tightened, but in earlier times there was a degree of confusion as to exactly what constituted a marriage. In the late medieval
period, it was generally expected that betrothal or a contract of marriage
would be followed by a ceremony overseen by the Church, but in four-
teenth-century Armagh 'formal contracts of concubinage' were drawn up
and observed. It is also clear that at this time marriage contracts were frequently prepared, and in Ireland, as in England, in instances of bigamy
'the church always upheld the earlier valid contract. This it did even if the
first marriage was made clandestinely and the second in church.' [64]
Official distinctions were drawn between contracts made in the present
tense and those made in the future, but confusion must often have
abounded over the difference between the agreement to marry and the
marriage.

Changes in social structure and the weakening of parental control over
the choice of marriage partner meant that by the early twentieth century
the agreement to marry was again becoming increasingly important to
young couples throughout the British Isles. The public statement of intent
which was made by becoming formally engaged, symbolized by the giving and wearing of a specially designated ring, gathered significance.[65]

Increased exploitation of diamond mines played a part in establishing
the diamond as the gem appropriate to symbolize the intention to marry,
and the engagement ring was sometimes popularly understood as an

Advertisement for engagements rings from *Veterinary Hygiene*, published Omagh, 1925. By this date, engagement rings, which began to become popular in the 1880s, were considered *de rigueur* by most aspiring young women, and to advertise in this publication suggests a shrewd marketing ploy. *UFTM archive.*

investment or insurance which might be cashed in in case of widowhood. In the late nineteenth and early twentieth centuries, advertisements for engagement rings appeared in many publications produced in the northern part of Ireland. One was even included in a handbook on Veterinary Hygiene published in Omagh during the 1920s; and, in 1894, one Belfast jeweller advertised having 'completed the mounting of the finest stock of Diamond Rings ever offered in Ireland, ranging from 40/-d. to £150'. While some of these settings conform to the fashion of the time, others are forerunners of styles which became popular for engagement rings in the present century. By 1900, increasing numbers of prospective brides expected a gem-set ring as a token of a promise to marry, and as the twentieth century progressed this practice became increasingly established.

4 The Wedding

In medieval times, attitudes to marriage ceremonial in Ireland were paralleled in many parts of Europe. While canon law began to be established, it was still popular to marry without the sanction of the Church, or at least without being present in a church building.[1] At this time too, the Gaelic way of life regularized by the Brehon court was still observed by many, while new ideas and attitudes often of English origin were being introduced in some areas of the country. Social and religious complexities continued to colour the picture of Irish wedding observance, and it is only within the last hundred and fifty years that the registration of marriage has been legally required. Ireland was, therefore, among the last countries in Europe to have marriage registration successfully imposed.

Some of the implications of this state of affairs may be inferred from the account of the trial for bigamy of one Abraham Black at Queen's County Assizes (now Co. Laois) in March 1845, only a matter of days before the 1844 Marriage Act came into effect. It was claimed that, in 1806, Black had married one Mary Anne Hayden. Some twenty-five years later he had also married a Margaret Larke, 'the said Mary Anne Hayden being then alive'. The evidence against Black included that of a Matthew Mansfield who 'knows the prisoner well, he was formerly married to Mary Anne Hayden ... they were married in the Church of Mountmellick by the Rev Mr Saurin, [Mansfield] was by at the time, and saw and heard the ceremony, to the best of his belief it was in 1809 or 1810, not of a Sunday, but on a clear, warm day ... '[2] Various other witnesses also swore that the marriage had taken place, but in the absence of written evidence, it was decided that the case was 'a monstrous one got up against Mr Black', who was acquitted. In this instance, a register had in fact been kept, but an entry for 1806 had been erased. Registers from earlier periods were sometimes maintained, but it was not until the 1840s that the practice was successfully enforced. Fewer difficulties beset the first Earl Annesley when in 1797 he married the wife of his brother's gardener, despite the technicality that she already had a husband.[3]

Apart from the question of registration of marriage, there were many complexities in the situation which prevailed prior to the 1840s. Connolly gives the following insight into some of these:

> Archbishop King, writing in 1723, accepted that 'the communion of saints' required him to take as valid the orders of Catholic priests who had conformed to the Church of Ireland, provided they could produce proof of having been ordained by a properly qualified person. The civil law also accepted the validity of Catholic orders in that it recognised marriages between Catholics celebrated by a priest as valid, even though marriages performed by Protestant dissenting clergymen were not.[4]

The importance of the 1844 Marriage Act and the tangled situations which it sought to address are reflected by a contemporary report in the *Belfast Newsletter*:

> The new marriage law on this day comes into operation. We fear that the measures necessary for diffusing the general knowledge of its provisions, and making actual preparation for its introduction, have not been resorted to by the proper authorities so promptly as was desirable. We question whether there be, at this moment, one place of worship registered, although no marriage can be celebrated where registration has not been effected. Our object is not to impute blame. However, the fact is as we state, and, further, instructions have only the other day been issued, and generally posted, for the guidance of parties seeking marriage. On account of the importance of the subject, we purpose furnishing, in this article, a distinct and popular view of the matters most needful to be known.
>
> It is to be remembered that the marriages by Roman Catholic Priests are not affected by this law. Such may proceed as formerly. We consider this renders the Bill defective, for there will be no permanent or national record made of any marriages that do not come under the provisions of the Act. Probably the Government excluded the Priests from the enactment, in order to avoid agitation for the repeal of the existing statute, which declares to be *null and void any marriage by a Priest between a Catholic and a Protestant*. We may have occasion to refer to this at another time. Meanwhile the above sentence, given in italics, should be well noted, inasmuch as we know, personally, instances in which such marriages, mere nullities according to law, have been wantonly ventured on, and encouraged.[5]

Even the provision of this Act did not ensure full registration of marriage, which was not to be achieved until several years later.

From the sixteenth century on, various attempts were made to regularize marriage practices in Ireland. During the 1540s, an Act for Marriages laid down:

> That from the first day of July past, in the year of our Lord God 1540, all and every such marriage as within this Church of Ireland hath or shall be so contracted betwixt lawfull persons, as by this act, we declare all persons to be lawfull, that be not prohibited by God's law to marriage, such marriages being contracted and solemnised in the face of the church, and consummate with bodily knowledge or fruit of children or child being had therein betwixt the parties so married, shall be by authority of this present Parliament ... deemed, judged and taken to be lawfull ...[6]

Cranmer's Second Edition of the Book of Common Prayer, which appeared during the following decade, 'had and continues to have a strong impact on the social order'[7] of the country. At about the same time, the Catholic Church was also seeking to establish greater regularization of marriage practice. The Tametsi Decree of the Council of Trent, promulgated in the 1560s, required that an authorized priest and two or more witnesses be present at a valid Catholic marriage ceremony. The synod of 1587 in turn promulgated this, along with other Tridentine decrees, but various factors, such as the delicacy of the structure of the Catholic Church in Ireland increased the difficulties of enforcement.

Among the provisions required to make a marriage valid was the 'publication' (or announcement) of the 'Banns of Marriage' for three successive Sundays by the Established Church. These announcements encouraged the expression of any doubts about the validity of the proposed marriage. Those Catholics who could afford to do so evaded the need to have the banns published by buying an appropriate licence.[8] While many may have chosen to seek ecclesiastical ratification, secular marriage continued to be the order of the day.[9]

Both the Catholic and the Established Churches appear to have experienced difficulties in their attempts to regularize marriage practices. This may have been compounded by a fear on the part of Catholic priests that the keeping of a register of marriages might constitute evidence to be used against them under the Penal Code, but it was also part of a general social picture in which ideas about marriage were still influenced at least to some degree by a way of life which had prevailed in earlier times.[10] As the seventeenth century progressed, 'the fundamentals of Christian Marriage' may have gained increasing ground, but in the mid 1630s Wentworth could write to Archbishop Laud:

> They are accustomed here to have all their Christenings and marriages in their private houses ... This breeds great mischief in the Commonwealth

... because these rites of the church are not solemnised in the Public and Open Assemblies, there is nothing so common as for a man to deny his wife and children, abandoning the former and betaking himself to a new task.[11]

This state of affairs was to persist for centuries. Two hundred years later, in the mid 1830s, the Rev. James Crook, Resident Priest of St Austin's in Manchester, told the Poor Inquiry that his migrant Irish parishioners frequently 'are not married at all in church, and no inducement will take them there. I always warn the female that the marriage is not valid in the eye of the law, and the man may leave her at any time. I have heard of cases where husbands have left their wives under these circumstances.'[12] The Rev. Daniel Hearne, Resident Priest of St Patrick's Church in George's Fields, also in Manchester, agreed. Hearne was himself a native of Co. Tipperary, who had been educated at Maynooth. Like the Rev. James Crook, he expressed concern that the 'law with regard to Catholic marriages in England tends to the most crying and shameful abuses'. He forthrightly declared, 'I do not make it a practice to exhort the parties to be married legally, and I never refuse to marry those of my own flock in whom I find no impediment.'[13] A similar stance was no doubt adopted by many other Catholic priests in England, where legal changes were made in 1837.

In mid seventeenth-century Ireland, the collapse of the authority of the Established Church as a consequence of Cromwellian policy led to additional difficulties in maintaining control of marriage practices.[14] A statute of 1653 authorized civil marriage, to be conducted by Justices of the Peace.[15] This appears to have been quite popular. By the end of the century, it was increasingly apparent that marriage legislation with a secular basis be passed, for the purpose of 'safeguarding of property'.[16] The tangle between Church and State has been succinctly explained:

Because of the distinctive features of the Irish situation in the matter of property, these laws were ... directed to regulating marriages between Catholics and members of the Established church conducted by irregular clergymen with a special eye on Catholic clergymen, because being in valid orders they could celebrate regular marriages except insofar as they were restricted by statute law.[17]

Several Marriage Acts were passed during the course of the eighteenth century, the purpose of that of 1745 being to annul marriages 'to be celebrated by any popish priest between Protestant and Protestant, or between Protestant and Papist'.[18] There may have been general concern to halt any extension of the Catholic Church in Ireland, and in the mid to late eighteenth century some steps were taken to attempt to relieve difficulties experienced by members of dis-senting Protestant sects. By the end of the 1700s, the position of Presbyterians had been improved, in comparison to that of the early part of the century. In 1716: 'Four members of Tullylish congregation [Gilford, Co. Down] were ... delivered over to Satan by episcopal authority for the high crime of being mar-ried by their own minister, the Rev. Gilbert Kennedy.'[19] It is likely that the offenders were punished by being imprisoned.[20]

In the late seventeenth century, certain Church of Ireland bishops began to protest that Presbyterian marriages were of dubious legality,[21] and in 1711 the clergy of Dublin decreed that public penance be required of anyone involved in marriages other than those solemnized by the Church of Ireland.[22] The prob-lem may have related at least in part to difficulties experienced over the need to publish the banns, although this could be done within their own congrega-tion. It seems that there were widely differing views on the need to comply with this requirement. Mrs Delany wrote approvingly in December 1752 of one young couple about to wed that 'they are to be asked in the church – Lord Limerick's daughter was – and so now it will be the fashion, and I think a very good one', [23] a remark which seems to imply a degree of difficulty in enforcing the need to publish the banns even among members of the Established Church. Presbyterians with a distaste for the public proclamation of the banns, but very fastidious about the legality of their union sometimes opted to be married by licence under the auspices of the Established Church, thus incurring punish-ment from their own congregations.[24] At the beginning of the eighteenth cen-tury, it was decreed that a Presbyterian minister who married a couple without a declaration of the banns should be punished by suspension,[25] but many disre-garded this, adding to the difficulties of controlling marriage practices.[26]

Even in the seventeenth century, some Presbyterian couples were happy to proclaim their intention to marry. The register kept by the congregation at Antrim records the purpose of marriage between 'Mr John Mare of county Down and Margaret Gilcrist of this Town' who 'were marryed Sept. 18th 1677'.[27] Several Presbyterian congregations kept registers during the seventeenth and eighteenth centuries. These record instances of the event of marriage, of 'pur-poses' of marriage (the calling of the banns) and of the 'purposes' followed after an interval which should have been of between two and six weeks by the mar-riage itself. It has been suggested that the purpose of marriage might be recorded in preference to the event itself in order to ensure that any 'Visitation Presbytery' would be satisfied that the regulations had been properly observed.[28] The payment of any necessary fees may also have been a consideration. In Templepatrick congregation, a fee of one shilling was levied for recording a purpose of marriage. For the marriage itself, the fee was eight shillings.

Throughout the eighteenth century, Presbyterian ministers encountered reluctance towards publishing banns on the part of their congregations, and attempts to call them to account had little effect. Early in the nineteenth century it was deemed sufficient to publish the banns on one Sunday instead of on three, and soon afterwards publication was made optional.

An Act passed in 1782 confirmed the right of Presbyterians to be married to one another according to their own form, and extended this right to other dissenting sects.[29] Following this provision, civil courts were prepared to accept the validity of marriages celebrated accordingly, irrespective of whether one of the involved partners was a member of the Established Church, but confusion eventually arose, apparently encouraged by the stance taken by a Church court. In 1840, a dispute over succession to an estate was taken before the Consistorial Court at Armagh. The decision reached was based on the view that the marriage involved was invalid, as it involved both a Presbyterian and a member of the Established Church.[30] This precedent was tested the next year, when a case of bigamy was brought before the Armagh Assizes. The issue was over the validity of the first marriage of the Episcopalian man accused, as this ceremony had been performed by a Presbyterian clergyman. The case was eventually 'extensively argued' before the Queen's Bench, and the final decision was that the first marriage had not been valid. This had far-reaching implications, particularly in the north of Ireland, where many marriages were founded on the belief that this difficulty had been resolved so many years before. Not surprisingly, Presbyterians felt particularly aggrieved at this calling into question of their rights, and the very legitimacy of many families was brought into doubt by the decision, adding to the need for the legislation eventually passed in 1844.

In addition to difficulties experienced as a consequence of relationships between the Established Church and other denominations, there were also differences of opinion with regard to marriage within individual religious groups. As an example, the urge to reform marriage practices among the Society of Friends might be considered. By 1800, modifications similar to those introduced in 1790 among English Quakers had been accepted in Ireland, but many members of the society wanted greater modernization. Two of those bent on reform, John Rogers and Elizabeth Doyle, decided in defiance of Lurgan Monthly Meeting to marry in March 1801 without observing certain established formalities, which they did in a room at Prospect Hill School, where Miss Doyle was a teacher. The couple had the permission of the school's headmaster, George Thompson, whose support of reform was soon to cost him his job.[31]

Many attempts of civil and religious authorities to take control of marriage practices met with varying types of resistance. In medieval Ireland, Church

Nigel and Naomi Green were married in Lisburn Cathedral in the mid 1960s. It was quite unusual for a photographer to intrude on the ceremony, even from a respectful distance. This image of bride and groom in church with attendants seems to epitomize the 'traditional' wedding, but is not typical of all denominations, and until the 1840s, a private ceremony at home was much more common. The bride's classical gown with lace overdress is a perfect example of one of the fashions of the decade. *UFTM L3180/5 and 6.*

rules of affinity were often disregarded, and many of those both Gaelic and Anglo-Irish who sought papal dispensation on these grounds waited to do so until after they had married.[32] In the post-Restoration era, Catholics having paid a fee to the Established Church were usually free to be married by a Catholic priest.[33] Some denominations frowned upon members who did not conform to their own marriage regulations. As late as 1860, Quakers marrying 'before a priest' might be subject to disownment, and even to attend a wedding other than one among members of the Society would be to risk severe punishment.[34] Although it had methods of endorsing them, the Catholic Church did not generally favour mixed marriage. The 1844 Act validated marriage of a Catholic to a Protestant if conducted by a civil registrar, although in practice such a marriage would probably be ratified before a Catholic priest. Legislation of the early 1870s validated mixed marriage before a Catholic priest, but such a marriage in a Catholic church was prohibited by ecclesiastical law. These could be held in the sacristy, and sometimes took place in the church itself. Although ecclesiastical law demanded that all children of such a marriage be brought up as Catholics, this was not strictly enforced until the *Ne temere* decree came into effect in 1908. Prior to this, it was common practice for sons to belong to their father's denomination, daughters to their mother's.[35] Despite the strictures of *Ne temere*, it was not unheard of for members of the Catholic Church to convert to Protestantism as a consequence of marriage.[36] In the case of mixed marriages among Protestant denominations, a common practice evolved of marrying in the church of the bride, after which the family adhered to the faith followed by the husband. On 8 January 1892, Annie Roy was married in Dunmurry, outside Belfast, as her marriage certificate describes 'according to the Form and Discipline of the Presbyterian church'. It may accurately be deduced that the bridegroom was Church of Ireland, as on 5 September 1927, one of their daughters was married, according to her marriage certificate, by 'the Rites and Ceremonies' of that denomination. Annie lies buried in Drumbeg Parish churchyard with the rest of the bridegroom's family.

There were many social pressures against marrying across the 'religious divide' between Catholic and Protestant. In an article published by the *Belfast Telegraph* on 30 June 1994, the Portadown-born broadcaster and television personality Gloria Hunniford recalled her wedding in 1961 to Don Keating, a Catholic. Gloria's father was a member of the Orange Order, which meant her parents could not attend the ceremony. Despite their absence from the event, a compromise was quickly reached and harmony prevailed, but this is not always the case.[37]

Many aspects of popular practice help to complicate the picture further, sometimes by taking advantage of the difficulties arising from attempts to reg-

ularize behaviour. In eighteenth-century England, irregular marriages conducted either by the clergy or by lay persons were common enough.[38] In
Ireland, this was the case both in much earlier [39] and in later times. The person
who officiated at a wedding without strictly being entitled to do so was known
either as a 'couple-beggar' or as a 'buckle-beggar'. A clear account of these
individuals has been supplied by Sean Connolly, who describes them as 'suspended clergymen and others who had taken up the business of celebrating
marriages as a means of earning a living':

> The majority of these couple-beggars were clergymen of either the Catholic
> Church or the Established Church. Some had been deprived of their offices
> on account of a breach of ecclesiastical discipline and had turned to clan-
> destine marriages as an alternative source of income. Others were Catholic
> priests who had conformed to the Established Church but had not been
> offered livings there. Others again may simply have been attracted by the
> money. Certainly the £1,000 reported to have been left on his death in 1737
> by Samuel D'Assigny, 'the famous couple-beggar', would have compared
> very favourably with what the great majority of Catholic clergymen in this
> period – and many of their Protestant counterparts also – could have hoped
> to end their lives with. D'Assigny, however, while regularly officiating in
> clerical dress, had never been in orders of any kind, and he was not the only
> layman to set himself up as a couple-beggar in this period.[40]

Among the irregularities countenanced by such individuals was the marrying
of people adhering to different religious denominations, particularly Catholics
to Protestants. In the 1820s, it appears one such couple-beggar was imprisoned
for doing exactly this. Undeterred, he continued to conduct marriages while
incarcerated.[41] When the renowned Dublin whore Margaret Leeson married
Barry Yelverton, whose father was later created Lord Avonmore, the ceremony
was quickly performed by a couple-beggar 'but not 'till the marriage articles
were properly ratified, signed, sealed and delivered, in the presence of my
friends'.[42] This marriage was so notorious that the bride's father-in-law soon
heard of it and persuaded her to terminate the arrangement in return for five
hundred guineas.[43] When Lord Glentworth, the son of Lord Limerick, married
an impoverished young woman in 1808, he took the precaution of following up
a ceremony performed by one Mr Murphy, evidently a buckle-beggar, with a
ceremony in Gretna Green. While a marriage performed by a buckle-beggar
might have been easily terminated in circumstances like these, the Scottish
marriage was accepted as valid.[44]

Some buckle-beggars seem to have regarded the calling as hereditary. In
1788, a Catholic church was built at Raloo in Co. Antrim:

The Reverend James McCarry, a friar, was the first priest. He was dis-
graced ... by having a female child sworn on him. This child, when she
came to the age of maturity, was tried at the Assizes for marrying people
in the absence of her father. Her father, after he was degraded became
what is locally called a 'buckle-beggar'.[45]

Although he might not appreciate the suggestion, it is tempting to relate to this
the late twentieth-century activities of Fr Pat Buckley who, despite having had
certain disagreements with the Catholic hierarchy, continues in a perfectly
legal if not entirely official manner to conduct certain religious services,
including marriage. He, too, is active in Co. Antrim, where, among other
things, he runs a support group for women who have been involved in intimate
relationships with members of the Catholic clergy.[46]

Deposed Presbyterian ministers and probationers [47] also occasionally acted
as buckle-beggars, and 'sometimes a minister who had demitted his charge
without being deprived of his office, did a very large trade in irregular marriages'.[48] Evidence from the Ordnance Survey memoirs suggests that, by the
1830s, at least in some regions, the official way of going about things had been
completely stood on its head: 'The Protestants prefer being married in their
own houses to avoid the bustle, noise and staring attendant upon a marriage in
church and therefore apply to the Presbyterian ministers.'[49] If Presbyterian
ministers were endorsing irregular marriages of this sort between non-
Presbyterians, this may help explain the increasing severity of the authorities
of the Established Church with regard to Presbyterian marriage in general. In
addition to clarifying the legality and validity of various religious forms of
marriage, the 1844 Act endorsed civil marriage by registrar. Popular attitudes
preferred a religious ceremony to a civil one, however, and in some areas
Register Office weddings were described as performed 'by the Buckle
Beggar'.[50]

The writer of the Ordnance Survey Memoir for the parish of Clonleigh,
near Lifford in Co. Donegal, composed in 1821, remarks: 'The marriages are
celebrated here usually in the church when the parties are of the Established
religion. The Roman Catholics and Dissenters are married in private houses.'[51]
Whether or not this distinction between denominations was widespread, the
preference for marrying at home, noted in the seventeenth century by
Wentworth as already described, was still strong in the nineteenth. Writing of
mid nineteenth century-Co. Kerry, the Halls explain: 'If the bride's father or
brother be a "strong farmer, who can afford to furnish a good dinner," the marriage takes place at the bride's house.' [52] Catholic weddings were also celebrated at the home of the officiating priest. In Co. Down in the mid 1830s, we

hear: 'Marriages are celebrated either at the house of one of the parties or more commonly at the priest's house (never at the parish chapel) on which occasion the priest receives 5s. for performing the ceremony and the Bishop 5s. more for his licence.' [53]

The Act of 1844 did not legislate for Catholic marriage, which was more subject to common and to ecclesiastical laws than to civil statute. In fact, the authorities of the Catholic Church were less than encouraging about regulations imposed by the state.[54] Strictly speaking, until 1870, a marriage performed by a Catholic priest between a Catholic and a non-Catholic was 'null and void'. [55] The National Synod of 1850 decreed that the practice of celebrating marriage, baptism and other services in private houses be discontinued. In order to enforce this ruling, it was decided that, if the regulation was overlooked, the right to a fee for performing the ceremony was forfeit. [56] The disestablishment of the Church of Ireland led in 1870 to another Act which clarified consequent matters of administration in relation to marriage and also dealt with aspects of the problem raised by marriages between Protestants and Roman Catholics. [57] A further amendment a year later made additional provision for intermarriage and established the legality of such marriages if celebrated by a Catholic clergyman.[58] In spite of earlier Acts and synodal decrees, situations which illustrated the need for the Acts of the 1870s could and did arise. The notorious case of the 'Yelverton Marriage' in the mid nineteenth century makes the point. Miss Longworth, a young Catholic woman of aristocratic background, was one of those who devoted herself to nursing the injured of the Crimea. In the course of this work she met and fell in love with the Hon. Major Yelverton, and they were subsequently married at Killowen near Rostrevor in Co. Down by Fr Mooney. The marriage was unsuccessful and Yelverton, heir to a peerage, married again. Unfortunately for Miss Longworth, who might have expected that precedence would have been in her favour, her marriage was the one finally declared invalid, but not before the case was brought in front of the House of Lords.[59] The Honorable Major Yelverton was the great-grandson of the father-in-law of Margaret Leeson, whose marriage had been so speedily dissolved in the previous century – coincidentally Margaret Leeson was also a Catholic.

In the late eighteenth and early nineteenth centuries, the question of the priest's fees was the focus of considerable attention. Among the objections registered by the Rightboy Movement was a dislike of paying priests' dues for weddings and other ceremonies.[60] Methods of paying the fee varied. Apparently at Catholic weddings in England, when the groom placed cash, symbolic of his worldly goods, on the priest's book, the fee would be taken and the rest given to the bride.[61] In south Armagh until the turn of the present century, the priest could augment the fee he received from the couple by 'selling the bridecake':

> [T]he priest arose, and went round with the bridecake, which he sold in pieces to the men and women present. Each one paid him for his or her slice, taking the piece of cake and dropping the money on the plate instead of it. When the priest had gone the entire rounds of the company, he took the proceeds from the plate, and put them in his pocket, and he shortly afterwards took his departure from the house. This habit of 'selling the bridecake' by the priest is very prevalent at weddings of poor Catholics throughout the north of Ireland ... the proceeds of the sale of the bridecake ... at this servant girl's wedding, I am told by an eyewitness, amounted to over £5.[62]

Priests were subject to considerable criticism for such habits, although their dependence on such fees for their income was widely acknowledged, and many commentators were in favour of the abolition of the system of paying dues, recommending that it should be replaced by 'an allowance from public funds'.[63] In their description of a Kerry wedding, the Halls remark:

> [B]efore he is married, [the groom] pays down to the priest the marriage fee according to his circumstances. The friends of both parties are also called upon to pay down something, and between their reluctance to meet the demand and the priest's refusal to marry them till he is satisfied, a scene, sometimes humorous and sometimes discreditable, often arises ... The cost of the ceremony is ... very considerable; and not unfrequently, the bride and bridegroom have to begin life within empty walls, their savings barely sufficient to recompense the priest for uniting them. We have indeed known instances in which Roman Catholics have been married by a clergyman of the Church of England, in consequence of the small expense of the ceremony there; being resolved to become 'one', and finding it utterly impossible to collect a sum sufficient to induce the priest to marry them; such cases, however are of rare occurrence.[64]

Many observers of the Irish social scene in the early nineteenth century comment on the difficulties which could be caused by the need to find fees for the essential ceremonies of baptism and of the churching of women, as well as for marriage.[65] In 1836, it was reported of the area of Clonlish in Co. Offaly:

> Labourers usually marry between the ages of 17 and 20. The first things provided are the priest's fee and the expenses of the wedding: they also endeavour to get a quarter of an acre of potatoes. They often marry before they have a cabin, or take lodgings or live with their parents.[66]

Some critics of the system of paying of dues hinted that priests actually encouraged early marriage in order to improve their incomes.[67]

This idea is echoed in a story from Co. Cavan, in which the priest supports
the wishes of the bride's family to proceed with a wedding although the bridegroom has certain reservations:

> 'They're very persistent,' he says, 'they have the wedding day appointed
> for such a day. I didn't want the wedding day at all,' he says, 'because I
> have no money, no marriage money, till I sell the pigs in the fair. I have a
> crowd of young pigs,' he says, 'be ready for sale, the fair day.' Fair day
> would be about a week after the wedding. 'And therefore,' he says, 'I
> don't want the wedding at all,' he says, 'because I've no marriage money
> to give you, except you marry me till I sell the pigs in the fair.' 'Oh, get
> married,' he says, 'it'll be time enough till the fair day, to you pay me the
> marriage money.'
>
> And Jesus the fair day anyway, all from about ten o'clock on the day he
> [the priest] was marching up and down the road from Curran's to the min-
> ister's gate watching for your man [the groom] to come. However, he
> came up the road on the jaunting cart, singing, half drunk, 'How are you,
> you old devil,' he says, 'you didn't mind the curse of the town with you
> anyhow, you're well ... you're well lined up with whiskey.' 'Oh I had a
> few, I had a few, Father, alright.' 'What kind of a fair was it?' 'The best
> fair ever I was at.' 'You sold the pigs?' 'I did sell the pigs,' he says, 'and
> by God,' he says, 'if I'd a hundred pigs I could sell them. I never was at a
> better fair in my life.' 'I'm waiting a long time, what about that marriage
> money?' 'What marriage money?' he says, 'Well damn me, Father,' he
> says, 'I'll treble your marriage money if you'll leave me the way you got
> me, can you do it? I'll treble it.' [68]

It seems that the plan backfired on all concerned.

It was believed in some parts of the country that charms could be used to
counter marriage vows. A jealous rival of the bride, probably a jilted former
sweetheart of the bridegroom, might answer 'I do not' under her breath when
the bride agreed to take the groom as her husband and to other important questions in the ceremony, each time putting a knot in a handkerchief. Michael J.
Murphy explains:

> [T]he 'charm' was said to fall on the husband. I've been told of girls who
> were killed because of this belief. I can't even hint how the practising of
> such a charm was discovered, but when it was discovered the girl was
> compelled, often at knife point, to undo each knot and to untie her words.[69]

Other charms, or curses might also be invoked, the intention being to cause sterility for the couple. Similar charms were believed to be used for other purposes, for example to condemn a house following an eviction.

The wedding of Arabella and William Ward, which took place at Killinchy on 27 March 1845, as described by the bride's mother in a letter to her aunt, Jane Mahon, is in very marked contrast to that of the Cavan couple, and gives a clear picture of a society wedding which occurred a few days before the 1844 Act came into effect:

> We had indeed a great gathering, and it was all allowed to be a brilliant wedding ... Captain Nugent met her at the Church door and led her up the Aisle and gave her away and she was followed up by her 10 Bridesmaids in the following order; her 2 sisters; M.A. Richards and E. Moore; Miss Forbes and little Louisa; all in pink. Then (in blue) Miss Reilly and H. Dillon; and 2 Miss Reillys. They formed a semicircle behind as she stood at the Communion rails. 2 sisters held her gloves, another her bouquet, another her handkerchief, another her Vinaigrette. Her old mother and Lady Bangor sat in the corner behind the pulpit, not being considered ornamental. The Church was crammed full and as the procession came up the Aisle they say the people all gave utterance to their transports of admiration and joy by an unusual clicking of their tongues (a noise for which there is no name) but the moment the service began there was breathless attention and every word was audibly uttered. Henry's voice trembled very much at first and he was very pale which put me in a fright but he soon recovered himself and you know how well and solemnly he reads the service. When it was concluded William raised the veil and in the true old fashioned style kissed the bride and handed her out of Church. It was really a beautiful sight and many I believe were present who joined with all their hearts in prayer for the Lord's blessing upon both.[70]

By the late nineteenth century, music made an important contribution to the ceremonial of many Anglican marriages, although at this date musical instruments were not to be countenanced in Presbyterian places of worship. Music had (and in general still has) no contribution to make to Quaker weddings. In July, 1889, *Irish Society* carried a report of the wedding of a young heiress, Miss Atkins, to Dr Joseph Boyd, which took place at St Patrick's Church, Monkstown, Co. Dublin: 'The exquisite wreath, the floral decorations and the choral service all contributed to make the nuptial Mass, performed by the Archdeacon of Dublin, the most imposing ceremonial of the kind that has been witnessed in this church for many years.' By the 1890s, reports of society weddings often include the fact that the 'service was full choral' and it had become popular for the bride to leave the church to the strains of Mendelssohn's 'Wedding March'.

The issue of the appropriateness of music, or of certain types of music at wedding services is still controversial. In 1990, the editorial of an edition of the provincial evening paper, the *Belfast Telegraph*, commented:

> A developing trend towards the playing of pop music at church wedding ceremonies has been exercising the minds of the Irish Catholic Bishops. They say that 'secular love songs' may be in order at the reception, but are out of keeping with the sacred character of the wedding ceremony itself. ... [T]he Bishops also expressed reservations about the use of the Wedding March and Ave Maria, neither of which they considered to reflect the richness of the religious service. There is no doubt that in an increasingly secular world, the religious significance of the marriage may be in danger of being overshadowed by the celebrations at the reception. In highlighting the sacredness of the wedding service, the Bishops will have struck a chord with many people. But a distinction should surely be drawn between pop songs and music such as the Wedding March, which is synonymous with the occasion and does not seem out of place in a church. Music has an important part to play in the service and can add to feelings of jubilation and celebration without diminishing its religious significance.[71]

The music played at church weddings has even given rise to an urban legend. The immensely popular 'Everything I do, I do for you', from *Robin Hood, Prince of Thieves* has played a part at many recent weddings. According to the story, one bride who wished to walk down the aisle to this accompaniment asked the organist for the theme to *Robin Hood*. She entered the church to the strains of 'Robin Hood, Robin Hood, Riding through the Glen'.

While the part to be played by music during marriage ceremonies may be the subject of some debate, there seems to have been less difficulty over the matter of decorating the church. When, in 1907, Miss Emily Acheson of Portadown married the Rev. John Irwin, MA, minister of Windsor Presbyterian church, Belfast, their wedding took place in First Presbyterian Church, Portadown, 'the chancel of which was tastefully arranged with palms and flowers'.[72]

If a marriage took place in church rather than at home, the problem arose of transporting the bride to church. Those who could afford to could travel by carriage, and the mother of the bride sometimes saw to it that this possibility was used to full advantage: 'We had posters [postillions?] to our brougham, and I made the bride sit with her back to the horses, as there was glass all round to show her off to the populace.'[73] In this account, the bride travels to church with her mother, to be met by her father and the bridesmaids. Her mother must follow the procession up the aisle and 'sit behind the pulpit' during the ceremony. Nowadays, of course, it is customary for the arrival of the mother of the bride, who enters the church alone and who sits in the front pew on the 'bride's side', to signal that the arrival of the bride herself is imminent.

Francilla Stevenson gives an account of a late nineteenth-century country wedding which took place in Drumclamph townland, in west Co. Tyrone. All the evidence hints at the splendour of the occasion:

[The bride was] the daughter of one of the most important church wardens. She taught in the Sunday School and was a member of the church choir and on the Committee of the Temperance Society. The church was decorated and the rector's wife played the Wedding March and the choir sang 'The voice that breathed o'er Eden', but I haven't the slightest recollection of how she was dressed. It was the only time I ever saw the carriage drive up to the church door and the wedding guests' cars allowed to come into the graveyard, other brides generally alighted at the church gate and walked into the church. When it was all over and the cars had departed, the graveyard looked as if a hurricane or whirlwind had blown over it or through it. The horses had trampled down the grass, and the carriage wheels had cut the grass verges and dug up the stones in the drive and I remember the verger lamenting about the destruction, and wondering how it would ever be brought back to its normal condition.[74]

The horse or horses which drew the wedding vehicle might be appropriately decked out. The collection of the Ulster Folk and Transport Museum includes a white crochet ear decoration intended to be worn by the horse which pulled the bride's jaunting car. An account from Co. Tyrone written in the mid 1960s reads:

I can remember 60-65 years ago seeing wedding parties passing our school. After the carriages 1-3 or 4 had passed (the horses wearing white glove-like covers on their ears from which tassels dangled) there would be a 'procession' of jaunting cars – a dozen or maybe more – with besides the driver on the 'dickey,' a fiddler playing merrily as the horses trotted by.[75]

The tremendous popularity of the bicycle during the late Victorian and Edwardian eras meant that it, too, was a means of travelling to a wedding. Around the turn of the twentieth century there was a fashion for 'Bicycle Weddings'. Bride, groom, best man and bridesmaid would travel to church on bicycles decorated with flowers in honour of the day.

Picturesque early twentieth-century bicycle wedding, Co. Fermanagh. Motoring veils must have been equally useful when travelling by car or by bicycle, and provided an interesting and fashionable means of veiling the face. *UFTM L3339/2.*

Couples also travelled to church on horseback, but perhaps the commonest means of transport was on foot. Mrs Delany describes the wedding of Dr Sandford and Miss Chapone in a letter written from Delville in early October 1764: 'All met here at eleven, the sun shone bright, and we proceeded in order through the garden to church.' [76] The bride and groom often travelled to church together, a situation which still obtained in many parts of Ulster in the mid twentieth century.[77] The idea that it was unlucky for the groom to see the bride before the wedding was slow to gain ground. Danaher describes how, in Donegal, the wedding procession walked to the church, the bride and best man walking at its head, immediately followed by the groom and the chief brides-maid.[78]

Although by the late nineteenth century the church wedding had become the norm, some weddings still took place, by special licence, at home. Certain cir-cumstances, perhaps the death of a close family member might dictate that weddings took place at home, but there is evidence to suggest that home wed-dings were considered rather stylish. Etiquette books offered advice on how the home might be prepared for a wedding:

An arch of flowers may be placed in the drawing room, under which the young couple stand, with the clergymen behind it. The bridal party enters as in church, and after they have been pronounced man and wife, they turn and face their guests, receiving their congratulations.[79]

On 24 June 1901, Eleanor Gilmore, then in mourning, wished to marry at home, and must have done so by special licence. White was an acceptable colour for mourning, but the fashionable dress of the couple repays examination. The groom, Robert Johnson, was a saddler with premises in North Street, Belfast. *UFTM L3036/5.*

The collection of the Ulster Folk and Transport Museum includes a beautiful gown of tan Irish poplin believed to have been worn by Miss Margretta Adams for her wedding to Robert Dunlop, which is understood to have taken place in the drawing room of Ashville House, Antrim, in August 1877.[80]

For various reasons, some couples decided to marry secretly. Paddy Gallagher's account of his own wedding, which took place at about the turn of the century, illustrates some of the considerations which might lead a couple to this choice:

> Sally and I decided to get married, but we did not want our parents to know it; I especially, as I should not leave them for another few years as my earnings were badly wanted at home. We got married on a Sunday evening in Dungloe. Sally had her sister Madgie for best maid and I had a cousin for best man. Sally went to her own home in the town with her sister, after the marriage. I went to my own home in Cleendra, and when I got a chance I packed up my clothes and slipped out after dark without telling any person. I stayed in the town with a friend of mine that night.
>
> I was up early next morning as Sally and I had arranged to go to Scotland. I waited at the corner until I saw her coming up the street with her shawl over her head. I was very happy, but when she came my length she was crying. I think I was crying too. When we got up on the side-car, who came round the corner only Sally's father. He reached his hand to Sally, and I am sure he gave her the last penny he had in the world ... He shook hands with me and said, 'I wish Sally and you every luck. May God's blessing be on you. I hope you'll be good to Sally.'[81]

Other couples may have remained living separately, on a semi-permanent or even a permanent basis. Both the following oral accounts relate to Co. Antrim. The first was recorded in the Ballinderry area, in the south of the county, the second near Ballymena, some twenty miles (32 km) to the north:

> They were cutting corn this day in the field, and womenfolk always had to tie it. It's cut with a horse drawn machine, and then it's cut in swathes and it had to be tied by hand. So this was the morning of her wedding day and she wasn't allowed to go to get married, nor they didn't know anything about this, the parents didn't know anything about this at all ... whatever way she'd met the man, it was kept a secret. But sure he was ordered to go to the chapel, and she went, got up early in the morning, went to the chapel, met her husband-to-be, and they got somebody, the sexton or somebody else, to witness it and she came home and back into the corn-

field and never said she was married, and she done the best. It came out later on, she reared her family and done alright. Well them days, they would have done things like that.[82]

There was one man around here and his mother and sister were at home and he went away and married a woman but he never brought her home you see, which was OK. And he used to go up, and I remember when I was courting myself and going on the bicycle you know, after the war, I married in '48, I used to see him going at the weekends to see his wife. She maybe lived maybe five or six miles from where he did ... but anyway his mother and sister grew old and died and he brought the wife and two daughters and son home then to the farm.[83]

Lack of space for accommodation, coupled with the possibility of friction between personalities were additional considerations, which, like financial constraints, might encourage couples to marry in secret and even to live apart.

Further oral evidence of the practice of married couples living apart comes from Co. Tyrone, and hints at some of the inherent difficulties:

There was a double match between two families, a man from one family married a girl from the other and vice versa, but because of the housing situation, they continued to live in their original houses. So in those days (do you have stations in your part of the country?) ... in our part of the country the priest goes and says Mass in a country house, and this is like an old custom ... they have a Mass in your house today, now the same happened again in October, and it would be at another neighbour's house in that district ... and they're called the Stations. So in those days the priest used to baptise children at the station houses ... and one of these families that I referred to brought a child to be baptised and, of course, the priest knew the conditions they were living in, and when he was baptising the child he says 'Did ye get it in the haystack?'[84]

Whatever may be the difficulties in interpreting accounts like these it cannot be overlooked that folklore provides hints of a practice similar to that identified on Tory Island by Robin Fox: 'At one time, I was told, at least half the married couples on the island would not be living with each other, but would be in their natal homes with parents or siblings' [85] The oral evidence provides a suggestion that such a pattern may have been more widespread, providing a practical compromise between filial responsibility and the need to establish a new family, while obviating certain other difficulties which might occur if the bride were to attempt to set up home with her husband's family.

One rather quiet wedding which, by the time it had taken place, had become something of an open secret was that of Miss Jessie Barr, who married Lieutenant Cecil in October 1901. The circumstances surrounding the couple so engaged the public imagination that the *Belfast Newsletter* carried detailed accounts of events leading up to and associated with the wedding, and with the ceremony itself, which was actually completed in less than five minutes. The bride, described as tall and very pretty, was a daughter of Mr John Barr, an insurance broker and agent, who was editor and publisher of the *Insurance and Financial Gazette*. By 1901 he had become JP for Tyrone and had exchanged his home at 29 Wellington Park, Belfast, for a house called 'Ardilea' at Greenisland. It was in the environs of Ardilea that the lovely Jessie met Lieutenant Cecil of the 4th Battalion of the Lincolnshire Regiment, who had been assigned to duties at Carrickfergus Castle. Lieutenant Cecil was the second son of Lord Francis Cecil, and therefore the grandson of the third Marquis of Exeter. He was also heir to a very substantial fortune. When the couple married, he was aged nineteen, she twenty-two. It seems that the bride's father was at least as keen for the marriage to take place as the groom's mother was to prevent it, although pressure from the young couple prevented him from insisting that they waited to marry until the groom attained his majority and a look in *Burke's Peerage* reveals that their first-born son made an appearance on 31 January 1902, a little more than four months after the wedding.

It seems that at some time before the wedding the prospective bridegroom took up residence at Ardilea with the Barr family, and the banns had actually been published twice in Jordanstown parish church before the groom's mother accompanied by a solicitor, visited the clergymen concerned, thus preventing the third reading. Accompanied by the prospective bride's father, the couple travelled to Edinburgh, where they were later joined by her mother. In order to fulfil the necessary requirements of residence, they stayed there for three weeks, and published the banns in St Cuthbert's, whereupon a Chancery writ was served upon the groom. The couple had by now excited such public interest that 'hundreds of strangers, actuated by gaping curiosity' [86] were present in St Cuthbert's for the reading of the banns, so the fervour engendered when Lord Blair Balfour refused to endorse the arrest of Lieutenant Cecil can only be imagined. The couple were married, not in St Cuthbert's, but in Morningside church, by this and other means evading as much public attention as possible. They still attracted publicity, as the lengthy reporting of their wedding illustrates. The attitude of the *Belfast Newsletter*, which presumably reflected local popular opinion, so far from being scandalized, was strongly supportive of the young couple and of the bride's family, as it was of the upholding of the independence of Scottish law so clearly reflected by the case.

The general pattern of emigration from Ireland had consequences for marriage behaviour, in that young men might set out, particularly for North America, and establish themselves there before sending home for their brides. There is evidence that these girls might either be sweethearts of their own choosing, or might be selected for them by their parents. A series of letters written home from Philadelphia to his parents and to other members of his family at Moycraig, Mosside in the parish of Billy, Co. Antrim, between March 1844 and June 1845 sadly illustrate the plight of such a young man in search of a wife:

> I think ... you will be willing to say he is still the same dutiful son and the affectionate brother, but not yet the loving husband, for alass I have not yet been successful in getting myself a helpmate nor do I want one in this country, for there is a sweet flower that has grown on the Carncullough hills whitch I shall labour to protect.[87]

It seems that the 'sweet flower' was unresponsive to any representations made by or on behalf of the groom, for a letter written the following August to his parents expressed a wish that his girl will write encouragingly to him.[88] By December he proposes:

> Perhaps I will go home in summer for them and bring so[me] young Lady alongst with me if I can find any one favourable to the propositions whitch I must shortly make to some of the dear little creatures, for I cannot live much longer alone.[89]

The young man was indeed in urgent need of a bride, for, some seven weeks after he wrote this letter, he married 'Miss Rachel Neill, formerly of Drunkenduct, Ireland' in Fourth Presbyterian Church, Philadelphia.[90] He deferred writing to his parents about the wedding for some months, until he could assure them of his happiness and 'also send to my dear mother a little parsel of my wife's hair and also a little of my own to remember her of us'.[91] As only Robert's correspondence survives, it is difficult to gauge whether he was under any degree of parental pressure to marry a girl from near his original home, but the news of his marriage was not greeted with the pleasure he had hoped. In a letter dated June 1845 to his brother Jonathan, he writes:

> [G]ive my warmest love to Father, Brother, Sisters and all friends tell them that without the state of their feelings and style of their letter change very much I must decline of any further correspondence, as I will consult the feelings and happiness of her I have chose to be my partner more than any other, and their letters were very far short of the affectionate congratulations I expected from them ...[92]

At least until the 1920s, some brides crossed the Atlantic from Ireland specifi-
cally to be married, and many young emigrant woman naturally married in
their adopted country. Others returned home to marry and settle in Ireland, having saved money while working in America.[93] The comparative wealth of emigrant family members affected Irish weddings in other ways, not least in that
this might pay for the bride's wedding ensemble. In some cases, this outfit
might be chosen and sent by the emigrant family member to the bride at home.
As far as Ireland is concerned, it is appropriate to consider the 'GI bride' phenomenon in the general context of emigration, although of course GI brides
came also from other parts of the British Isles, of Europe and of the world if
occupied during the latter years of the Second World War by American soldiers.
Some 2,500 GI brides came from Ireland, representing approximately 4% of
all these brides coming from the British Isles and approximately 3.5% of the
grand total of approximately 72,500 spouses and their dependants shipped to
America in the mid 1940s.[94] Before an American soldier could marry a non-
American, it was necessary to obtain the permission of the superior officer, and,
in order to qualify to be transported to the United States after the war, certain
requirements were made of such a spouse. These included a letter from the husband requesting that the bride be transported, stating her intended destination
and that the couple were legally married. Statements had also to be made in the
cases of children, and it seems that some widows may have travelled to the
families of their late husbands in the USA. Some procedures for the trans-
portation of GI brides were already in place prior to the passing of an Act on
28 December 1945 (Public Law 271, 79th Congress) which 'facilitated the
entry into the United States of alien wives, husbands and children of citizen
members of the armed forces,'[95] by removing many of the then usual immigration requirements for the people concerned.

Belfast was among the European cities to which officers were sent to
'process' brides wanting to travel to join their husbands in America. By 5 April
1946, approximately 1,000 brides had sailed from Belfast, and it was hoped
that all war brides would be transported and settled by June of that year.[96] In the
event, in early July 1946, a total of almost 9,500 women and children still
required shipment from Britain to the USA.[97] Between 28 December 1945 and
the end of the American Fiscal Year on 30 June 1946, 783 wives and 11 children, a total of 794 people, had travelled from Eire to the United States under
the scheme. A total of 1,098 people – 1,082 wives, 15 children and 1 husband
– had travelled from Northern Ireland. Incidentally, only one dozen husbands,
compared to more than 60,000 wives, travelled from the British Isles under this
scheme, two more coming from Scotland, and nine from England.[98]

The first American troops to arrive in Belfast disembarked at Dufferin Dock on 26 January 1942.[99] As may be gauged from the numbers of local girls who found husbands among their ranks, they were very popular. Their generosity is well remembered, along with their access to consumer goods. One woman, recalling her Belfast childhood in the 1940s, remembered how several American troops, men and women, were stationed in a large house, across the road from her mother, who felt sorry for them being away from home and treated them to some of her home baking. The little girl returned home from a Sunday walk to discover a large box, dressed like a cinema usherette's tray, filled with sweets the like of which she had never before seen, having been brought up with rationing.[100] However, they were not universally popular, and from some they attracted the reputation of being 'overpaid, oversexed and over here'. Although many were to marry local girls, some Ulster parents did not favour them or consider them to be suitable prospective husbands:

At morning service one Sunday there was an American soldier in our pew ... he was stationed at Newcastle, Co. Down. He had come up to Belfast, uninvited, to spend the day with people in the area, where he had been before. Apparently they said they were going off for the day, he being left on his own, wandered up to Malone Church ... My wife invited him to lunch ... I know the people who had disappointed [him] and in due time I mentioned the incident to the head of the house. I did not ask any questions but as there was a daughter in her late teens, I think the family were playing safe. This was always a tricky situation where there were girls at an impressionable age in the household. I heard one case where marriage was contemplated. The girl's father raised the question of the future and the reply he got was – if it did not work out all right they could get a divorce. The friendship ceased.[101]

In the 1940s, divorce had still to become acceptable in Northern Ireland and this response must have been deeply shocking. It should be said that many GI brides rose to the challenges facing them, and enjoyed happy and enduring marriages, and their stories add a touch of romance and even glamour to the way in which the war years have been remembered. GI brides are held in great affection, and return visits home are special occasions which are often picked up by the local press.

During the war years there were, of course, many civilian marriages. Conscription was not enforced in Northern Ireland, but many young men did in fact join and take pride in joining the Armed Forces. One bride from Banbridge, Co. Down, who married in December 1941, gives an insight into the constraints under which courtships were conducted, and the circumstances which might arise if one's prospective bridegroom was a soldier:

We had arranged the wedding for the 20 December at 11 o'clock ... and he
was to come home on the Friday. And he was down in Kent ... So he came
up and got as far as Stranraer. And when he got to Stranraer, the morning
boat was full, so he didn't get on it. And the afternoon boat filled up very
quickly too, before he could get on. They said, 'Oh, no more.' They were
told to go back to a reception camp or something that they could sleep in
at Stranraer. And he went up to the Sergeant Major in charge of loading
the boat, and he said to him that he was getting married the next day, in
the morning, and could he not get on, because the wedding would have to
be cancelled. He could never get to Banbridge in time for it. So, 'Well son, .
I'll see what I can do.' So, half an hour or so later he came back, and he
shouted, 'Where's that young man who's getting married in the morning?'
And he said he was absolutely avalanched with people, with men running.
But he picked Wilfred out of the crowd, because Wilfred was six foot
three, you see, so you couldn't really miss him. So he picked him out and
he got on the boat with a lot of boos and hissing from the rest of the people, because they would have had to have stayed to the next morning, you
see.

   But oh, I was glad to see him coming in because we must have had con-
fectionery that day, and I was serving in the shop and a lady came in with
her son ... I knew her. And I said, 'When did you come home, Larry?'
'Oh,' he said, 'I came home this morning.' And I said 'Did you come off
the Stranraer boat?' He said 'Yes.' Well, my heart sank. I thought 'Where
has Wilfred got to, and what am I going to do?' Because, you see, people
didn't have telephones and things like that in those days. But we were so
busy in the shop that I just didn't have time to do anything about it. And
then Wilfred came in, about 4 o'clock, and oh, I was glad to see him.[102]

Some brides strove for more ceremonial weddings, even during the war years,
but in doing so they ran the risk of being considered frivolous and flighty by
relatives and friends.

   It is much more difficult to gain such intimate perceptions of experience during the First World War, an event which was to become deeply engraved in the
imagination of generations of Ulster people in the twentieth century. A tribute
to Ulster soldiers published in 1919 states: 'Between 4th February 1914 and
November 1918, 75,000 men voluntarily enlisted in the army in the North of
Ireland' (interpreted as including the counties of Donegal, Monaghan and
Cavan).[103] The tribute goes on to state that: 'The Graveyard of Ulster in France
and Flanders is very large.'[104] In fact, two thirds of those who recruited were to
lose their lives in the four years of conflict,[105] leaving many Ulster women widowed or without the prospect of finding marriage partners.

Contemporary postcards give an inkling of the emotions experienced by couples separated by the war. Miss Minnie McCombe of Bessbrook received an unstamped, undated postcard from her sweetheart George, stationed at Bordon Camp, south-east of Aldershot. Available to him and his peers was a printed 'Soldier's Letter to his Sweetheart' which expressed for him his sentiments in verse, leaving him a place to sign that these sentiments were fully endorsed. He was then free to write a jaunty message, 'I believe there is a war on, do you not?'[106] Less jaunty were two cards sent by an unnamed soldier to his wife, Martha, both of which show the same loving couple, the young man in uniform. On one occasion, Martha is assured that the card 'Leaves me A.1. only I am fed up here'.[107] Another, perhaps sent later, can have reassured her of little but his love, for the message reads:

> Dear Martha, I hope I will soon be home now, Dear, as my heart is yearning to see you Dear and get a few X. but I hope that will be soon any way Dear, and then I will be content, but not till I am home to you Dear. Your Loving Husband, with best love, Dear XXX. [108]

Expressions of emotions caused by love thwarted by war and conflict may also be found in folk-songs, and in general, in Ireland as elsewhere, love is the most popular theme of folk balladry.

By the mid twentieth century, the practice of rehearsing weddings was becoming increasingly established. In June 1971, a local newspaper strongly recommended rehearsal of the ceremony, and offered helpful tips on the etiquette of such matters of seating for the meal at the reception. It warned:

> There are many jokes told about wedding days and marriage ceremonies. It is possible for the best man to forget and mislay the wedding ring ... But if everything is well rehearsed and the ceremony planned to the last detail, you can be sure that everything will go smoothly.[109]

Rehearsals also help to reduce the risk of marrying the groom to the bridesmaid, a worry which beset some couples in earlier times.

Perhaps the most significant change which has occurred during the two decades since that piece of advice was given is that it is now much more common for the couple to exchange rings. The exchange of rings is generally understood as symbolizing a more equal partnership and if for economic reasons only one ring, for the bride, is available at the time of the ceremony, another will often be bought for the groom as soon as possible. This idea is not as new as it may seem, for in medieval times a woman of material substance might present a ring or a similar item to her bridegroom.[110] In late twentieth-century Ireland, some recalcitrant husbands who choose not to wear their rings may now find their wives taking a similar stance.

The wedding ring is perhaps the symbol most strongly associated with marriage. It provides lasting physical evidence of the fact that the ceremony has taken place. According to widespread ceremonial usage, it is actually by means of the wedding ring that the marriage is effected. However, this is not the case, even among all Christian denominations. Although nowadays a ring may be received by a Quaker bride or rings exchanged by Quaker couples in the course of the wedding ceremony, the vows which the couple exchange do not refer to a ring, and the ring is not therefore an integral part of the wedding ceremony. The physical symbol that the marriage has taken place is the Certificate, signed in the course of the ceremony by the couple and their attendants, and afterwards by their guests. These Certificates would afterwards often hang in Quaker homes, although in the past a Quaker bride might have been given a wedding ring after if not during the ceremony itself.

In former times, the wedding ring was not considered an essential element in marriages among reformed Presbyterians or 'covenanters'. A Co. Antrim account remarks: 'The ceremony of marriage was extremely simple. My aunt ... states that a wedding ring was often not worn, neither was an engagement ring.'[111] A wedding ring might not be worn for economic rather than symbolic reasons. Although rings of gold or of other precious metals were often given as wedding bands in the past, as they are today, such rings were beyond the means of many. Rings made of other materials, wood or even rushes, were sometimes used. As early as 1217, the giving of rush rings was condemned by the Bishop of Salisbury, concerned that a ring of such fragile material might betoken only a temporary contract.[112] In Co. Kildare, late in the seventeenth century, one bride received a wedding ring 'made of a small twig of osier handsomely plaited' which was blessed 'with two crosses and a short prayer'. However, the bride did not keep this ring on her finger:

> The ring was taken off by one of the young women who I suppose was a sort of bridesmaid, and tied on one of the strings of the bride's purse which hung at her girdle, and it is worn there or in the bridegroom's hatband until it is either broken or lost.[113]

It seems that until the eighteenth century, married women did not wear wedding rings as a matter of form.[114] Since very ancient times, the ring has been used as a token of love and commitment,[115] but, despite attempts at regularization by Church authorities, even when a wedding ring was worn as such, it was not always worn on the 'ring finger', or the fourth finger of the left hand. It is often said that this finger was chosen to carry the wedding ring because of a belief that a vein connected it directly with the heart, but there is evidence that in the early eighteenth century a bride was free to choose the finger on which she would wear her wedding ring.[116]

Some poorer couples might borrow a wedding ring in order that the ceremony might be properly performed. One Tyrone man, whose mother was house-keeper to a priest recalled:

> My mother was the housekeeper in the Beragh parish, there was a new priest ... ordained then, and my mother was just widowed at the time, and she went to him as a housekeeper. And the weddings at that time was at 8 o'clock in the morning. And manys a one came to the church without a wedding ring. And Fr McGrath used to say to my mother, 'We're having a wedding this morning, give us your ring in case.' And I remember my mother saying, she says, 'That ring of mine has married dozens and dozens of people.'[117]

Rings might also be hired, and it has been claimed that in parts of Ireland 'it is believed unless the wedding ring be golden, the marriage lacks validity. If the people are too poor to purchase the circlets made of precious metal, hoops of gold are hired.'[118] It was claimed that a Munster shopkeeper considerably aug-mented his income by renting rings to couples to use during the wedding cere-mony.[119]

Some brides were married by having the loop of a door key, either to the new home, or to the church, slipped on to the finger. This was usually a matter of expediency for those who could not afford a more expensive ring, but it could carry greater implications of stigmatism, as sometimes it was understood to mean that a couple who had been living together were pressurized into mar-riage by the priest.[120] The practice of using a key as a wedding ring was also known in other countries.[121]

By the late nineteenth century, the wedding ring had become more com-monplace, and, as we have seen, the engagement ring was beginning to gain in popularity. The custom of having a ring mark both the agreement to marry and the wedding itself echoes a practice of much earlier times, when a formal cer-emony of betrothal could be overseen by the Church. At this time, some cou-ples favoured the 'gimmal' ring, of two or more separate but interlocking bands, one of which was received by the bride at the betrothal, the second kept by the prospective husband, and a third band possibly kept by the priest. The reunited bands would eventually form the bride's wedding ring.[122] Some gim-mal rings feature the 'fede' device of clasped hands,[123] occasionally holding or concealing a heart or hearts.[124] An elaboration of this device is found in the Galway 'claddagh' ring, in which the heart is surmounted by a crown. The claddagh ring was apparently worn as a wedding ring, but it could be passed from mother to daughter.[125]

In the absence of an actual wedding or betrothal band, some couples sealed an agreement to marry by a visit to the Holed Stone at Doagh, in Co. Antrim. Standing one on either side of the stone, they would join hands through the circular hole in the stone, thus effectively using it as a type of ring. As recently as the 1960s, some local couples continued to observe this custom as a part of their marriage preparations, and interest has recently been expressed in reviving the tradition.

During the second half of the twentieth century, the fashion for wearing an 'eternity ring' has become increasingly popular. In appearance, this is something of a blend of the wedding and the engagement rings, as it is a metal band in which precious stones are embedded. Earlier examples are often full hoops of stones, although more recent examples feature half hoops, the rest of the ring being of metal. These rings, received by a wife from her husband, symbolize a reinforced commitment, and are often given on the occasion of a wedding anniversary, or perhaps to mark the birth of a first child, particularly a first son.

The eternity ring had a forerunner in the keeper ring, which was especially popular in the nineteenth and early twentieth centuries, when it even passed into balladry. Isabella Green's version of the well-known ballad 'Bonny Barbara Allen' includes the verse:

> Will you look up to my bedhead
> And there you'll see it hanging,
> A guinea gold ring and its keeper too,
> I bought for Barbara Allen.[126]

Keeper rings featured in jewellers' catalogues in the Edwardian period, and as early as 1827 one was bequeathed in a will.[127] *The Ladies Book* explains: 'Some husbands who like to observe these pretty little fancies present their wives of a year's standing with another ring, either chased or plain, to be worn on the wedding-ring finger, and which is called the keeper.[128] Alice Ward, who was married in 1869, recorded that, immediately after she had signed the register, her new mother-in-law 'came and kissed me, and gave me a turquoise guard ring'.[129] Like the eternity and engagement rings, the keeper ring was to be worn along with the wedding ring, and there is some evidence that mourning rings may at least occasionally have also been worn in this way.[130]

The wedding day is and has been the focus of many different traditions. It is considered unlucky to marry in May, perhaps because of the association of this month with the Virgin Mary, though this may be 'a superstition known to many but observed by few'.[131] It is often the case with such 'traditional beliefs' that knowledge of them may do little to prohibit or restrict action, but they may function as useful safety valves or scapegoats. One young Belfast woman who was married on 1 May and widowed a few years later sometimes cited the tradition as the reason for her tragedy, without investing it with profound or consistent faith. A bright, sunny day is auspicious for a wedding and for rain to fall on a bride is considered unlucky.[132]

But perhaps the most influential wedding tradition of the twentieth century is related to photography. As cameras became more available, it became increasingly popular among the wealthy to record the event with a relatively informal photograph. By the end of the nineteenth century, some affluent couples engaged a professional photographer to attend them for the day, but far more common was a visit to the photographer's studio. Early in the present century, this visit would often not be made on the wedding day itself, but several days later, the couple dressing up again to have their finery recorded, and this may help to explain why so many brides seem not to carry bouquets. As photographic processes became quicker, it became popular for the couple, along with their attendants, to visit a studio on the way to their reception, and even in the 1950s, some couples had their wedding photographs taken in this way. By this time it was more popular to have the photographer present to take photographs of notable moments, such as the bride's arrival at church, or the newly married couple signing the register. Fashionable locations began to be found in which to have a wedding photograph taken. In the late 1930s, one such location was the roof of the Midland Hotel in Belfast, irrespective of whether the reception was actually being held there.[133] By the mid 1960s, some clergymen were prepared to permit photography from a distance within the church during the actual ceremony. Increasingly, the event of a wedding has become dominated by the need to record it, so that the document may even take precedence over the occasion. With the coming of the video camera and camcorder, an inartistic wedding procession may come down the aisle more than once in order to improve the aesthetic quality of the film, and in extreme cases the entire event may be rerun if the film is considered unsatisfactory.

The Jewish community has long been represented in Northern Ireland, and since the mid twentieth century there has been increasing immigration, particularly of members of the Chinese and Indian communities, bringing with them many influential traditions, most notably those concerned with food and its preparation. Among the important events concerning local ethnic communities is the recent establishment of a Hindu temple in Belfast, at which weddings and other ceremonies may take place. The traditions associated with these ceremonies may be creatively blended with more familiar local customs, and have much to offer to enrich the local community. In 1971, a Hindu wedding which took place in Portadown was an event of such rarity that it was reported in substantial detail by the local press. On that occasion, the actual ceremony took place in a garage. Today, Hindu couples wishing to marry in the temple may travel considerable distances, some coming to Belfast from the Irish Republic in order to celebrate their weddings.

Distinctive traditions are believed to be characteristic of weddings among the Irish Travellers. Many Traveller weddings are arranged, or 'matched' marriages, although these are often concerned less with the transference and inheritance of property than with 'solidifying kinship vows and social relationships'.[134] Travellers may often marry earlier than members of the settled community, and bridal virginity is considered to be of tremendous importance.[135] Many Traveller women now aged approximately forty were married by the time they were fourteen or fifteen. Their matches were arranged although they were free to reject a partner if they wished. They did not receive engagement rings. By the 1990s, it has become more usual for Traveller women to delay marriage until they are eighteen years old, even if they have been 'matched' at fourteen or fifteen. Girls now receive engagement rings, and some bridegrooms now propose marriage to their brides before seeking parental permission to wed. Large families have been especially favoured by Travellers, and among the men a large progeny is the best proof of virility.[136] The way of life of Travellers may increase stresses on marital relationships, so that, while the family unit may have great symbolic importance, some women have deserted their husbands.[137]

Among Travellers, marriage is considered to be the passport to adult status, a matter which is often claimed to be typical of Irish society in general.[138] Further investigation shows that, especially for women, adult status was indeed more generally conferred by marriage. One etiquette book, published in 1890 in London and New York, explained to the new bride that she would take precedence over unmarried women, even those older than herself.[139] In polite society of the late nineteenth century, marriage conferred adult status on the bride, irrespective of her age, a matter which would come to be seen as typically Irish and which would long be retained among the rather conservative Traveller community.

5 Dressing for the Day

Given the wide range of cultural influences, social, religious and economic, it is not surprising that there are huge variations in the ways in which people dress and have dressed for weddings. Some weddings were quiet, even secret occasions, and to dress specially for these would be to run the risk of revealing that the event was about to take place. Many people undertaking such a marriage would not have had access to special clothing, even if they had wished to wear it. At more ceremonious weddings, attention was and is focused on the bride, who will usually dress in the best clothes available to her. If possible, these would be new and fashionable, at present conforming to the latest appropriate style for bridal wear, but in the past to contemporary trends in street or every-day fashion.

As a generalization, it is true to say that, although special features of her dress and accessories more or less 'bridal' might set her apart, it was not until the mid twentieth century that the 'wedding dress' itself began to be governed by a specific vogue. Until quite recently, a wedding gown was usually a rather special version of contemporary fashion, rather than a distinctive and ritualized form of dress. While some brides may choose not to conform to this image, for many today the ideal is the 'traditional' wedding gown, white and veiled. In 1991, an analysis of spending on weddings calculated that the average amount paid in Northern Ireland for a wedding gown was £569,[1] although some brides are prepared to buy gowns costing in excess of £3,000.[2] Some brides have always been prepared to pay for a very special wedding dress. In 1953, one young Lisburn woman bought a very fashionable bridal ensemble from an expensive Belfast shop at a total cost of £55 4s. and paid a further £21 16s. to dress her bridesmaid. At this time, a young girl starting work as a typist might hope to earn between 35s. and £2 per week.[3]

White, described in the 1590s by Spenser as the colour 'that seemes a virgin best', [4] was sometimes worn by Irish brides. A guest at a wedding held in Glenwherry, near Ballymena, in 1812, recalled his experiences of the ceremony, which took place in the same earthen-floored room where the table was already laid for dinner: 'I was introduced to the bride. She was a modest-looking girl about seventeen. She was dressed in a white calico gown and ribands, and had a fan in her hand.' [5] In 1835, it was stated that brides from Magilligan, in north Co. Londonderry would choose to be 'dressed in white if it can be procured'. [6] at around the same time in nearby Dunboe, 'white is the colour for full dress at parties and other meetings', [7] but whether white was chosen for wedding wear because of this fashion, or whether white party dresses were the consequence of the fashion for white wedding gowns it is difficult to judge.

Though popular enough, white was not the universal choice of brides. The appearance of a late seventeenth-century Kildare bridal couple was described:

> The bride was clad in a red frieze petticoat and waistcoat with green tape about the skirts; on her head she wore a white hood of linen, for they do not wear the kercher until they are married, and she sat in a dark corner of the room with two or three other young women about her. The bridegroom was a strapping young fellow with a grey frieze suit on; he had brogues on his feet, and [li]ned leather gloves, and a long neckcloth about his neck, as long as any of our steenkirks, and a blue ribbon in his hat.[8]

The bride's outfit was very typical of women's dress in late seventeenth-century Ireland, the groom's of a style growing in popularity among contemporary Irishmen.[9]

Surviving examples of nineteenth- and early twentieth-century Irish wedding dresses illustrate that these follow contemporary fashion, and the impression is that at this time white was often chosen by those who found it a practical and wearable option. Many brides selected dresses of good quality fabrics in an extensive range of colours. The collection from the Ulster Folk and Transport Museum includes three wedding ensembles, all dating from the late 1850s, and each worn by an Ulster woman, one by a member of the wealthy middle class, one by a daughter of a comfortable farmer and one by a woman of the artisan class. All these outfits are of silk, and all are interpretations of the same basic style. The artisan bride wore a black mantle featuring bell-shaped sleeves and fringing, made up of numerous fabric fragments, some quite tiny; her skirt was a very fully gathered affair of shot purple silk. The bride herself was the daughter of the lightkeeper on Rathlin Island, off the north-east Ulster coast. Her bridegroom was an island blacksmith. The farmer's daughter

James Heron and Sarah Harris, 'both of full age', married on 23 July 1874 in St Peter's Church, Drogheda. The bridegroom was at that time a subconstable in the Royal Irish Constabulary, and the son of a farmer. The bride's father was a vintner. Her brown silk dress and the couple's family Bible, received as a wedding present, form part of the collections of the Ulster Folk and Transport Museum. *UFTM L4023/2.*

chose a one-piece dress of blue and grey check silk, with a full, crinoline skirt and with fringed bell-shaped sleeves, the bodice being very typical of the current fashion. The bridegroom at this wedding was a civil servant. The wealthiest bride of the trio wore oyster coloured silk, again trimmed with fringing and featuring a full crinoline, the bodice having sloping shoulders and bell sleeves. All the dresses were intended for subsequent wear. The bodice of the dress worn by the wealthiest bride was detachable, and when removed revealed a *decolleté* evening top, a feature of other contemporary wedding gowns.[10]

As fashion moved from the crinoline to the bustle, the shape of wedding gowns also changed. In the last three decades of the nineteenth century, many Ulster brides chose two-piece outfits. This must often have increased the wearability of the gown by teaming the skirt with alternative bodices or with blouses. Local women seemed to have combined a taste for fashion with a strong practical streak, and Ulster dressmakers were obviously adept at copying and producing the latest styles for their clients. Good quality fabrics and fashionable styles were available even to women living in fairly remote regions of the province.[11] The dress worn by Jane Eliza Sprott for her wedding in 1912 illustrates an interesting approach to newly available synthetic materials. The dress itself is of rayon, the lining of silk.

Surviving wedding dresses from the second half of the nineteenth century show that various tones of mauve gained great popularity with brides at this date. One gown, of purple silk and velvet, made in Belfast and worn *c*.1875, is understood to have been the costume of a bride in mourning. Its rather sombre colour would certainly have made it appropriate. 'Mourning was almost a national pastime in the nineteenth century', it has been remarked,[12] and this rather nostalgic and elegiac sensibility may have influenced the popularity of lilac tones for wedding gowns, irrespective of whether the bride was actually socially impelled into this choice. In fact, because of its range of symbolic associations, white would also have been considered a perfectly acceptable colour for wear by a bereaved bride.[13]

At this period, some brides favoured extremely formal gowns, especially for society weddings in major cities such as Belfast and Dublin. Constance Pitt-Bremner, who married in September 1893, was described thus: 'The youthful bride looked lovely in her magnificent gown of white satin with court train from the shoulder, of brocade, which was borne by her little brother, dressed as a page.'[14] Some four years earlier, a Miss Edie, whose wedding at Monkstown church, Dublin, was described as '[o]ne of the most fashionable events of the week', wore a dress the front of which was draped with Limerick lace (i.e. finely hand-embroidered net), while the back, of ivory poplin, featured a court train.[15]

For less formal wear, browns, greens, blues and other colours were also chosen by brides at this time. One late nineteenth-century bride from west Tyrone left a lasting impression on the observant Francilla Stevenson, who was then training to be a schoolteacher in the area:

> Four purple pansies on a brown straw hat worn by another bride stand out in my memory. They were so real that it seemed as though they had been freshly plucked from the garden that morning and left on the hat. She wore a brown suit with beige accessories and this brown hat.[16]

Brides who chose not to wear white often wore hats or bonnets trimmed with flowers or feathers, and, at a slightly earlier date, the crinoline would often have been accessorized with a paisley shawl. Many brides found that the wedding day provided the perfect reason for acquiring one of these beautiful and desirable garments, and the collection of the Ulster Folk and Transport Museum includes examples of such bridal shawls.

Contemporary fashion continued to influence the appearance of locally worn wedding dresses in the early twentieth century. The distinctive but perishable silk and gauze creations of the first decade gave way to a no less typical style of dress which enjoyed great popularity in the late Edwardian period and until shortly before the outbreak of war. By this time, women's clothes permitted much greater freedom of movement, and had become much more practical, as they moved away from the bound and corseted elegance of the late nineteenth century. Hemlines also began to rise, and in the 1920s short wedding dresses were almost universal. Although some were identifiably 'bridal' in appearance, many were elegantly fashionable day or street dresses. Coffee-coloured fabrics, especially silk and georgette, were very popular. In the mid 1920s, some local brides favoured a dress and tunic combination, often embroidered and of woollen fabric, which in style echoed contemporary interpretations of Celtic Revivalism.

With the 1930s came the true 'ritualization' of the wedding dress. It was at this time that it began to develop clearly distinctive features which set it apart from every-day wear. It has been pointed out that, in England, the tradition of the white wedding became established in this decade,[17] and the same is true of developments in Ireland. The slender elegance familiarized by images on the cinema screen was interpreted in sleek gowns,

Mr and Mrs Todd with bridesmaid Sarah Roy and best man Harry Adair. The wedding took place in St Patrick's Church, Coleraine, on 4 December 1904. The bride's magnificent dress was of fine madras cotton in silver grey, heavily lined and boned, with lace insertions and trims. The colour of the bridesmaid's dress has been forgotten, but it is trimmed with lace and carries a fashionable modesty inset with collar. Coleraine milliner Miss Hutchinson made the wonderful hats, which were in a cream and were extravagantly trimmed with ostrich feathers. *UFTM L4065/10.*

often bias cut, favoured by many brides. Romanticism was often expressed by giving wedding dresses a vaguely medieval character, popular at this time throughout the British Isles.

The stringency of the war years that followed was registered in Northern Ireland, which by then was a political unit set apart from the Irish Free State or Republic. British policy regarding Northern Ireland meant that there was no conscription here, but this did not prevent huge numbers of people from volunteering for service, which incidentally affected many wedding plans.[18] The neutral Irish Republic provided a haven for amateur smugglers. Bus and train trippers returned to Belfast and to other towns in the north laden with delights such as butter and sausages, goods in short supply at home and likely to be in demand for any kind of celebration. Waistlines suddenly thickened as lengths of fabric, the means of producing a coveted gown, were wrapped around bodies and concealed under loose coats for the journey home. Some brides took the risk of acquiring fabric for a wedding gown in this way, rather than submit to the restricted choice available at home, and a visit south improved the possibilities of an enjoyable reception.

The choice of a wedding gown during the war years was often governed by austerity. There was, of course, the question of availability of goods, but, to an extent, austerity was also a state of mind. Some brides were influenced by a general feeling that to pay too much attention to decking oneself out in an obviously 'bridal' manner was frivolous and inappropriate to the spirit of the times. Many young women therefore dressed quietly, often in a good quality suit or 'costume' which could be guaranteed to give wear for several years. A Banbridge woman who married a serviceman describes how her wedding ensemble, a brown wool dress and jacket, the jacket trimmed with fur, was acquired:

> We went to Brands & Normans, and I can't remember whether I tried on any others or not. Can't remember that, but this little Frenchman ... came out with a pointed beard, and I thought this suit fitted me beautifully, but it didn't according to him and he took it in here and let it out there and I went back a week or ten days later for it ... It fitted me like a glove. It did, and I wore it all, everywhere I went during the war, even wore it to my sister's wedding reception, the dress of it ... You had coupons for it. You had coupons for everything.[19]

Some of the necessary coupons she received as wedding presents from the neighbours.

Similar stringencies were experienced by other war brides, and the same spirit of austerity may have influenced many young women to put practical concerns first when choosing a wedding gown. Photographic and other evidence shows that fine wedding gowns were aspired to by girls of many social classes, but there was also pressure against dressing in this way. One undated oral account dealing with life in the early twentieth century in the Donegall Pass district of Belfast explains:

> You didn't have big white weddings in those days. You always wore something you could wear afterwards. You'd get married in a suit, or a coat and a dress, and you didn't have to buy for the bridesmaids like you do now, because you didn't have the money.[20]

The 'costume' was a popular and practical choice for many brides, both before and after the war years. In 1936, a young couple from Inishmore, on the Aran Islands off the coast of Co. Galway, were described:

The bride was a small woman who had been to America and, having saved some money, had come home for a holiday. She was dressed in a blue costume, thin stockings and light shoes; she wore a necklace, and her appearance was in strong contrast to that of the other women. It is hard to realise how she could remain contented with life in a cottage on the island, but such marriages frequently occur and always turn out well. The bridegroom was a magnificent specimen of manhood.[21]

American money often provided a wedding outfit for the Ulster bride. Sometimes the cash, sometimes the ensemble itself might be sent by a sister or another relative who had emigrated, to dress a girl left at home.

Suits or similarly practical outfits are sometimes chosen by brides today, for first or for subsequent weddings. Although they were very popular during the war years, they were not the universal choice. Even during this period, some brides refused to be cheated of the chance to dress up in a special gown. Peggy Waite, a Belfast woman who married an American soldier in 1944, describes her experiences:

My father was recalled to active service in the Indian Army on 1st September 1939 – my Mother and I followed him there in June 1940. We stayed in India till November 1942. My father was killed on June 4th 1942 at the Battle of El Alamein, Libya. So we decided to come back home to Northern Ireland. Upon our return we were given additional clothing coupons since our wardrobes consisted mainly of light weight clothes suitable for hot climates and we would need warm garments to replace them. As you may know in those days we spent our coupons for clothes with great care. I was able to use some of the coupons that I had saved to buy material for my wedding gown and bridesmaid dresses. My gown was made by a local seamstress. I made both of my bridesmaid dresses and the headdresses.[22]

Rationing, and with it strictures on wedding gowns and other goods, continued after the war, but one girl, who married an RAF Warrant Officer in January 1946, was determined to turn her back on past events and went to some lengths to do things in the way she wanted. She managed to buy fabric appropriate for a wedding gown from Robbs, a Belfast department store, and had outfits made for herself, her adult bridesmaid, child bridesmaid and page boy, all at the Cripples' Institute in the city. Her own dress, of cream satin, features a very full, five-gored, floor-length skirt with a fitted bodice. The bodice features a V-neckline and long sleeves, ruched at the shoulders. She also wore a head-dress of ostrich feathers and a bor-

Mr and Mrs Hesbrook married in Banbridge Methodist Church on 20 December 1941. The bride's brown fur-trimmed wool dress and jacket from Brand's and Norman, Belfast was bought with clothing coupons given by her neighbours. *Below*, GI bride, Margaret (Peggy) Waite married American serviceman Harry Cummings in Belfast on 31 March 1944. The white bridal gown was unusual at the time, the neckline prefiguring the styles of the 1950s, while the large bouquets are reminiscent of the 1920s and 30s. Only the bridemaids' headdresses seem of their own decade. *UFTM L3122/8 and L3197/8.*

rowed veil. As goods were still in short supply, her dress itself was subsequently borrowed by another bride, although the original owner had agonized over her decision to favour a white gown of this type. She remarked, 'When I think over it, like, I should just have made do, and had a wee, short dress.'[23]

Barbara Cartland would have sympathized with her predicament. Some years after the war ended, she wrote of her experiences as a Welfare Officer, acquiring 'once worn' wedding dresses for the use of brides in the services:

> By the end of the war I had bought over five hundred wedding dresses and the girls in all three services could be married in white ... [F]or thousands of war brides, the wearing of a wedding dress, even someone else's and borrowed for only a few hours, made all the difference to the happiness of the day.[24]

During the war years, many Ulster brides chose to wear white gowns, a proportion of them borrowed from sisters, cousins or friends. The newspapers of the time carried photographs of veiled, white-gowned young women, many of whose bridegrooms wore military uniform. Some Belfast brides wore military uniforms themselves. One Belfast bride who married in 1943 wore an off-the-peg full-length white wedding dress with shoulder-length veil. Originally from rural Co. Down, many of her neighbours had little money for new clothes, so coupons were surplus to their requirements and she received several as wedding presents, enabling her to have a special dress. The gown was passed to another bride who wanted a white wedding which might otherwise, in 1946, have been beyond her means.[25]

With the 1950s, the ritualization of the 'traditional' wedding dress became increasingly established. Some dresses, especially those of the early 1950s, featured beadwork echoing the gown worn by the then Princess Elizabeth in 1947. The fashion was for 'blush pink', a very subtle shade favoured in preference to chalk white. Some dresses featured collars flatteringly turned up at the back of the neck, a style which begins to appear with some of the specially made wedding gowns of the 1940s. When rationing ended and fabrics again became widely available, dresses could be made more extravagant. Brocades became popular, and skirts fuller. The 'picture dress' was worn by some brides, and was popular for bridesmaids.

By the late 1950s, the vogue for the 'traditional wedding' with the typical bridal appearance had become so well-established that it could incorporate a raising of the hemline without being challenged by it, and for a while some wedding dresses again were influenced by contemporary street fashion. Bouffant dresses, worn mid calf-length or shorter, sometimes of brocade, sometimes of machine-made lace or of other fabrics, became popular and were worn by many brides. These dresses were sometimes in pastel shades rather than in white, although this was often considered rather daring. The bouffant style remained popular until the mid 1960s, when those who wished to wear a short wedding gown usually selected a mini-dress, again under the influence of contemporary street fashion. One Banbridge bride, whose wedding dress was bought in Etam's, Portadown, wore a white mini-dress. Her bridesmaid's dress, in exactly the same style, was navy blue. Although extremely short, the dresses were several inches longer than the girls usually wore, in view of the formality of the occasion.

Throughout the late 1950s and 1960s, there were brides who chose to dress more classically. Some were influenced by the ideas of Sybil Connolly, and wore Irish wools and laces. In the 1960s, brides increasingly opted for sheath-like dresses, sometimes Empire line, with high mandarin or rolled collars and long sleeves. This basic style remained popular throughout the 1970s, and was suddenly and dramatically ousted by full, crinoline-skirted dresses which copied the gown worn by Lady Diana Spencer for her wedding to the Prince of Wales. Despite the sad outcome of that marriage, the influence of her image continues to dominate the silhouette of many gowns of the early to mid 1990s, although other styles are also now popular.

In recent years some Ulster designers have created bold wedding gowns, usually for export, although some local brides have been daring enough even to wear red, which until quite recently was (and for many still is) the hallmark of the scarlet woman in bridal terms, and others have swapped their satin pumps for Doc Marten boots, although these, too, are often in white satin, sometimes complete with sling-back heels. Ironically, in earlier times deep red was considered an acceptable alternative to mourning dress for a widow attending the wedding of her child.

The 1990s have seen an increasing fashion for themed weddings. The dress of the bride and her bridesmaids may reflect an interest of the bride, so that, for example, a passion for horse riding may encourage a certain style of dress and accessories. (Report has it that one English bride took this recently to an apotheosis by actually having her horse as bridesmaid, complete with dress, but it is not known if any Ulster bride has yet followed suit.) Increasingly, the waistcoat worn by the bridegroom and his attendants will mirror the colours of the gowns worn by bride and brides-

Hemlines rose quite high in the 1960s and 70s, as the mini skirt chosen by Jennifer Evans for her wedding conducted on 14 March 1973 in Banbridge illustrates. *UFTM L3917/9.*

maids, and these colours will be picked up and reflected by wedding guests, particularly in the dress of small children attending the wedding, and in the colours of favours and other items used at the reception. The motor-cycle wedding is an extreme example of the themed ceremony. The bride may sometimes choose to dress in white with flowers and veil, although, as she arrives on a motorbike, she is likely to favour leather as a more practical choice.

When catering for romantic tastes, local dress designers often choose to draw on antique gowns for inspiration, so a bride who wants a distinctive look can find 1920s-inspired dresses, or lavishly trimmed and bustled gowns to rival those of the 1880s. The allure of boning and lacing has also

Biker wedding conducted by the Registrar in Bangor Castle, mid 1980s. *UFTM L3825/10.*

been rediscovered. Their appeal was not lost on those who advertised and sold corsetery a century ago. The Army and Navy Stores, purveyors of all manner of fascinating and sometimes astonishing goods, advertised a wide range of women's underwear, including corsetry, in their catalogue for 1898. One corsetry line, a boned, back-lacing basque which extended from bust to hips and across the abdomen, was entitled the 'bridaline'. Exceptionally, it is illustrated, not as modelled by a young woman in a camisole, but in its own right beside the figure of a gowned and veiled bride.[26]

Between the early nineteenth and the mid twentieth centuries, more was contributed to the ritualized appearance of the bride by her veil than by her gown. Although her dress was often stylish enough to be obviously 'bridal', it could also be worn on other occasions, and in style it bore a close relationship to everyday dress.[27] While fashion may often have attempted to dictate otherwise, brides have long chosen to veil their faces for their wedding ceremonies. An engraving of Youghal church, published *c.*1840, features a procession, apparently bridal, headed by a man and a woman whose arms are linked. The woman's face is veiled, although she appears to be leaving the church on the arm of her new husband.[28] Not all veiled brides unveiled their faces immediately after the wedding ceremony, but how many bridegrooms, like William Ward, have 'raised the veil and in the true old fashioned style kissed the bride'?[29] The bride in this instance wore a veil which reached to beneath her knees. Although at various times fashion may have recommended that a bride dispensed with a veil, or did not wear it so it covered her face, the image of the draped, concealed figure has long had a hold on the imagination.

By the 1920s, brides who chose to wear veils generally favoured anchoring them low on the forehead. This style, usually associated with that decade, had begun to make an appearance shortly before the outbreak of the First World War, and became increasingly popular with brides in the closing years of and immediately following the war. Many brides at this time wore hats, and these usually followed contemporary tastes in fashion for headgear. If veils were chosen, they were often very long and voluminous, as if in compensation for the shortness of the gown. When in the mid twentieth century the hemline of the wedding dress was raised again, the fashion was for short, bouffant veils which almost echoed the shape of the dresses.

Hats are usually worn by brides whose outfits are chosen for subsequent street wear. From time to time it has also been fashionable to team the 'traditional' white wedding gown with a hat. Some brides when wearing a hat with a serviceable wedding ensemble take advantage of a hat veil, thus hinting at the symbolism of bridal attire. Early in the twentieth century, the motoring veil was selected by some brides as a fashionable way of veiling the face. Practicality must also have influenced their choice, as this style was favoured by some bicycling brides.

Fashions in bridal head-dresses have also changed with time. The floral chaplet often selected by nineteenth-century brides was again popular in the 1980s. The twentieth century has seen many different styles, including the close-fitting Juliet cap and the large single flower sometimes called the 'Miner's Lamp'. One of the most distinctive types of head-dress was the tiara chosen by Princess Marina and copied in the 1930s by brides in Ulster, as it was in other parts of Britain. One woman who married in Warrenpoint in 1939 wore a coat and dress with a hat which echoed the sunray shape of this head-dress.

Other accessories, including embroidered or otherwise decorated shoes, garters (often blue) and other garments have from time to time been popular with local brides. Many wear and have worn gloves, and usually the left glove or the pair will be removed so that the bride may receive her ring. Alice Ward described how, having dressed for her wedding in 1869, she took time to 'put powder in my glove to make the ring slip on well'.[30] Some girls in the early 1950s may have complied with the rather extreme advice offered in a contemporary etiquette book: 'The fourth finger of the left hand glove should be ripped to receive the wedding ring.'[31]

Like veils, handkerchiefs could be made or trimmed with lace. Local handmade laces, especially Carrickmacross and Limerick, have often made important contributions to the ensembles of brides throughout Ireland and beyond. White embroidery, so characteristic of textile decoration in the north of Ireland, has often featured on brides' handkerchiefs. Handkerchiefs specially decorated, to be carried on and to commemorate the wedding day, were popular in the mid to late nineteenth century, and have recently caught the attention of local retailers. There is some debate as to exactly when the idea of wearing 'something old, something new, something borrowed and something blue' began to be observed in Northern Ireland, but it was becoming established before the middle of the twentieth century.

The bouquet is often an important part of the bridal ensemble. Arabella Ward carried five white camellias, presumably arranged in the posy style then popular.[32] In 1869, Alice Ward's bridal bouquet was described by her sister: 'Mrs Forde had sent from Seaforde a lovely bouquet of half-open camellias done up artistically with sweetherb and surrounded with maidenhair fern.' [33] For brides' bouquets, nineteenth-century etiquette books recommend white flowers only, thus tacitly acknowledging their contribution to the purity of the 'bridal' image.[34] Orange blossom, symbol of fertility, increased in popularity throughout the first half of the century. Coloured flowers were also often featured in bridal bouquets.[35] At least one late nineteenth-century Belfast bride carried a bouquet that included montbretia.[36] By the twentieth century, flowers of mixed colours were favoured by many brides, although others continued to favour all-white arrangements.

Photographs provide useful information about the changes in shape of bridal bouquets. The posies of the mid nineteenth century gradually gave way to the much larger arrangements often favoured by late nineteenth- and early twentieth-century brides. Although the fashion was followed by many women, for others, individual preference obtained. When Annie Savage of Laurel Hill married the Rev. James Mulligan in September 1910, she wore a fairly simple though very fashionable gown and a floral wreath without a veil. Her photograph shows her carrying two flowers, apparently roses, one light and one dark in colour.[37] Some local brides of the 1920s observed the fashion for flowers 'cradled like a baby in the crook of the arm, rather than carried',[38] while some others appear to have dispensed with flowers altogether. The dominant theme for bouquets at this date was for the enormous, the height increased by ferns, the scale by trailing foliage and dangling ribbons, so that they often appear to provide a mobile means of concealment for the short-skirted brides. Bouquets of this type remained popular in Northern Ireland during the 1930s, even with floor-length, ritualized wedding gowns. Trailing ribbons and greenery held their place, although some other styles also appeared, including bouquets in an elegant, open, rather spiked arrangement.

After the Second World War, smaller, sheath-shaped bouquets became very popular, to be succeeded by a return of the posy. More recently, very large shower or 'teardrop' bouquets have once again become extremely popular, while 'over-arm' bouquets or less formal hand-held arrangements are also fashionable. A trend noted by some florists in the 1990s is for crescent-shaped bouquets.

Ribbons, bouquet holders and other devices have also gone in and out of fashion with the passage of time. In the late nineteenth century, one etiquette book advised that 'posies should be tied with long ends of the very richest white moiré or velvet ribbons. The bouquets are either enclosed in lace paper or in white satin bouquet holders, trimmed with blonde and pearls.'[39] Although the bouquet makes a major contribution to the ritualized appearance of the bride, some have chosen not to carry one. In Northern Ireland, a Bible, often bound in white, is frequently chosen by brides as an alternative to a bouquet.

The tradition that the groom pays for the flowers carried by the bride and her attendants is long established. In the late nineteenth century, it was thought proper that the bridesmaids' flowers should be delivered the day before the wedding, but that the bride's should arrive on the day itself. By this time, it was also popular for the groom to give presents of jewellery to the bride and her attendants. Contemporary accounts of weddings often give detailed descriptions of bouquets, mentioning that they were the gift of the groom, and sometimes gifts of jewellery are also described. The bridesmaids at the wedding of Constance Pitt-Bremner to Edward Rouviere Day in Dublin, in September 1893 'wore gold bangles, with C.R.D. intertwined'.[40] When, later the same year, Mr Hugh Law, son of the Lord Chancellor of Ireland, married Miss Charlotte Stuart of Bogay House, Londonderry, he presented her five bridesmaids with handsome pearl bracelets.[41] Some five years earlier, gold brooches were given by the groom to another pair of bridesmaids at a wedding in Stillorgan,[42] while another set of five were each given a 'gold pencil bangle'.[43] Contemporary advertisements of gifts suitable for bridesmaids sometimes quote discounts if numbers of any item are to be bought.

Some brides received quite extravagant-sounding gifts from their new husbands. Alice Battersby, who married early in 1890, wore jewellery of 'pearls and gold, the gift of the bridegroom'.[44] In June of that year, Helen Watson's 'tulle veil of unusual size was gracefully fastened by diamond pins, the gift of the bridegroom'.[45] The Rev. John Irwin gave his bride 'a pearl and diamond necklace', her five attendants 'carried bouquets of carnations and roses, and wore gold bracelets', also as a result of his generosity.[46] The bride's mother and mother-in-law might also choose to deck her in expensive jewellery. The practice of giving gifts to the bridesmaids may be related to a custom which was noted in England during the 1640s:

> Their use is to buy gloves to give to each other or their friends, a pair on that day; the man should be at cost for them, but sometimes the man gives the gloves to the men, and the woman to the women, or else he to her friends, and she to his.[47]

It is still the custom for the bride and her attendants to be given gifts of jewellery by the bridegroom.

It has been argued that the ritualized appearance of the bride in a 'stereotypical bridal gown' serves to distance her from rather than to unite her to her husband. To dress like this, one writer claims '[w]hile desexualising the bride, did more to emphasise her femininity and bonds with other women. It was not unusual for brides to wear their mothers' or sisters' dresses, thus reinforcing a familial rather than conjugal identity.'[48] This point may hold even more true of the ritualized, symbolically bridal dress of girls and women undergoing rites of passage other than marriage, recognized by means of religious ceremony. For their confirmations, young girls, especially of the Anglican Church, often appear veiled and in white. In February 1881, *Harper's Bazaar* featured a selection of appropriate dresses then available in America, all demurely high-necked and long-sleeved. As illustrated, these gowns are worn by young women, all veiled and carrying prayerbooks.[49] Little Catholic girls are often dressed in a similar manner in order to make their First Communions, usually at the age of seven. Prior to the Second Vatican Council of the early 1960s, it was customary for young women who wished to embrace religious life as nuns to dress as brides for the ceremony of Reception, at which they took their first vows. Often, the dresses they wore for this ceremony were actual wedding gowns, suitably restrained in style, which had been handed in to the convent to be used in this way. (Surplus gifts of this sort were sometimes cut down and made by the sisters into First Communion dresses to be returned for use in the local community, or into other appropriate items.) Occasionally, a nun might have a dress specially made to be worn for her Reception, but second-hand gowns were much more usual. Especially if entering an enclosed order, some young women were accompanied for this ceremony by child attendants dressed as pages and bridesmaids.[50]

The symbolic importance of dress was not lost on the reforming Quakers of the early nineteenth century. Quaker couples wishing to marry were expected to attend several Meetings prior to receiving permission. Among the objections to these regulations was the fact that more pre-marriage appearances had begun to be used as opportunities to dress up in a showy, fashionable manner,[51] which ran counter to the basic tenets of Quaker philosophy.

Among other denominations, the showy quality of new wedding garments was so well appreciated that the Sunday after a wedding was actually known as 'Showing' or 'Show-off Sunday'. In many country churches it was the practice for men and women not to sit together. In a centre-aisled church, men would often sit on the right, women on the left. An echo of this distinction is still preserved in wedding ceremonies, when friends of the bride are seated on the left, those of the groom on the right. In the past, on the Sunday following a wedding the bride, groom and their attendants dressed in their wedding finery would all sit together at the front of the church. In instances where a marriage occurred at home, this gave an opportunity to reaffirm the fact that the ceremony had been observed by means of a public appearance at church. It was also an occasion when ideas about fashion could be transmitted to a community, and when changes in style could be observed and evaluated. The custom was also known across the Atlantic, and was familiar in some English churches. The bride and groom would sometimes arrive after the service had started, and might stand and turn round in the course of the sermon, to ensure that everyone had a chance to admire them.[52]

As transport became more available during the nineteenth century, honeymoon journeys became increasingly popular, and consequently Showing Sunday began to decline. Some couples chose to travel by train, and this meant that the timing of a wedding became increasingly critical. The account of Emily Ward's wedding in 1861 helps to illustrate the problem which might confront a bride:

Young woman about to be received into the enclosed Order of Poor Clare, Belfast, 1930s, attended by her bridesmaids and pages. She is leaving the Sisters' dwelling to go to the church, which she will enter as a member of the laity. After making her vows she will leave the part of the building which is open to the public and make her way to the entrance of the nuns' choir, where she will be silently welcomed by the sisters holding lighted tapers. She might easily be mistaken for a conventional bride leaving home on her father's arm. Her gown is most likely to have been given to the convent by a member of the public, and would have been worn by a succession of young women for this solemn event. *UFTM L3210/12.*

Breakfast lasted from 1 p.m. till 2.30. She had a rush to be ready for 2.30, leaving the table at 2.15, but she was quite in time to catch the train for Belfast and Dublin. She drove away in a blue silk cashmere shawl and white bonnet with maize rose buds and lappets of Honiton behind.[53]

In order that the departure would not be delayed, some brides chose to be married wearing an outfit suitable to be worn when travelling. According to the report of Kate McClay's marriage to John Pollock in Christ Church, Strabane, on 3 June 1890: 'The bride was very tastefully attired in a brown travelling costume ... After the ceremony, the happy couple left Strabane by train for London, via Belfast and Liverpool.' [54] Some brides were careful to ensure that they had enough time to exchange their wedding gowns for travelling outfits. The ensemble was often an important feature of the trousseau and was reported in newspaper accounts. Today, the choice of an outfit to be worn when departing on honeymoon is still an important one for many brides. The going-away outfit, something which may be worn on many occasions subsequent to the wedding, today fulfils the requirements placed on many less ritualized wedding gowns of the past.

When access to transport was very restricted, only the wealthiest couples expected to spend the early weeks or even months of their married lives on 'wedding journeys'. By the 1830s, these had begun to be known as 'honeymoons'.[55] In the mid nineteenth century, newly wed couples enjoyed increasing freedom to travel unchaperoned.[56] Alice Ward describes how she departed on honeymoon in January, 1869:

> I retired, dressed myself in grey silk, rabbit fur coat with long fringe, white bonnet and roses, and soon after it, at about 3.45, the carriage and ... postilions came round. I passed through a file of bridesmaids, popped in, Nugent after me: slippers were thrown and we were off, with grinning postboys looking back, and no one else inside. We pulled down the blinds when we got beyond the cheering and went full pelt to the Quoile, where they refreshed, and again at Crossgar, and we behaved very well inside, drove quietly through Saintfield in the dark, and arrived at the house at 6.10.[57]

The expectation that a honeymoon would provide an opportunity for travel increased during the nineteenth century, but not all couples felt entitled to view a honeymoon as a trip to be devoted entirely to pleasure.

One Ballymoney man, recalling the wedding of his grandparents, which took place in Finvoy Presbyterian church early in the 1860s, explained:

The honeymoon was spent on the farm of a sister of the bride about 7 miles away. Among the luggage my grandfather took was a parcel done up in brown paper. When asked what it was he said it was his wearing boots. He wasn't going to waste time going about dressed. He was going to help his brother-in-law on the farm while his bride helped her sister in the house.[58]

To 'go about dressed' means to wear one's best clothes.

Increased access to transport did not make the possibility of a honeymoon trip an option available to all couples, but it did often mean that, after the ceremony, many couples could spend the rest of the day at the seaside or in town on a shopping trip. Their attendants would usually join them for the day. Some couples visited unfamiliar cities, perhaps coming to Belfast for the first or only time. Portrush, Bangor and Newcastle were among the coastal towns which were very popular for these trips. Many people still remember seeing young couples promenading, their primary purpose being to show off their wedding clothes. These couples would usually return home to a big party attended by all their friends who had spent the day working as usual.

The attendants, particularly the bridesmaid or Chief Bridesmaid, usually play important supporting roles to the bride during her preparations and on her wedding day. Like the bride, bridesmaids are usually distinguished by their dress. The idea that the bridegroom should not see the wedding dress until the bride appears at the ceremony has been extended to allow great secrecy about a bride's gown. This now extends also to bridesmaids' dresses. A belief has developed that prior to a wedding it is unlucky for a bride to reveal details of the outfits to be worn by her attendants.[59] Among the Travelling community, the bride's chief female attendant is often referred to as the 'best woman'. In the past, many brides and grooms travelled together to their wedding ceremonies so the belief that the groom should not see the bride before the ceremony could have little relevance. The two accounts of the wedding of Alice Ward in January 1869 seem to suggest that this belief was known, if little observed, at that date. The bride herself wrote in her diary that, helped by 'Emily and Louisa', she dressed in '[w]hite satin, orange flowers [i.e. blossom] and Honiton lace; [was] ready at 10.20 and presently I was summoned down to Pa's room to sign. The first person person I saw and went to was my precious little Nugent'.[60] Her sister Charlotte, who also kept a diary, records the incident as follows: 'A covered car drew up and there issued forth Mr Anketell for signing the papers. ... After the signing Alice retired to dress, which office was performed by Emily and Louisa.' [61] The natural conclusion is that the bride's own account is the accurate one, and that her sister has modified hers, perhaps to accord with the idea that the bride and groom should not have encountered one another before the ceremony, although perhaps the bride was too excited to remember all the events of the day in strict sequence.

Like the bride, the bridesmaids generally receive their flowers as a gift from the groom, a tradition which has long been established. To mix red and white flowers is sometimes considered unlucky, although some brides have chosen bouquets of this sort. The attendants who escorted a Miss Jellett up the aisle on her wedding day in June 1890 'carried posies of cream and scarlet flowers tied with ribbons to match'.[62] Although etiquette books sometimes advised against it, many bridesmaids at this date and throughout the twentieth century have carried baskets of flowers, sometimes of substantial proportions. Even more outrageous were the ribbon-bedecked shepherdesses' crooks topped with bouquets which were carried by the seven bridesmaids who attended Helen Reilly Barbour at her wedding on 26 June 1908. She married the ill-fated Thomas Andrews, managing director of Harland and Wolff shipyard, who four years later was to perish on the *Titanic*. Not content with flowery crooks, Helen also had her bridesmaids wear huge, flower-bedecked hats, and corsages embellished the bodices of their dresses. Large bouquets could prove difficult for bridesmaids to manage, particularly when the bride also carried an elaborate and extensive arrangement. Women who performed this role in the early to mid twentieth century frequently recall how awkward it was to keep hold of their own flowers and to take responsibility for the bride's bouquet to enable her to receive her ring. These large bouquets were often heavy, which made keeping two under control additionally challenging.

Hats were a popular feature of bridesmaids' outfits, especially in the decades before and immediately after the turn of the twentieth century. The outfits of the young women who attended Miss Jellett were clearly described in the report of her wedding: 'The bridesmaids wore extremely pretty dresses of soft cream llama with rows of satin merveilleux ribbon, and most elegant and picturesque hats of clear fancy straw trimmed with cream ostrich feathers and delicate gauze ribbons.' Light-coloured gowns were often worn by bridesmaids at this date, although bolder shades were also popular, and it was fashionable for bridesmaids' outfits to combine white or cream with more dramatic colours. Charlotte Ward, one of nine attendants at the wedding of her sister Alice in 1869, described how she 'was in the "uniform" of the bridesmaids, white with cerise'.[63] For her wedding to Mr Paget Reeves of the Leinster Regiment (Prince of Wales's Royal Canadian), his bride Harriet wore white corded silk with orange blossom and a lace veil: 'She was attended by five bridesmaids who wore white pongee silk dresses with scarlet vests and shoes, and posies of scarlet and white flowers, with streamers the colour of the regiment.' [64] A Miss Powell, who married a Mr Lawson in 1888, wore ivory duchess satin trimmed with Carrickmacross lace, while her bridesmaids wore 'electric grey, with sashes and vests of ivory watered silk, and hats to match'.[65]

Some brides chose to reverse the usual pattern, and to dress themselves in darker colours than their bridesmaids. Annie Beamish of Skibbereen wore 'a beautiful and elaborately fashioned gown of rich brown silk with the bouffant sleeves now so much in vogue' for her wedding in April 1893. Her hat, veil, and gloves were all en suite, and she carried a bouquet of white flowers. Alice Beamish, chief bridesmaid, wore 'a somewhat lighter tint of brown silk', and the second bridesmaid a 'tasteful gown of grey corduroy cloth, with sleeves of white silk'.[6]

In the early to mid nineteenth century, it was quite usual for a bride who veiled and dressed in white to be attended by bridesmaids dressed in much the same way, although this fashion was occasionally challenged. The girls who attended Sarah, a niece of Fanny Burney, at her wedding in 1821, wore coloured dresses.[67] There were ten bridesmaids at the wedding of Arabella Ward in March 1845. The first six in this procession wore gowns of pink, and the following four dressed in blue.[68] Constance Pitt-Bremner, married in Dublin in 1893, had six bridesmaids who occasioned the comment by a reporter: 'A novel feature of the bridesmaids' frocks was that each wore a paler shade of yellow than the preceding.' [69] While many brides have stipulated that their bridesmaids must wear identical or almost identical gowns, others have allowed considerable freedom of choice, perhaps suggesting little more than a general unifying style of dress and allowing the girls to make their own selection.

Extant wedding and bridesmaids' outfits worn in nineteenth- and early twentieth-century Ireland, especially in the north, clearly illustrate a point which emerges from a study of contemporary accounts of weddings, as they show a keen interest in changes in fashion. By implication, these dresses also illustrate the often very considerable skills of local dressmakers, and show that good quality fabrics were available to many women. Reports featuring descriptions of wedding dresses, especially in the nineteenth century, may concentrate on the more affluent members of local society, but surviving dresses worn by the wives of small farmers and by women of the artisan classes show that they, too, had a taste for fashionable styles. They also had access to the skills and fabrics which enabled them to dress in stylish clothes, at least for special occasions.

The fashion for veiling bridesmaids was well established in the early nineteenth century. In more recent times, veiled brides have chosen to have their bridesmaids veiled too, but this has been a matter of individual choice. Imaginative use has often been made of hat veils for bridesmaids as it has for brides.

The main duty of the bridesmaid or maids may seem to be to provide an attractive foil for the bride, but they have other functions and duties to perform. Jobs were found for at least five of Arabella Ward's ten attendants to perform during the wedding ceremony: 'Two sisters held her gloves, another her bouquet, another her handkerchief, another her vinaigrette.' [70] It must have presented quite a challenge to the bride to reach the altar without dropping some of this paraphernalia. Bridesmaids often help the bride to dress and, if necessary, ensure that her train and veil are properly arranged. Ideally, they are on hand with moral support if she feels nervous before the ceremony. Nowadays, a good bridesmaid will usually help with wedding plans and to entertain guests at the reception. A poorly chosen bridesmaid may add considerably to the bride's responsibilities and worries. There is a belief that it is unlucky to act more than twice as a bridesmaid, expressed in the saying 'Three times a bridesmaid, never a bride'. Towards the end of the nineteenth century, widows planning a second marriage were advised not to have bridesmaids, but to be attended by a sister or a friend.[71]

The modern fashion for child attendants, flower-girls and page-boys, was also very popular at weddings a century ago. When a Miss Edie was married in Monkstown church, Dublin, in January 1889, '[h]er nephew, Master Jackson who was dressed as "Little Lord Fauntleroy" walked directly after the bride as a page'.[72] Miss Jellett, who was married in St Peter's Church, also in Dublin, the following year, was 'attended by two lovely little boys in pages' attire of crimson plush'.[73] Miss Rock, who married Prince Raoul de Rohan of Bohemia in Dalkey on 17 October 1888, took a sporting chance when she chose to dress a two-year-old page in a sapphire blue velvet frock with a trim of Irish guipure lace. The child also sported a large Beefeater's hat with long white ostrich plumes.[74] Pages again featured at weddings during the 1930s, when the term sometimes applied to child attendants of either sex.[75] Child attendants were also referred to at this time as 'trainbearers'. Noreen McIlhagga, who married in St Columba's parish church, Belfast, in 1934, was attended by three adult bridesmaids and by two children, a boy and a girl, both of whom carried cushions, possibly for rings. Page-boys at late twentieth-century weddings are sometimes given responsibility for carrying the rings on a cushion, and this may be among the items specially prepared for the bride by her dress designer. It is often advised that these rings are symbolic, rather than the actual ones required for the ceremony, and that they are secured by ribbons, as the temptation to swing the cushions about or to drag them on the ground is one some pages cannot resist, whether or not they are encumbered by ostrich feathers.

Available evidence suggests that, throughout the nineteenth and twentieth centuries, Ulster bridegrooms have conformed to the fairly drab conventions which have long governed men's clothes here. Some have sported top hat and tails, often under duress, but many have worn unremarkable lounge suits. In the mid twentieth century, grey 'morning suits' are often preferred to black dress suits. Colour has been added to many local weddings as a result of the strong Scottish connections of some families. Appropriately qualified bridegrooms have sometimes chosen to dress in kilts, and to have their attendants and supporters similarly garbed. More recently, colour has begun to make its way into formal dress for bridegrooms, as elegant waistcoats in extravagant patterns and fabrics increase in popularity. Some locally based dress designers are beginning to make grooms' waistcoats in fabrics to match or to complement the gowns chosen by their brides. Perhaps the day will come when local grooms will be as interested in dress as the early eighteenth-century Co. Laois gentlemen, Pole Cosby, who wore on his wedding day 'an embroidered silver damask waistcoat with a grey cloth suit embroidered with silver and lined with white satin'.[76] A number of bridegroom's waistcoats of the nineteenth century are preserved in the collection of the Ulster Folk and Transport Museum. One, of very fetching figured satin, is inscribed on the lining 'My darling husband's wedding waistcoat'.[77]

As with brides, some grooms were restricted by circumstance and lacked the money to dress in formal, much less in flamboyant styles. A story from Co. Tyrone helps to illustrate the point:

A man from Foygin, Donaghmore, acquired a very good coat. It is believed he received this special coat from uncles who had earlier emigrated to New York. The coat was so special that he never wore it himself, except when he was getting married. For at least twenty five years after this (1870s–1890s) all the neighbouring small farmers would go to him to borrow the coat for their own marriages. The practice fell into disuse because it became a liability for a young man to be seen going to visit in the house, as the neighbours automatically concluded that he was planning marriage.[78]

By the mid nineteenth century, the bridegroom's coat was an important part of his attire. The very loving Alice Ward, who married her 'precious little Nugent' on 5 January 1869, described how he appeared that morning, 'looking so much too dear in his wedding coat and blue tie'.[79] Uniform dress is an option for grooms in the services, and it was worn by many bridegrooms marrying during war years.

As the nineteenth century advanced, the role of the bride's mother during the wedding ceremony seems to have become more established, and with it her way of dressing has become increasingly important. In February 1896, *Harper's Bazaar* featured an illustration entitled 'Toilette for a bride and for the mother of the bride'.[80] The latter is a very fashionable two-piece, the jacket having enormously puffed sleeves and, like the skirt, carrying a design worked in bands of embroidery. When Princess Louise married the Earl of Fife in the summer of 1889, the gowns were acquired in Dublin, from Mrs Sims of Dawson Street. The outfit worn by the bride's mother, the Princess of Wales, was also made by Mrs Sims, and was described in great detail by a contemporary report:

> It was composed of magnificent pearl grey satin, brocaded in silver. The back of the skirt forms a long train, and the front is draped with exquisite grey crepe lisse, richly embroidered in silver and finished with revers of satin edged with silver galors. The bodice is trimmed to correspond.[81]

When the form of wedding ceremony demands it, the bride is usually 'given away' by her father or by another senior male relative or friend, whose clothes are usually in harmony with those of the groom and his attendants. One Co. Down bride who married in the 1940s recalled how her father dressed for the occasion in his usual style, dark-suited, but with a collarless shirt and without a tie. At his neck he wore a neatly folded muffler or scarf. On only one occasion did he wear a 'collar and tie', that being the day on which another of his daughters was received as a Sister of Mercy.

Nowadays, receiving a wedding invitation may either provide an excuse or impose a need to acquire a smart new outfit, as wedding guests are expected to dress up in honour of the occasion. In the past, there was often a marked difference in the dress of the wedding party and that of the guests, who might be in every-day wear. The Loughinisland photographer Thomas Gribben caught this distinction in his picture of Brigit Dornan and Eddie Martin on their wedding day in the 1930s. Dressed in their wedding garb, bride and bridesmaid especially stand out from the assembly in their ordinary dress.[82] At a much more formal but approximately contemporary Belfast wedding, guests dressed in a style in keeping with the event. There was a stylish reception at Belfast Castle, and senior female guests wore floor-length, long-sleeved gowns and carried bouquets. Guests at the Dalkey wedding of Miss Rock to her Bohemian prince in 1888 were observed to choose either morning or evening gowns for the event.[83] Some of Constance Pitt-Bremner's guests in 1893 were described in considerable detail. The bride's mother 'displayed a handsome toilette of blue velvet and satin with jet bonnet; a bouquet of pink roses'. One widow 'wore white lace flounces and fichu on a black gown and carried a large white bouquet'. Costumes ranged from the entirely black outfit worn by one guest to the white satin and crepe 'trimmed with old Brussels lace' of another.[84]

Such accounts were no doubt carefully studied and the outfits copied as closely as possible by guests at slightly less fashionable events. Even in the 1950s, etiquette books advised considerable formality of dress for wedding guests, especially for the mothers of the bride and groom, who 'usually wear dresses the same length as members of the bridal party ... For a formal afternoon wedding, floor length dinner gowns should be worn, with long or short sleeves.'[85] Although in the late twentieth century the rules seem more relaxed, guests at a wedding will usually dress much more formally than for every day. Women generally include hats and gloves in their selections of accessories, and corsages, sometimes pinned to a clutch purse, are popular. There are, of course, exceptions. On *her* wedding day, keen motorcyclist Lynn Gourley of Bangor, Co. Down, wore black leather and blue denim. All the wedding guests travelled, like the bride and groom, on motorcycles, which dictated the style of clothing worn.

Many factors influence and have influenced the appearance of all those participating in and attending wedding ceremonies. Changes in fashion have helped to determine the style of the wedding and other gowns. Social and cultural issues involved may include religious and class differences, and these are all overlaid by personal preference. While the veiled and white dressed bride has long been an easily identified figure, during the second half of the present century she has become much more ritualized and 'traditionalized'. There are those willing to spend thousands of pounds in the attempt to achieve a perfect 'traditional' wedding. There are others who, choosing simpler options, may fit as easily into a recognizable historical pattern.

6 Celebration, Prank and Disruption

'You're not losing a son but gaining a daughter' is regularly quoted in relation to marriage in Ireland and, as in the past women often set up home with their in-laws, it was often charged with literal as well as with figurative meaning. It may also express some of the anxieties over the strains in and possible fissuring of existing family bonds as a new unit is established. The gathering of families to attend and to help celebrate a wedding gives opportunities to establish new family connections and to reinforce existing bonds symbolically if not always actually. The wedding party expresses the unity of the family and gives an opportunity for restating and strengthening of its ties. This is especially true in the case of marriages among the Irish Traveller community. Family members go to great trouble to ensure that they are present to help celebrate the event of a marriage, and their behaviour at the wedding celebration is of great interest. Rather than sitting as subdued observers, guests may wander around and talk to one another while the ceremony is in progress, and even bridesmaids may leave their places near the couple to mingle with the guests. Kinship ties are expressed with similar intensity among Travellers at funerals and, on a lower key, in times of sickness of a member of the family.

Wedding feasts have been popular in Ireland since ancient times, and are referred to in Irish heroic literature.[1] Nineteenth-century sources sometimes lay stress on the popularity of parties and celebrations. 'Lavish expenditure and unlimited hospitality characterised marriage feasts in the olden time' is a typical comment.[2] Contemporary accounts of early nineteenth-century life in Ulster remark on the enthusiasm with which wedding feasts were celebrated.[3] These celebrations were governed by various factors, but, as a general rule, wedding parties were held in the home of the bride or of her sponsor. The trend for holding a reception at a hotel or similar venue has grown increasingly popular as levels of affluence have risen in the present century. In the mid twentieth century, it was usual to host a formal meal to be attended by friends and family.

Speeches were made, toasts drunk and the guests dispersed after the couple departed on honeymoon. The current trend is to arrange a fairly formal meal complete with toasts and speeches to be attended by family members and close friends. The younger members of this party usually stay on with the bride and groom for an evening dance attended by a wider circle of contemporaries, which in some respects represents a return to earlier patterns of celebration.

The letters of Mary Delany help to provide a picture of wedding festivities among the gentry in the mid eighteenth century, and of those who came into their orbit. Her accounts of the marriage of her kitchen-maid in December 1751 provide a useful insight into the nature of the relationship between employer and servant, as well as giving details of the celebrations themselves. In a letter from her home at Delville dated 14 December, she describes how her maid Sally told her of her wedding plans:

> She is to be married this evening, had bespoke a supper in the neighbourhood; but that I can't allow. The Dean will marry her himself; they are to have their wedding-supper and lodging here, and I shall soon lose my pretty cook. Her lover is a mason, settles above two hundred pounds on her, lives at Clogher, an old widower, and she has known him fifteen years![4]

Despite her concern over finding a suitable replacement, Mrs Delany found time to write another, undated letter, some days later:

> Last Sunday Sarah Hipwell [Sally] was married at Glasnevin church, by the Dean of Down, to Robert Rames, mason; I gave all the maidens and men new white ribbon favours, and we all marched and made a gallant show through the garden, D.D., Mrs Don., and I at the head of the company, to the church, as soon as the bell began to ring, and the ceremony was over just before the congregation came, and I gave them for dinner as much beef, mutton, and pudding as they could devour. Fourteen people dined in Smith's room (beside the servants of the family) and now the bride is packing up to go away today.[5]

A few years later, another Sally, Miss Chapone, god-daughter to Mrs Delany, came to live at Delville. She fell in love with the Dean's librarian, Daniel Sandford, a young clergyman. It was to be ten years before this couple could marry, and after their wedding they continued to be part of the Delany household. Mrs Delany described their wedding celebrations in a letter to her niece:

When breakfast was over the company dispersed for a little while, some to different rooms, some to the garden, and breakfast things removed, all met again and music took place. I tried and recollected some of my old tunes to set the rest agoing, then the Mr Hamiltons brought fiddle and flute and played some very pretty sonatas together. Mrs G Hamilton plays very agreeably on the harpsichord, but particularly excels in country dances and minuets, which she plays so distinctly, and in such firm good time that it supplied the place of an excellent fiddler. Dinner at four.

Here's my bill of fare: turbot and soles, remove ham. Force meat, 2 partridges, 2 grouse. Pies, Rabbits and Onions, sweetbreads and crumbs. Salmagundi, Soup, Boiled chicken. Collop veal and olives. Pease. Cream Pudding. Plumb crocant. Chine of mutton. Turkey in jelly. Hare. Lobster Fricassee. Desert – nine things, six of them fruit out of our own garden, and a plate of fine alpine strawberries. ...

Coffee and tea at seven, one cribbage table in a corner of the room which is pretty large, and three couple of dancers to Mrs Hamilton's playing. At half an hour after nine the prayer bell rang and we went to chapel, after that a salver with bridal cake ready in the parlour, the coaches at the door and the company went away at ten.[6]

Salmagundi, a dish with mixed ingredients, often included chopped meat with anchovies and eggs.

Similar fare to that available at the feast in honour of the wedding of Miss Chapone was also served at the wedding dinner given in honour of Thomas Wakefield Junior and Mary Anne Willcocks, who were married in the Meeting House of the Society of Friends at Rathfriland on 16 October 1817. Their party was held at Topsyturvey (more properly Rostrevor House). The menu for the meal included soup, turbot, calf's head, sirloin beef, French beans, haricot, stewed sole, ham, roast ducks, rabbits, giblet pie, potato loaves, pigeon pie, Scotch collops, roast tongue, turkey, trout, and oyster pie. Served with these were lobster sauce, butter, sweet sauce and winter salad. The seating plan for the event also survives. The groom's father appears to have sat at the head of the table, with the bride at his right hand. Next to her sat the bridegroom.[7]

By the second half of the nineteenth century it was becoming increasingly popular to send out printed wedding invitations, which were usually distributed two to three weeks before the wedding. Charlotte Ward describes the invitations sent out on the occasion of the marriage of Robert and Maud Ward in June 1878: 'We busily set to to write and send all the invitations for the wedding breakfast. About 50 went. The card is printed in silver and is quiet and neat with a little picture of a church in the corner.'[8] Charlotte also gives some information about an earlier wedding party which was held in honour of her sister Alice in January 1869. This event took place in the family home, Strangford House in Co. Down. On the morning of the wedding, members of the family were compelled to breakfast 'on the landing, the table being already laid downstairs for lunch'.[9] Late in her account, Charlotte refers to this lunch itself as 'breakfast', and gives this lively description:

> At one, everyone was taken down to the breakfast except we nine bridesmaids and the young gentlemen ... We were wild enough to please anyone, and champagne flowed ... I sat next Walter and Francis and Henry Price, and alarmed Francis Price by stealing a tart off his plate when he was not looking.[9]

Although the Temperance Movement influenced some people to avoid it, alcohol, especially whiskey, was an important component of many wedding parties hosted by the less wealthy. One such party, held in the Glenwherry region of Co. Antrim in 1812, was described in considerable detail:

> A table was decently laid out for dinner ... After the ceremony was over, the whiskey went round, and we then sat down to dinner. It was a very abundant one, not ill dressed, – nor, considering the condition of the people, ill served. The priest was grand carver, grand talker too, and grand laugher. I was seated at his right hand, and if I were not comfortable it was not his fault, for no person could be more attentive. The moment dinner was over, the table was removed, and the company began dancing. The music was a fiddle and dulcimer. The dances were reels of three and four – when one person got tired, another instantly started up in his or her place, and the best dancer was he or she who held out the longest.[10]

The meal associated with a wedding celebration is still sometimes known as the 'wedding breakfast'. This term was quite loosely applied and could be used to refer to a relatively informal meal, although some etiquette books of the late Victorian period distinguish between the lavish, formal and expensive 'wedding breakfast' and the much less formal and costly 'wedding tea'.[11] In 1892, William Buszard, an established caterer based in London's Oxford Street advertised that he supplied 'Wedding Déjeuners, Receptions, Dinners and Ball Suppers'.[12]

By the turn of the twentieth century, the exotic-sounding 'Déjeuner' was available to Irish wedding guests. At a wedding in south Armagh at about the turn of the present century, those present enjoyed a 'déjeuner' in the company of the priest who had married the couple:

> He sat at the head of the table, and handed out 'tumblerfuls' of wine, which he handed round to the females present, each of whom approached the priest and made a curtsy as she took her tumbler of liquor from his hands. To the men who were present, the priest handed 'cups and tumblerfuls' of whiskey.[13]

Various names were used to refer to fashionable wedding parties of the late nineteenth century. When Miss Ethel Mary Walker and Lord Bradbourne were married in June 1890, the bride's father, Colonel Walker, hosted a 'reception' at his home.[14] After a Dublin wedding that same month, Mrs Jellett gave for her daughter 'a very large "at home" at her residence, 69, Palmerston Road'.[15] By about 1900, the 'wedding reception' was sometimes recommended as a less formal and expensive way of celebrating than some of the more elaborate festivities.[16]

Whatever the degree of formality involved in a wedding meal, catering for it was an important consideration. An account referring to early twentieth-century Castleblaney in Co. Monaghan records how a few neighbours might stay back from the actual ceremony to help with the cooking for the party.[17] Descriptions of meals of this sort state that roast meat, particularly chicken was prepared. Guests might be offered boiled chicken on some occasions. Meat was usually accompanied by vegetables and boiled potatoes. An account from Warrenpoint in Co. Down mentions 'fried ham, bacon, eggs and sausages. Hot tea was also served ... Tipsy cake was often the dessert. It was sponge cake well soaked in sherry and was served with custard.'[18] Soft drinks, and sometimes buttermilk, were often available to those who preferred them to wine, sherry, beer or whiskey (illicit or otherwise).

In the bigger towns, as well as in country areas, catering for wedding parties was often done at home, especially among the less affluent. An undated, but early to mid twentieth-century account from the Donegall Pass area of Belfast reflects this:

> You'd have the reception in the house, a cup of tea and sandwiches and things like that, and somebody might have brought a bottle of wine, and somebody else might have brought Guinness or beer in. If somebody got married and you went to the wedding, you brought something with you.[19]

With rationing, special circumstances obtained for wedding catering during the Second World War. A woman who married her soldier bridegroom in Banbridge Methodist church on 20 December, 1941, recalled:

> I remember we got currant loaves from somewhere, I hadn't a wedding cake. We had currant loaves from somewhere, and I remember I had quite a blister there [on my hand] with cutting these loaves and putting them out on the tables. And we had saved some sugar, and baked, and we had a roast of beef from the butcher's [we must have had] and we cut all that up, and we had a dining room behind the shop, and then a living room, and quite a big kitchen at the back, so we were able to accommodate everybody who came.[20]

Toasting the bride and groom, and other members of the wedding party, is often an important element of the celebration. This version of a popular and widespread toast was recalled from Co. Antrim:

> Health and life to you
> A woman of your choice to you
> Land without rent to you
> A good harvest every year
> From this day out.[21]

Speeches are also important, especially as part of more formal wedding celebrations, and have persisted in spite of the challenge they have sometimes presented to those charged with making them. One late Victorian etiquette book rather prematurely suggested that the custom appeared to be in decline 'and it is probable that in time it will be altogether discarded'.[22]

Perhaps the most conspicuous component of the modern wedding feast is the cake. This is usually a multi-tiered edifice, most popularly comprising three sections, of very rich fruit cake, white iced, although sometimes the icing may conceal a plainer type of cake. The cake is a powerful symbol of the feast, and is shared not only by those physically present at the event, but by guests prevented for whatever reason from actually being there. The custom of sending out pieces of wedding cake to absent friends was well established in the nineteenth century, and, then as now, little boxes could be bought in which to pack and post off a slice. Like speeches, this practice was considered unfashionable by some late Victorian etiquette books, but *Irish Society* commented in May 1890: 'Brides pride themselves on the beauty and digestibility of their wedding cakes, and enjoy the work connected with the preparation of boxes in which small portions of the cake are to be carried to distant friends.'

The cake's symbolic significance is further emphasized by the ceremonial manner in which it is cut. During the twentieth century, it has been usual for the bride and groom to join hands over the knife and to cut the first slice together, but the custom of their feeding cake to one another is seldom observed in Ireland. Although it is often considered unlucky to receive a knife as a wedding present, a special knife is sometimes used to cut the cake and is afterwards kept as a souvenir. When GI bride Peggy Waite, the daughter of a soldier, married in 1944, she cut her wedding cake using her late father's sword.[23]

One etiquette book published in 1890 makes no reference to the groom's part in cutting the cake, advising: 'The bride cuts the first slice, for it is one of the duties which belong to her'.[24] Many nineteenth-century Irish brides were quite literally in no position to cut their own wedding cakes. *Irish Society* explains why:

A wedding breakfast is very seldom given now, as all the marriages take place as a rule about one or two o'clock, and people are supposed to lunch before they go. Refreshments are served like an ordinary 'at home' during the afternoon, with the addition of the wedding cake and champagne, which everyone present is supposed to partake of. This cake is cut over the bride's head. It is then cut up in small pieces and handed around on a plate, champagne in glasses being passed around at the same time.[25]

Papers relating to the Ward family of Strangford in Co. Down provide clear examples of this tradition in operation. Anne Ward describes in a letter how this was done at the wedding of her daughter, Arabella, in 1845:

[W]e returned to cut the cake which was very large and being all white contrasted well with a wreath of rose coloured Camellias (which Nanny got from Mount Stewart) laid on the cloth round it. The tray was held over her head by Robert Ward and Hugh Montgomery and Janet Reilly being the tallest Bridesmaid and having drawn the bouquet lot plunged the knife in and then the other Bridesmaids labour began of which I hope you reaped part of the benefit this morning.[26]

When Arabella's daughter Alice married in 1869, the bride recorded in her diary: 'Maude cut the cake over my head.'[27] More details were provided by Charlotte, Alice's sister:

Soon up came the cake and three gentlemen held it over Alice's head as she sat in a chair while Maude manfully stuck a knife into it. Then William Trench being trustee cut it up into enormous wedges and the Prices sat at the table and packed it up for giving away: all the young ones busied themselves packing it up in the air, crumbling the ground dreadfully.[28]

Mrs Delany's description of the wedding party she gave for Dr Sandford and his bride Sally Chapone in October 1764 shows that cake was an important element of the wedding feast at that date, but, while the cake involved was evidently a special one, there are no details of its appearance or of how it was cut.[29]

Among the surviving illustrations of nineteenth-century formal wedding cakes are two of edifices constructed to be shown at the International Exhibition held in London in 1862. Both were triumphs of the confectioner's art. One stood four, the other five feet (1 and 1.5 m.) tall.[30] In 1892, Buszard's of Oxford Street advertised gloriously decorated 'cakes of any magnitude always ready', the prices for which ranged between one and sixty guineas.[31] In 1895, Harrods advertised ornamented wedding cakes ranging from 4 lb. to 50 lb. (2 to 23 kg.) priced at 1s. 6d. per pound. [32] Towards the close of the century, *Irish Society* commented that 'wedding cake is not actually a necessity at a quiet wedding, but it is usual, no matter how small or quiet the wedding'.[33] Late nineteenth- and early twentieth-century wedding cakes were often composed of two or more layers, each of the same shape, but of decreasing size, iced together to form a single unit, rather than separated by pillars or other supports. The wedding cake of the Marquis of Kildare, an Irish peer, and Lady Caroline Leveson Gower, who were married in Staffordshire in 1847 was reputed to stand four feet (1 m.) tall. It was a single layer of cake, decorated with harps and shamrocks, and supported on pillars.[34]

However, there were many brides at this and at earlier dates whose 'cakes' bore little resemblance to the magnificent structures usually described as wedding cakes. An account from Magilligan, in Co. Londonderry, composed in 1835, explains: 'When the bride is seated at the table, a cake (sometimes of oatbread) is brought and broken on her head, and distributed among the guests. This is called the bridecake.'[35] Cakes of this sort continued to be used as bridecakes, and to be broken over the bride's head, until the present century. The tradition was known in countries other than Ireland, and apparently was familiar to eighteenth-century Londoners. It was the duty of Samuel Pickering, who in

1751 gave away the bride at a Fleet marriage, to break 'the biscuit over her head'.[36] 'In Scotland, shortbread was sometimes used.'[37] The cake crumbs symbolized fertility and plenty to the couple, and are echoed by the custom of pelting them with rice, petals or with paper confetti.

Whether elaborate or not, wedding cake formed part of the meal eaten at celebrations held in south Armagh at about 1900, as 'the priest arose and went round with the bridecake which he sold in pieces to the men and women present'.[38] This practice may relate to the custom of levying a collection on the friends of the couple, to augment the fee, ascribed to priests of the mid nineteenth century.[39] Guests who were to attend this Armagh wedding brought their presents to the bride's home the day before: 'Instead of being of a useful nature, the gifts consisted of quarts of whiskey or a pint of whiskey and a pint of wine.'[40] The practice of guests contributing to the wedding feast was widespread among the less affluent members of society, and was reminiscent of the practice of contributing to the supper given in association with a wake. In some areas, contributions might be levied from guests, especially if the refreshments proved inadequate as the evening wore on. An account from Boa Island in Co. Fermanagh tells how the supply of alcohol was 'augmented by what was known as a "cess" being held when drink ran out, and more being sent for to the nearest public house'.[41]

An account of a bridegroom's arrival at his wedding on Rathlin Island shows that, in certain circumstances, the refreshments might be needed before the celebrations had even begun:

He was to be married on the island, and he came in his own boat, and it so happened that there were a gale of wind blowing the day he was due to arrive, this was the groom himself in his own boat. And they were all watching for him, and the sea was so bad in fact, they couldn't see a sign of him and all of a sudden out of the breakers this boat appeared with a sail on it, but I think it was from the south-east or the wind was, and he couldn't just make it right to Church Bay, because to go from Ballintoy to Church Bay you're going more or less maybe nor-east, I don't know but you'd be heading too much into the wind, and his boat just couldn't get in and he had to go on out round by the west lighthouse into a wee port there called Stackabouy, that's next the bird rocks, and the people saw him going there and they all followed him along the cliffs and helped him to pull the boat up. I mean the sort of beach that he landed on, if he had landed himself the boat at least would have been smashed on the breakers, but there were so many people there to meet him that they just literally lifted the boat out of the water and saved it, and he'd brought some whiskey and stuff for the wedding. And I believe by the time they'd reached the top of the rocks there was nothing of it left! And they would have to have gone down to the same pub as is today, only it would have been the grandfather would have had it in those days. He had to go there and get some more for to carry on with the wedding.[42]

By sharing in the celebrations which helped to mark a wedding as a special event, those involved helped to express the fact that the day was of importance to the wider community as well as to the couple and their immediate circles. They also expressed good wishes to the couple for the future, a matter given practical expression by means of wedding presents. Newspaper accounts of late nineteenth-century society weddings often include lengthy lists of the gifts received by the couple. When they married in September 1893, Constance Pitt-Bremner and Edward Rouviere Day received more than two hundred gifts. Their household furniture was given by the groom's parents, and they received many other household items, including several pieces of table silver. Of the presents listed, few were of personal gifts to the bride although she received an ostrich feather fan from one of her guests.[43] The list of gifts received by Charlotte Stuart of Londonderry, who also married in 1893, shows that she was given several personal presents, including pieces of jewellery and a 'worked toilet, nightdress and brush bag' in addition to a quantity of household items.[44]

In the course of the twentieth century, household gifts increasingly replaced personal items as appropriate wedding presents and, by the mid twentieth century, urban Ulster brides expected to receive household items only. Personal presents continued to be given to country brides, and there are interesting points of contrast between the lists of gifts received by two brides who married in the early 1950s. The first bride married a farmer and lived in Leitrim, near Hilltown, in Co. Down. Her wedding presents included several of cash. Among the household items she received were a silver teapot, linens, tableware, a tilley lamp and 'a beautiful statue of the Child of Prague' (this statue is often given as a wedding present; it betokens prosperity to the young couple). She also received a pair of silk stockings, 'magnificent kid gloves', a nightgown, a blue scarf and several other personal gifts. Her wedding outfit and accessories were the gift of a sister who had emigrated to Canada. Her close contemporary, a sophisticated middle-class bride, lived in Lisburn. She, too, received wedding gifts of money, but no personal presents are included on her list. Instead she was given a wide range of household items, many of them modern electrical appliances, including a toaster, a coffee percolator and an 'electric alarm clock'. As an echo of the tradition of the contribution guests might make to the refreshments for the party, her wedding cake was received as a gift.[45]

In earlier times, beds and bedding were items of sufficient significance to be mentioned in wills. An account from Fivemiletown, Co. Tyrone confirms their importance to the act of setting up home: 'Bed and bedding being hard to get in the olden days ... a bride was often given bed and bedding as part of her dowry. This gave her time to gather up feathers and make blankets for a second bed.'[46] Patchwork quilts often formed an important part of the bottom drawer, and girls frequently received these as wedding presents from their mothers. In addition to, or perhaps instead of, making their own, they might benefit from quilts made by their mothers, either newly prepared or from existing household stocks.

The weddings of those of high social status have long been marked by public presentations. Gifts of Ulster linen have traditionally been made for members of the British royal family. When Lady Helen Stewart married the sixth Earl of Ilchester on 25 January 1902, the ladies of Belfast presented the bride with a robe of Carrickmacross lace accompanied by an illuminated address. One etiquette book of the late nineteenth century advised rather grandly that illuminated addresses should be sent only 'when the present is given by tenants or upper servants'.[47] Such advice does not always reflect more general practice. When a Miss M. Rattray married on 24 June 1881, one of her gifts was an illuminated poem with a dedication to the bride,[48] but the servants of Castleward behaved with propriety when they presented the Hon. Bertha Ward and her groom, Mr Robert Kennedy, with an illuminated address 'and handsome family Bible' in August 1883. From the working men of Castleward, the demesne of the bride's father, the couple received a barometer and an ormolu clock.[49]

Wedding gifts could provide the means of helping to cement commercial as well as social relationships. One Co. Antrim pharmacist who married in 1918 received a letter of congratulations and an accompanying gift from the company of Evans, Sons, Leschner and Webb. In the mid twentieth century, jewellers sometimes gave tokens such as little sets of silver teaspoons to couples purchasing wedding jewellery, a practice recently revived by some retailers.

Retailers of household items today readily make use of the wedding present list, and some offer incentives to couples in order to encourage custom. The issuing of a list of desired wedding gifts has become increasingly widespread in the last decade or so, but it was not entirely unheard of even in the nineteenth century. One piece of advice on giving and receiving wedding presents comments on the problem of duplicates, remarking how difficult it is to avoid them 'unless we adopt the fashion of the American bride who calmly wrote out a list of things she would like and scratched each item through as it was presented to her'.[50]

The practice of displaying wedding gifts is still very important, although one late nineteenth-century etiquette book advised: 'Wedding presents are no longer exhibited on the day of the wedding, ticketed and labelled with the names of their givers like dry goods in a shop window'.[51] Nowadays, to ensure the display of wedding gifts, to give prospective guests a chance to meet prior to the wedding itself and perhaps to entertain friends who will not attend the actual formalities, pre-wedding parties are often held. Several such parties may be necessary, adding considerably to the contribution of the bride's mother, and extending the influence of the wedding over a number of weeks of preparation before it actually occurs.[52] When these parties are solely of women they may give an opportunity for the exchange of ribald jokes and stories in the presence of the bride.

In the mid twentieth century, the North American custom of giving a 'shower' was fashionable, but whereas in the USA this custom seems to have grown in popularity and to be extended, for example to pregnant women who may be 'showered' with the gifts for expected babies, it does not seem to have retained its appeal locally. A 'shower' was usually arranged by a friend, who would invite other acquaintances of the prospective bride to attend. She would then be 'showered' with gifts, usually small, utilitarian items such as dusters and dishcloths, which would be useful in her new home, but which would not qualify as wedding presents proper.

These pre-wedding parties are usually in addition to, not instead of, 'stag-nights' and 'hen parties'. The stag-night has become increasingly popular in the course of the twentieth century. An all-male gathering which marks the groom's departure from the circle of single men, this event is sometimes held the evening before the wedding, although it has become more popular to hold it some evenings in advance of the actual event. The stag-night offers an opportunity for licensed disruption, which may take various forms and which may occasionally provide a cover for malice. Advice on conducting stag-nights has sometimes been offered by twentieth-century etiquette books, and more recently a few have begun offering suggestions about the parallel hen party. The hen party for women friends of the bride has become increasingly popular with changes in the role and status of women. Stag-nights and hen parties may involve the consumption, sometimes of substantial amounts, of alcohol. At the very least, the bride or groom will be subject to teasing, and sometimes to excesses of disruption if not of consumption, good reasons for ensuring there are a few days between the party and the wedding.

Disruption may even interrupt the wedding formalities. A bridegroom is playfully kidnapped and carried from his reception at a Belfast hotel, late 1950s. *UFTM L3179/12.*

A degree of disruptive behaviour may also characterize the wedding reception, so that the bride and groom may try to leave this party as unobtrusively as possible, if they plan to depart immediately on honeymoon. Precautions may be needed to ensure that there are no attempts temporarily to kidnap either party, or to subject the couple to other forms of teasing. Their suitcases may be tampered with, or various forms of decoration applied to the car in which they are to depart. Increasingly, couples delay going on honeymoon until the day or a few days after the wedding. This change also reflects a change in the character of the wedding reception, when the formal event, including a meal, speeches and the cutting of the cake, may be followed by a dance. The dance is usually attended by the bride and groom, any guests at the formal celebrations who wish to stay on, and a wide circle of the couples' contemporaries who may not have attended the formal ceremony.

A wedding may trigger disruptive behaviour on the part of those formally invited to attend, or among the community at large, reflecting the wider relevance of the event of a wedding. The prospective bride's last day at work may be marked by a mixture of celebration and teasing, after which she may find herself ridiculously dressed, daubed with flour, tied to a tree or lamppost, or similarly abandoned.[53] This practice has been quite common, at least since the 1970s, and is generally marked by raucous good humour on the part of the participants. The victim usually complies with resigned if not equal amusement, although some who may have fared unfortunately may alarmingly call to mind the tarring and feathering endured by some young girls as a punishment for courting British soldiers, especially during the 1970s.

Prospective bridegrooms may experience similar treatment, and past experience has led some firms to operate bans on pre-wedding pranks. Despite a ban, one such incident which occurred in the summer of 1994 went disastrously wrong when a young man tied to a lamppost was doused, not with water as his colleagues thought, but with undiluted caustic soda so strong it caused 75% burns and carved a hole in the pavement where he had been standing.[54] Stories abound of stag-night pranks which became over-exuberant causing broken limbs for the bridegroom, or resulting in his being sent off on the last boat to Scotland and finding himself in Stranraer on the morning of his wedding.

Another form of teasing, which seems to be highly localized, is currently observed in the region between Newtownards and Greyabbey on the Ards peninsula of Co. Down. Slogans are painted on the road, often at the gateway to the groom's family home, sometimes at the church or at the new dwelling to be occupied by the couple. This custom has been intermittently observed at least over the last two decades, and the graffiti may be visible for several years, until they are obliterated by wear or by resurfacing.

In earlier times, some forms of disruptive behaviour were equally localized. One practice was typical of the southern coastal region of Co. Down:

> Along the Mourne coast, particularly in Annalong, it was the custom to hoist the flags on ships and boats in the harbour to mark a local wedding. This was always observed when a fisherman or a member of a fisherman's family was being married. The bridegroom was traditionally required to provide some money to buy a drink for the person who lowered the flags after the ceremony – 'to take down the flags.' Since the sailing schooners ceased to use the harbours this custom has died out, although it was revived [in 1966] when the daughter of a local fishing-boat owner was married in Annalong.[55]

The idea that disrupters may be 'paid off' is a component of many of these traditions. Often, the route to be taken to the church by either bride or groom would be blocked in some way, so that a fee would be paid in order to have the obstruction removed. Sometimes, the couple would scatter money, perhaps as a symbolic invitation for all to join in their celebrations, perhaps also to pre-empt disruption. The groom might also scatter money at the church before going in to the ceremony.[56]

Other methods were employed in the attempt to outwit would-be pranksters or importuners. One description records how 'routes were kept quiet to avoid roads being blocked',[57] and another, written of Keadymore, Mountnorris in Co. Armagh in the mid 1960s, remarks:

> Very often the road was barred by thorns, etc. Within these last two years in this district, church gates have been locked, brides and bridegrooms have been kidnapped, until local clergymen had to protest at the length to which these tricks went.[58]

In some areas, the bride did not return home by the same path along which she travelled to church, even if this meant undertaking a longer journey. This might have helped to avoid tricksters, but it also meant that the bride did not retrace her steps, so perhaps she symbolically as well as literally travelled a new path according to her new status.

One very popular custom associated with weddings was the holding of races, either on foot or on horseback. These were run by guests from the church to the home of the bride where the party was to be held after the ceremony. If the race was on horseback, it might be quite a dangerous event, and the excitement was heightened by the fact that women rode pillion. William McMenamin recalls these events in Co. Donegal: 'Long ago in the parish of Glenfin, guest couples (wife on pillion) left church after a wedding, on horseback, and raced to see which couple arrived at the bride's home first. Winners got some award, such as poteen.'[59]

Such races were sometimes for legally distilled whiskey and some-times, more soberly, for broth. Occasionally the prize was a garter belong-ing to the bride. Similar races were popular in many parts of Europe and in North America, as well as in the rest of the British Isles. Florence Harrison of Castleblaney in Co. Monaghan remembers how a certain man might be selected to meet the couple returning home after the wed-ding with a bottle of whiskey:

> He 'treated' them from the bottle and before the bottle was finished he took it by the neck and dashed it against a stone on the roadway with the intention of smashing it and scattering the contents. If by any chance the bottle did not break by the fall it was not considered a lucky omen and by some it was deemed to be a sign of a childless marriage.[60]

In other areas, the bride herself was expected to smash the empty bottle won in the race to her home.[61]

The author of the Ordnance Survey Memoir for Magilligan remarks: 'If the marriage is extraordinary, the wedding is announced by lighted torches, cheering, firing of musquetry and playing of musical instru-ments.'[62] Any or all of these practices seem commonly to have been observed at many weddings in the past. One Ulster account recalls: 'Neighbours often fired shots in the air as bride and bridegroom were on their way to church', and adds ascerbically: 'If the bridal couple were not too young the shooting was more enthusiastic.'[63] The following oral account, recorded from a storyteller who lived near Portglenone, docu-ments an occasion when such shooting became over-enthusiastic with tragic results:

> A man and a woman, they got married down here at the chapel, this is the Greenlough chapel, down there, you know? And ... they were walking up the road here after getting married, and he had a ... big tall hat ... And they would have shot at the weddings at that time ... And there were one or two walking up behind them, and they had

guns with them, and one boy says to the other 'wait to you see me blow the hat off the boy.' And he put up the gun, and he took the skull and all off him.[64]

Shooting after the bridal couple is well remembered in country areas, and occasionally is still practised today. In the summer of 1992, would-be guests at a Co. Tyrone wedding found themselves in hospital instead of church when a shotgun to have been fired after the bride as she left her home discharged earlier than planned in the kitchen. Pellets hit the legs of several guests, including the bride's mother, who as a consequence sadly missed the ceremony.[65] In the past, enthusiastic shooting was some-times a mark of the popularity of the couple, and tallies of shots fired might be kept. An account from Co. Londonderry published in 1802 asso-ciates shooting after the bridegroom with local weddings among the 'Scotch' rather than the 'Irish' communities, and remarks:

> The groom and his party vie with the other youngsters who shall gal-lop first to the house of the bride; nor is this feat of gallantry always without danger, for in every village through which they are expected they are received with shots of pistols and guns. These discharges, intended to honour the parties sometimes promote their disgrace if to be tumbled in the dirt on such an occasion can be called a dishon-our.[66]

The wedding processions of the more affluent were sometimes hon-oured by the local community, who often garlanded the path to be taken from the bride's home to the church. When Miss Lowry of Pomeroy mar-ried Major Alexander in the spring of 1888, the town was 'en fête' for the event.[67] In August 1883, the Hon. Bertha Ward of Castleward married Robert Kennedy of Cultra:

> All was festivity for the occasion. Flags gaily floated from all the houses and prominent places in the district. The entrances to the demesne and the avenue from Castle Ward to the church were spanned by triumphal arches of evergreens, displaying the arms of the Kennedy and Bangor families and the mottoes, 'God bless the bride and bridegroom,' 'A welcome to Ballyculter for the bride and bridegroom,' etc.: and everywhere were expressed wishes of contin-ual happiness and prosperity. The tenantry on the estate and on that of the bridegroom joined heartily in the celebrations, turning out in large numbers and assisting in the tasteful decorations.[68]

When in 1869, after her marriage, Alice Ward travelled to the parental home of her new husband, the couple 'made a great entry into Saintfield, with arches, flags, mottoes and cheers; the horses were taken out, and we were drawn from the gate'.[69] Well-wishers frequently pelted newly married couples with rice, confetti or rose petals, and some had flowers strewn in front of them as they left the church.

Some wedding parties were disrupted by the arrival of uninvited guests, who might expect to share in the celebratory meal. This parallels the behaviour normally associated with the celebration of death in Ireland. Everyone was expected to attend a wake, the period of three days between death and burial, during which people called to pay their respects to the dead, and to smoke, eat, drink and socialize. If uninvited guests arrived at a wedding celebration, they were often treated as if they had every right to be there, although on some occasions they were 'cold-shouldered' or encouraged to leave.

The most dramatic interruption of traditional wedding celebrations was that of the arrival of the strawboys. Although strawboys were better known in more southern areas of Ireland, they were to be seen at weddings in parts of Co. Fermanagh until the 1960s. Their name was derived from the fact that they wore costumes of straw similar to those worn by Christmas Rhymers, and their arrival was often thought to betoken good luck to the young couple. Certainly, to exclude from a party a group of high-spirited young men in disguise might well have been to invite bad luck. The strawboys expected to join in the revelling and perhaps to dance with the bride. If they considered they had been well treated, they unmasked and made a bonfire of their costumes in the yard. Dancing then symbolised the integration of the couple in the community. If they were poorly entertained, the costumes would be thrown up into the highest trees surrounding the place where the party had been held, and left there to rot as an inauspicious omen. In some areas, uninvited guests might arrive disguised, but not in straw. One account records: 'Ragamuffins dressed in old clothes generally played tricks before they entered the house : they [stayed] together with the guests to the small hours of the morning – say to 7 a.m. before leaving.'[70] Parties which did not break up until dawn or after are often referred to in oral tradition and it seems that lengthy parties often followed a wedding.

It is probable that the arrival of uninvited guests was seldom entirely unexpected, and prudence dictated that they should be treated well. A report from the Newry district says that disrupters 'generally stayed outside, and I've heard of them reaching a briar through the window and

catching the bride by the hair of her head.[71] Other tricks involved block-
ing the chimney in order to make the room in which the party was being
held fill with smoke, a prank which was also often played at Hallowe'en.
Sometimes more potentially dangerous pranks were organized, as this
reminiscence from Gortin in Co. Tyrone illustrates:

> A trick sometimes played at the bride's home while the festivities
> were at their height by locals who weren't invited to the wedding; a
> metal box of a cart would be corked at one end. Then it would be filled
> with rock powder and a fuse cord inserted in the other end which
> would also be corked ... This bomb was carefully left near the front
> door and the fuse lit, when those doing the job fled for their lives to
> some hidden spot where they could hear the explosion. Sometimes
> there would be a guest in the know who would report results later.[72]

While pranks like these were and are often put down to high spirits and
good humour, community involvement of this kind also provided the
opportunity for malice and the expression of jealousies and resentments.
That these, too, might be brought into focus by marriage is expressed by
Sandy McConnell, writing of Bellanaleck in Co. Fermanagh and describ-
ing how '[a] woman on her knees prayed bad prayers' against a couple
about to be married.[73]

Evidence of the custom of formally bedding the bridal couple can be
found in Nicholas Brown's poem 'The North Country Wedding', first published in 1722:

> The stocking thrown, the posset next came on,
> in slow procession by a matron borne,
> who with full many an olive branch had decked
> the good man's table; whilst he, nigh her side,
> with breeches wide displayed, the bed approached,
> and thrice in magic compass round their heads,
> the wide containers of his manhood waved:–
> 'Be ye', says he, 'as in our time we've been
> the joyful parents of a numerous brood.'[74]

Brown was a native of Fermanagh, and the poem appears to relate to the
Fermanagh/Tyrone region.

The tradition of flinging the stocking, forerunner of the modern practise of throwing the bouquet, was very widespread. An account from
Magilligan in Co. Londonderry composed early in the nineteenth century
records a variation on the theme:

Before the party disperses, they form themselves into a circle and
run around the room. The bride standing in the centre with her eyes
muffled, a stocking filled with oatcake is put into her hand. The person the stocking first strikes will be the first married.[75]

In common with other local sources, this account makes no reference to
the couple being formally accompanied to their bed chamber.

The bride and groom often travelled to their new home immediately
after their wedding party. The Halls give a somewhat idealized description of such a journey as observed by them in the south-west of Ireland,
towards the middle of the nineteenth century:

We had scarcely ... entered the county of Kerry, when we encountered a group that interested us greatly; on enquiry we learned that
a wedding had taken place at a cottage pointed out to us, in a little
glen among the mountains, and that the husband was bringing home
his bride. She was mounted on a white pony, guided by as smart looking and well dressed a youth as we had seen in the country; his face
was absolutely radiant with joy; the parents of the bride and bridegroom followed; and a little girl clung to the dress of a staid and

Young Kerry woman being led on horseback from her parents' home to the house
of her bridegroom, mid nineteenth century. From Halls' *Ireland*, vol. 1, p. 165.

sober matron – whom we at once knew to be the mother of the bride, for her aspect was pensive, almost to sorrow; her daughter was quitting for another home the cottage in which she had been reared – to become a wife.[76]

An account from Castleblaney in Co. Monaghan explains how the bride might expect to be greeted when she arrived at the groom's house:

On arrival at the groom's house a woman (who had been arranged with to do it) met the bride as she came up to the door, and handed her the tongs from the fire. This gesture signified that a new woman was in control of this fireside in future.[77]

As the fire symbolized the heart of domestic activity, to be given control of the fireside meant having control over all the workings of the home. According to Anna Sexton, the tongs were handed over to the bride by her mother-in-law: 'It was frequently a symbol only as the old lady rarely surrendered her authority so easily.'[78]

No evidence of early examples of the practice of the groom carrying the bride over the threshold have come to light, although Lageniensis reports: 'On coming home to her new dwelling, the bride must not step over the bridegroom's threshold, but her nearest relations were required to lift her over it, by locking their hands together, when she sat over their arms and leant upon their shoulders.'[79] Occasionally, the bride did not accompany the groom immediately, but waited for a few days after the wedding before travelling to her new home. A Co. Antrim account explains:

The ordinary run of the country did not go away on honeymoon. After the party which lasted most of the night, the groom returned to his own home but the bride remained at her father's house for a few days or perhaps a week or more, and then quietly and without ceremony went to her new home.[80]

To delay for a few days may have helped some couples avoid falling prey once more to pranksters, although many couples were denied this chance. An account from Co. Fermanagh illustrates that a high-spirited group of friends might escort the couple on their journey: 'A crowd usually accompanied the couple to their new home, and this was called the 'drag home' as sometimes the horse was taken out of the vehicle, and it was pulled by the guests.'[81] Alice Ward's account of her arrival in Saintfield, quoted above, illustrates that the 'drag home' was observed at various social levels. Its popularity persisted into the present century, and some couples returned home by rail from honeymoon to discover a crowd of friends waiting to 'drag' them home in a cart from the station. This would often lead to an impromptu party in their new home. The exuberant and noisy convoys of cars which characterize the journey of wedding guests from ceremony to reception at present-day weddings, particularly in the west of Ireland, are reminiscent both of the drag home and to an extent of the races held after weddings in the past.

When the 'drag home' occurred on the night of the wedding, it helped to ensure that, although there was no formal bedding ceremony, the couple did not retire uneventfully. Their bed was often interfered with. An 'apple pie bed' might be made up, the bottom sheet folded back giving the impression that all was well, but making it impossible to lie down until the bed was remade. Briars or frogs were often placed between the sheets, and someone would usually be posted beneath the appropriate window, in order to report back on how any such surprise was received. The potential for embarrassment was increased by placing epsom salts in the chamber pot under the bridal bed.

For many couples, adjusting to their new routine began the day after the wedding. Many immediately returned to work, and some young women found themselves negotiating their position in the new household while others were responsible for organizing and directing servants. It is often considered typical of rural Irish society that marriage brought about an enhancement of status, but this was equally true of more sophisticated circles. Immediately after her young sister Lydia's wedding, the fictional Elizabeth Bennet was to observe the bride 'with anxious parade, walk up to their mother's right hand, and hear her say to her eldest sister, "Ah! Jane, I take your place now, and you must go lower, because I am a married woman."'[82] A more modest newly married woman might find: 'It startles her when the servants call her "ma'am", or when she has to take precedence of some unmarried lady older than herself.'[83] She might be afforded the luxury of a transitional period during which she might continue to be referred to as a bride, giving her a chance to adjust to her new role and status, but for many married couples, especially in past generations, the reality was summed up by Lageniensis: 'Then, forgetting frolic, they settled down to their ordinary occupations.'[84]

7 Life in the Home

Marriage enhanced the status of individuals, both male and female. This is often considered to be typical of Ireland, but, as we have seen, it was also a feature of society elsewhere, being true, for example, of England in the sixteenth and seventeenth century.[1] In the eighteenth century, the term 'Mrs' was sometimes used by friends addressing unmarried women, as a mark of respect.[2] Wives of doctors were sometimes referred to as 'Mrs Dr'. The idea of respectability, which was of fundamental importance to the middle classes, helped to associate social standing with the married status. Among the poorest classes, the married enjoyed greater credibility and were more likely to be regarded by those in authority as 'deserving' than were the single, a point which may sometimes have encouraged pauper couples to legitimize their unions.[3]

That being said, there is evidence to suggest that, among both the urban English working classes[4] and the Irish poor, marriage was unlikely to enhance one's status in the eyes of one's peers.[5] For those who were homeless, dependent on begging or on casual labour, marriage may have carried little relevance, although, even when couples were separated or women deserted by circumstances exacerbated by poverty, they often knew the whereabouts of 'spouse or partner'.[6]

The attitude to marriage held by the poor helps to reinforce the view that marriage was fundamentally concerned with property, access to or the ownership of which was more likely to guarantee a settled life and provide a basis for aspirations to respectability which marriage in turn enhanced. It has been argued that in certain circumstances refusing to marry a partner actually extended a woman's rights, at least in the domestic sphere. The lack of legal recognition of the rights of married women could well place them at a great disadvantage in relation to their husbands, whereas if they did not marry their bargaining power was enhanced. Men too perceived that they stood to gain from not being married, one being quoted as saying, 'If I married her, I should never be sure of my tea.'[7]

Certain advantages in not marrying were also perceived at higher social levels, although in order to maintain the appearance of respectability, those enjoying sexual relationships while dispensing with the formalities of marriage had to keep such matters secret. In May 1862, the *Dublin University Magazine* commented on the plight of middle-class mothers who 'are now wailing over daughters they cannot get off their hands, and sons who prefer clandestine domesticity to a respectable settlement in life'.[8] It continued: 'There are other means of securing most of the advantages of matrimony without any of its disadvantages, and this without incurring any social disapprobation. Why, under these circumstances, men may as well remain in a condition of nominal celibacy.'[8] Clearly, many different types of relationship between men and women were played out against the backdrop of Irish society at various levels, not to mention in different periods, making it very difficult to generalize about the experience of marriage and of life in the home. Ireland is no exception to Lautman's statement on marriage and family in Western society:

> We have an idealised image of the family, which we believe provides unconditional solidarity, homely affection and a satisfying place for a moderate amount of sexuality. Continually obliged to admit that our image does not correspond to reality, we find that we can give it more substance by projecting it into the past. Thus the family serves both as a haven and a symbol. It is a rallying point for ideologies ... [T]he traditional western family ... is a myth that never corresponded to any reality.[9]

The actual experience as opposed to the idealized view of Irish family life is increasingly being made subject to scrutiny.

In early Irish society, there were clearly defined sets of circumstances in which a woman could separate from her husband without forfeiting her property and receive compensation from him. These included neglect or abandonment, violence, ridicule, failure to give the wife 'full rights in domestic and other social matters' and 'giving her a love potion before marriage'.[10] In more recent times, some Nonconformist sects have been prepared to countenance divorce,[11] and 'self divorce' was an option availed of by some.[12] It has been remarked that divorce settlements in early Irish society were as preoccupied with property as were the marriage settlements themselves.[13] One of the consequences of the Tudor plantations of Ireland was that the capacity of married women to hold land was substantially curtailed.[14] Scholars have identified as characteristic of much more recent times a 'preoccupation [not only] of keeping land within the family but also keeping it under male control'.[15] A woman's dowry was no guarantee of any rights to her husband's property, and in some circumstances this could create difficulties for childless widows who might discover that they had no claim on property owned by their late husbands.[16]

Childlessness and property are intertwined in the question of inheritance. Failure to provide an heir meant that the line was discontinued, and responsibility for the inability to conceive was usually attributed to the woman.[17] This might undermine not only the position of a widow, but that of a childless woman – or even one who had daughters but no sons – whose husband was still alive. One Thomas Knox of Dungannon, for example, in 1700, had 'expectations of his present wife stepping off the stage in hopes to have a son and heir by another'.[18] Even in the present century, a childless woman might be repudiated and, although her husband could not remarry while she remained alive, he 'could give over his land to his brother in return for a fortune and a stipulation that his brother would marry and produce an heir'.[19] The emphasis on producing an heir is echoed in fairy belief. Theft (or sometimes substitution) of children is a characteristic of Irish fairy belief, and male children were considered to be at greater risk than females. Little boys were often dressed in skirts,[20] and, while there were strong practical reasons for this, it is often explained by reference to fairy belief, as a mechanism for tricking the 'wee folk' into misunderstanding the sex of a child.

In some economic and social circumstances, children were a mixed blessing, a liability until old enough to contribute to the family income.[21] Women sought to limit family sizes,[22] and there is growing evidence for the practise of infanticide.[23] On the blessings side, older children helped to rear younger brothers and sisters, and in the mid twentieth century a measure of child-care was provided by allowing children to play in fairly large groups, those not quite old enough to join in sitting in push-chairs near a group which included older sisters (and occasionally brothers). Children as young as seven might provide immediate supervision, themselves not straying too far from home.

Poverty sometimes compelled a couple into separation, either temporarily or long term, and even families with a relatively stable home base might be separated for a while, as able-bodied men from some areas engaged in migratory labour. Wives of the very poor were generally responsible for begging in order to maintain the family, and often travelled to regions were they would not be known and recognized when resorting to this means of raising a living.[24] It has been argued that many families were compelled into separation in the aftermath of the Famine of the 1840s, support for this view coming from the claim of an official from Co. Kerry 'that many fathers had emigrated using prepaid passages and dumped their families in the workhouse, only to marry again, soon after their arrival in America'.[25] Officials in Limerick apparently guarded against this: when, in 1852, one Thomas Hackett sought assistance to go with his two children but without his wife to North America, he was refused permission until she gave up her position in domestic service and travelled with him, on the grounds that otherwise she might subsequently become 'a burden on the rates of the Union'.[26] Women, too, had access to assisted passages to North America, and employed strategies of temporary desertion in order to qualify for such help. Some women abandoned their children to give themselves the opportunity to establish themselves in better circumstances, and once they had achieved this they either paid or applied for assistance to pay to have their children join them.[27]

Marriage was not necessarily a guarantee of a stable domestic environment, especially for those living on or below subsistence level. None the less, couples, including poorer ones, did marry and attempt to set up home together. Many did so in the same dwelling already occupied by the parents of the bridegroom. Despite the ritualized handing over of authority to the new housewife,[28] a bride's position in her new household 'had to be carefully negotiated'.[29] Some needed to iron out a mode of co-operating with mother-in-law in a well-established routine. Many another young woman found herself in a household in which she became wife to one man and housekeeper to several others besides. A young woman who began married life with her husband's family in a Co. Down town, *c.*1970, describes her situation:

> I moved in with his family, now there was three men and me. I sort
> of was threw in at the deep end there too. You know, working after a
> crowd of men. And it was hard, going into a crowd of men ... There
> was me, his brother, his father and himself, and I was stuck in the
> middle of it ... I know at the start, now I sort of took over the house,
> where cleaning and things is concerned. You end up doing that, and
> then regret it after it, for you know you should have worked it out at
> the start, who done what.[30]

Households previously run by sisters of the groom might present brides with quite other sets of complications.[31]

Public sector housing did not become widely available in Northern Ireland until the mid twentieth century, although some housing was accessible to farm labourers, at least in certain areas, by the beginning of that century. Some couples had the means to set up home independently, and this option was not entirely restricted to the wealthy. It is worth remembering that, in the mid nineteenth century, a considerable proportion of the population of Ulster, particularly in the west, lived in one-roomed houses.[32] 'House' might be a rather too elevated name for the structures of rubble or turf, perhaps not tall enough to permit their occupants to stand up, in which within living memory some people sheltered. Thomas Reid, who travelled in Ireland in 1822, described buildings in the region of Ballygawley as being 'constructed by placing long sticks in a starting position against a high back and covering them with scraws'. Reid commented on how a young Tyrone couple were provided with a new home:

> I happened to pass near a place where five men and a young female were regaling over a bottle of whiskey, for the purpose, so they said, of 'christening Donald's castle.' This Donald had been married the day before, but having no house to live in, four good natured neighbours volunteered their services to assist him and his bride to construct one. They accordingly had assembled at day-light this morning and in thirteen hours they completed their task: the 'castle' was finished and the newly married couple were to sleep in it that very night!
>
> Green heath composed the bed, a row of sods was to serve as a pillow, and Donald's 'big coat' with Sally's cloak had to answer for bedclothes.[33]

Traditional accounts of houses built in a day for newly married couples, and of earthen floors being 'danced in', are widespread in local folklore.

In rural areas, having moved into her new home, the bride was expected to observe a 'month's mind'. This was a period of a month following the wedding, during which she was expected to stay at her new home without paying a visit to her parents. Some accounts suggest that to make such a visit any earlier would bring bad luck, and most agree that the bride should break with her parents for at least that time, in order to become accustomed to her new circumstances. Before taking their brides to their new homes, some bridegrooms stayed with them in their own parental homes for a few days, perhaps to lessen the impact of the loosening of family ties. In Co. Tipperary in the early nineteenth century the ceremony of bringing home a bride was apparently known as the 'hauling home'. The groom, accompanied by his neighbours, all on horseback,

could expect to be 'pelted with cabbage stalks by the mob'.[34] Throughout
the British Isles, some couples did not live together after marriage.[35]

A Co. Antrim poet describes in one of his verses the mixed feelings,
romantic and practical, of a man who lacks confidence to court the
woman of his choice, despite his belief that she would 'marry the first one
who takes her':

> I went home and sat down on the aul fir log
> At the back of the kitchen door
> For the piles of ash and dirty dishes
> Was nearly blocking the floor.[36]

Some women must have faced lives of domestic drudgery, and research
has revealed that, for many, confinement to the home was more prolonged than for the 'month's mind'.[37] Some very young brides of much
older husbands found themselves to be subject to the authority of long-
standing female hired helps whose presence in their homes predated
their own, and whose influence on husbands could be strong.[38]

Not all accounts of early married life subscribe to the picture of misery.
Sean Crawford tells of a custom observed in south Co. Down:

> In Aughnamoira there was a custom known as a 'Bride's Play'. It
> took place, I think on the Sunday after the married couple return. As
> far as I can recall the bride ran out of the field and was chased by the
> male members of the party. She, of course, got a good start. When she
> was caught she may have been kissed, but I can't swear to that and
> my only evidence is 'hear-say.'[39]

A description from Fanad in Co. Donegal tells that friends would sometimes hold parties for newly-weds. These might continue for several
weeks after the wedding. Prolonging the festivities in this way seems to
have been more popular in urbanized or more fashionable society than
in rural areas. Middle-class brides could expect to attend receptions, one
given by parents, a subsequent one by parents-in-law, on their return
from honeymoon. Brides were advised that their dress for these occasions should be 'dark silk, as rich and elegant as means permit, but without any bridal ornaments'.[40]

Couples were expected to send out cards as soon as they had settled in
their new houses, and friends were warned: 'If you do not receive a wedding card, do not call upon a newly married couple. There is a tacit understanding that only those receive them whose acquaintance they wish to
retain.'[41] Another contemporary etiquette book several times repeats a

warning that a bride should not visit anyone who has not first called on her: 'After everyone has called upon her, the bride will have to return their visits, leaving her card with her At Home Day written under her name or across the left hand corner of the top'.[42] The collection in the Ulster Folk and Transport Museum includes a card case believed to have been given as a wedding present to one young woman, *c*.1880.

Just as uninvited guests might attend a wedding party, some married couples might suffer unwanted guests in their new homes. Sean Connolly comments on the collection of May Balls, or of substitute money, alcohol or other items, which were demanded each spring from couples married during the previous twelve months, remarking that these levies were sometimes claimed very violently, so that in 1782 the Bishop of Ossory decreed:

> Those who in future demanded the customary tribute from newly married couples, as well as those who gave it, were to be punished by being excluded from the Sacraments. In addition, the couple's first child was to be baptised only in the parish chapel ... and the churching of the mother ... was to be delayed for thirty days.[43]

As there were restrictions on the behaviour of the unchurched mother, the final prohibition would have made life very difficult for anyone affected by it.

Churching was the religious ceremony through which women were socially reintegrated after childbirth, and it was of particular importance to women in the Church of Ireland and the Catholic Church. One Church of Ireland woman explained:

> Whenever I was having the baby, I knew, like, where the baby was coming from, but I didn't really know. You know, you'd pains and what have you, and they used to say, 'It's like hell, you know, but you forget about it.' And the neighbours used to say, 'Oh, you'll have to go and get the grace of God about you, you know, after having a baby, the bed and all you come out of.'[44]

The 1549 Book of Common Prayer of Edward VI included 'The Order of the Purification of Women', which required the recently delivered mother to kneel down 'nigh unto the Quire door' to give thanks and to make offerings including a Crisome, the white vestment put on to a baby at baptism by the priest. The priest's prayers during this purificatory ceremony mention the 'great pain and peril of childbirth'.[45] This ritual was later known as 'The Thanksgiving of Women after Childbirth, commonly

called the Churching of Women'. In this form, it includes Psalm 116, one
verse of which runs: 'The snares of death compassed me round about, and
the pains of hell gat hold upon me', an apt description of the experience
of labour which also expresses the peril of childbirth for both mother and
baby, and which, to judge from oral evidence collected in the twentieth
century, appears to have helped to form and inform popular opinion and
traditional belief for hundreds of years.

Despite the change in emphasis from purification to thanksgiving, the
idea that the churching ceremony was a cleansing process continued to
influence the thinking of women themselves. One Catholic woman, referring to her own experience in the mid twentieth century, explained:

> 'You didn't enter anybody's house, you know, you never went to any-
> body's house until you got your churching done.'
>   'And why was that?'
>   'Well, I was always told it was, a woman went through the pains of
> hell, and once you go through the pains of hell, then you've got to be
> brought back into Church again sort of style, you know. About the
> churching, I was speaking to my own mother, and she said that was
> your first trip, was to the chapel. And it was every day you could go,
> at any time. – Or sorry, no, there was a particular time, say two
> o'clock in the afternoon, the priest would have come into the chapel
> and if there was anyone there that had had a baby, that wanted
> churched, there was a special blessing and what have you, laying on
> of hands. And this was to clean you after producing the devil himself.
> It was baptism cleaned the child. – Baptism cleaned the child, but not
> the mother.' [46]

The activities, particularly of Catholic women, were very curtailed
between the time of childbirth and the observance of churching, as one
Belfast mother shows in her account of her experience earlier in the
twentieth century:

> 'And sure [now] they're into the bath, after the babies is born. We
> couldn't get washing our faces. I had hair at that time down my back.
> If I only had had the sense even to put two plaits in it, or even one
> plait. When I got up, I wasn't able to comb my hair, I was taking it in
> wee bits by wee bits, to get it combed.'
>   'And you weren't allowed to comb it until you were churched, is
> that right?'
>   'No. Not at all – I was near dead to see the [nurses] would get their
> heels getting out, till I would get over to the chapel to get churched.

You see, you couldn't have done a thing at that time, to you got churched. And they weren't out of the district, Maggie was over in St Peter's, and another old doll beside me, she was there too. And at that time you were churched at the very bottom, [near the door] and you knelt on the tiles. And she was up like a bird, I could hardly get off the floor. Big Andy, the sexton, was there, with the priest, he said, "Look at that, away out," he says, "didn't take her." Hers was born the same night as mine, hers was born that Saturday night, too. She lived in the next street to me. I couldn't rise off the tiles. I got up. I got on home. I got then I could make my own dinner, and make the dinner for everybody come in. And do my own washing, and all the rest.'

'And you weren't allowed to do any of those things till you were churched?'

'Not till you were churched. Nobody could, you couldn't make nobody a cup of tea. Did ever you know the like of it?'[47]

Although this period of prohibition might have given a new mother time to recuperate after childbirth, it could place her under great restrictions even in regard to the food she could eat. As recently as the 1960s, some clergymen did their best to encourage women to be churched and there was a belief that mother and baby would thrive better if the appropriate ritual was observed. More recently, the significance of the churching ceremony has radically declined, and in the Catholic Church the ritual has been incorporated into the ceremony of baptism.

A live child of the Catholic Church or the Church of Ireland was expected to be baptized soon after birth. Traditionally, the first visit ought to be for baptism. Godparents took the children for christening, and therefore would be chosen before the birth of the child. It was sometimes considered unlucky to chose an engaged (or perhaps a childless) couple to stand as godparents, in case this blighted their own chances of parenthood. Among some Presbyterians, there was a fear that infants would not thrive if they were not baptized. Elaborate christening gowns were often prepared for baptism and passed down through families. Another custom observed in some parts of the country is described by a Co. Armagh woman:

We had an aunt who was a maternity nurse ... and she said that in a few houses there was a box placed outside the door, if they were at the top of the house and she came out through the door with the new-born babe in her arms, maybe to bring downstairs to show to the grandparents or something, she had to step up on a box first of all, so that the first step the child took was up in the world, whereas if she had gone down the stairs it would be going down in the world ... And another one was putting a sixpence in its hand, the very first.[48]

The custom of putting silver money into the hand of a new-born baby on the first visit is still often observed.

For the most part, stillborn children, at least since the turn of the century and in Belfast, were buried in the family grave or in an old grave, without the funeral service. According to oral accounts, the father would take the body, generally in a cardboard box, to the cemetery, where the gravedigger would open the grave. An older tradition held that unbaptized children were not entitled to burial in consecrated ground; however, lay baptism was often administered even in the case of a still birth, in case there was imperceptible life in the child. Recently, the burial places set aside by the Catholic Church for stillborn children are increasingly receiving recognition, a matter which is often of great comfort to the bereaved mothers whose children may have lain there for years.

⟵ Baby Linen.—Detailed List. ⟶

Lawn Shirts, Trimmed Lace	9d., 1/-, 1/6, 2/-
Longcloth Night Gowns, Trimmed Work	1/6, 2/6, 2/11, 3/9, 4/6
Nainsook Monthly Gowns, Trimmed Insertion and Lace ...	4/6, 5/6, 5/11, 6/9, 7/6, 8/9, 9/6
Cambric Slips, Tucked Skirts	2/9
Cambric Slips, Trimmed Work	3/6, 4/6
Robes, with Insertion Bodices and Trimmed Skirts	10/6, 12/9 to 21/-
Robes, High or Low Necks, fully Trimmed Embroidery or Lace ...	21/-, 25/- to 3 gns.
Flannel Day Wrappers	3/9, 5/6, 6/6, 8/6
Flannelette Night Wrappers, White and Pink	2/9 to 3/9
Welsh Flannel Night Wrappers	2/9, 3/3, 3/9 to 5/6
Flannel Pilchers	1/9, 2/9
Mackintosh Pilchers	1/3, 1/6, 1/11
Turkish Towels, per dozen	3/11, 4/11, 5/6 to 8/6
Woven Swaithes	9d. and 1/-
Flannel Head Squares, Embroidered Silk	2/11, 3/6 to 6/6
Wool Boots	6d., 9d., 1/- to 3/-
Bibs, Quilted and Embroidered	1/-, 1/6, 2/-, 2/6
Bibs, Embroidered and Trimmed Lace	2/6, 3/6, 4/9
Mackintosh Aprons	2/-, 2/9, 3/6
Mackintosh Sheeting, per yard	2/6, 4/3
Cashmere Christening Cloaks	21/- to 3 gns.
Cashmere and Silk Hoods	4/6 to 19/6
Washing Hoods and Hats	from 3/6
Knitted Wool Hoods and Hats	2/9, 3/6, to 9/6

Early twentieth-century layette list of items available from the Bank Buildings, Belfast. *UFTM archive.*

Labour was a dangerous time for both mother and baby. Women in child-birth and new-born children were considered to be among the favourite targets of the fairies. Certain precautions were necessary to deny access to a new-born child. These included rocking a new-born infant, particularly a male child, in horse's harness prior to putting him into a cradle, wrapping a male baby in his father's trousers and never leaving a cradle unattended unless the fire-tongs were placed upon it. The link between fairies and the dead seems to relate to people dead, as it were, out of their time, whose proper place is therefore neither among the living nor the dead. Pregnancy and childbirth are, and have long been surrounded by traditional customs and beliefs. One account tells of a well educated Belfast woman, of childbearing age between the wars, who believed that her first child was stillborn because she wore a green dressing gown to hospital when she was to be delivered. It is considered unlucky to wear green in any circumstances, and the colour is particularly associated with the fairies. There are strong beliefs that the actions of the mother can have physical consequences for her unborn child. Birthmarks, for example, were believed to result if a pregnant woman witnessed any bloodshed, while a slight accident to the expectant mother could result in damage or disfigurement to the child. If a pregnant woman saw a hare and omitted to tear her shift, it was believed that her child would be born with a harelip, or cleft palate. Traditonal beliefs and customs also suround the vulnerable newborn, so that for example, it was often considered lucky to borrow a cradle for a first-born child. Nowadays some people consider it unlucky to bring a new pram into a home until the child for whom it is intended is born. In extreme cases, some people leave all preparations for the new arrival until after the birth.

Childbirth and child care were intensely female concerns. During labour, men were with few exceptions, expected to keep well away, and this often applied equally to any arrangements for adoption which may have been necessary. One woman described arrangements made for the adoption of an illegitimate baby girl in Belfast after the Second World War:

> They took her home out of the hospital, she brought her round to me. And my man was sitting there ... but he went out and stood at the door. And the child was lovely ... [S]he says. 'I want rid of it.' ... Well, I told Mary then to go up to where [a certain woman] lived ... So that woman kept it.[49]

Other arrangements which might be made for illegitimate children included their being brought up by maternal grandmothers as if they were sisters of their actual mothers. Some were simply abandoned to be cared for in the workhouse, where they would become the charges of wet nurses, circumstances which did not enhance their expectation of survival:

> [T]he minding of foundling children was the least desirable of all occupations. Women outside the workhouse had to be paid an attractive wage to act as wetnurses. Pauper women within the workhouses had to be cajoled with a daily jug of porter to undertake the task ... which was lower in prestige than washing the dead or cleaning the workhouse toilets.[50]

It has also been suggested that infanticide or at least deliberate and fatal neglect of children might be practised. The children of women who entered Magdalen asylums, institutions which in the nineteenth century were dedicated to the reclamation of 'fallen women', were likely to be handed over for adoption.[51] Oral accounts attest to the fact that women might attempt by various means to procure abortions.[52] This was true of married women whose capacities for child-rearing were already severely stretched by the numbers of children in their care, although some duties were usually delegated to older daughters.

Attitudes to illegitimacy varied according to several factors including geography, historical period and status. Some individuals were more sympathetic than others, and it has been suggested that in some areas, for example Tory Island, illegitimacy was not considered a stigma.[53] It has been argued that Catholic women were more inclined to chastity than their Protestant counterparts, and rates of illegitimacy in Ulster in the mid nineteenth century were higher than in any other region of Ireland, making them more comparable to contemporary rates in England.[54] Of the south of Ireland during a later period, another commentator remarks: 'Pregnant but unmarried women were usually exported, like the criminals, to England',[55] and it has been suggested that some Dublin houses featured concealed basements which could be rented as virtual prisons in which unmarried pregnant girls might be confined.[56]

There are wide differences in opinion as to whether contraception was practised in the Irish countryside[57] during the last two centuries and some historians believe that both infant mortality and contraception helped to keep the size of nineteenth-century pauper families relatively small.[58] Folklore attests to some knowledge of contraceptive methods, including *coitus interruptus*, and also provided remedies which might be tried by barren women.[59] Fertility and its absence were generally considered to be matters for which women were solely responsible, although one mid eighteenth-century toast honouring a new-born child acknowledged 'The lady on the straw and the gentleman that made her so'.[60]

Reticence is often considered to characterize the Irish attitude to sex. Married Irish women of the 1960s are quoted as remarking 'He's very good, he doesn't want it often', 'I'm lucky, I don't mind it', or expressing other, similar sentiments.[61] Many scholars have been in broad agreement on this idea, but some have found evidence of other codes of conduct. Women mill-workers in Belfast were perfectly capable of ribald behaviour and of teasing young men alongside whom they worked.[62] One blushing north Antrim bride, who married early in 1739, was less than reticent on her wedding day:

> We hear from Dunluce, that a comical Marriage lately happened there, between a couple from Finvoy near Ballymoney, as follows: the Bride unfortunately happened to fall very drunk; who immediately after the Priest had ended the Ceremony, called out with a loud voice, *go to Bed, go to Bed*, and was heard at a considerable Distance off, to the great Shame of the Bridegroom, who to prevent her Cries, and make her quiet, went to bed with her, but as she was going she fell down Stairs and broke her Nose; With much ado she got to Bed, still crying, *go to Bed*, and the Bridegroom having laid her down, went back to his Company. An arch Wag then in the House took the Opportunity to lying down with the Bride in the Bridegroom's Absence, who, unhappily going to see his agreeable Bride, found the honest Fellow in Bed with her in a very loving Manner, which sight caused the Bridegroom to fall into a Swoon, while the arch Fellow got off; the Bride also got up and ran after him still crying *go to Bed*, who fell a second time down Stairs and was thereby much hurt, having lost much of her Blood. Her Husband is in great Trouble for the Harm his Spouse had so innocently met with.[63]

The nineteenth-century Co. Down poet Robert Huddleston included in his manuscripts various ribald allusions along with accounts, perhaps fantasized but revealing none the less, of outrageous sexual encounters.[64]

Prostitution was a fairly common profession for women inhabiting larger Irish towns in the nineteenth century, and many refuges were established to provide temporary or permanent accommodation for women who no longer wished to pursue this way of life. Margaret

Leeson's memoirs give a colourful insight into the rather elegant life of a society prostitute during the eighteenth century. Mrs Leeson, also known as Peg Plunket, eventually succumbed to venereal disease, but not until she was almost seventy years of age and had repented of her excesses, remarking of her charitable contemporary, 'Had Lady Arabella Denny lived ... I would have given all I possessed to the Magdalen asylum, and retired into it myself.'[65] Mrs Leeson's profession was far from being condoned by contemporary society: as a young woman she attempted a reconciliation with her family, but on visiting one of her sisters, 'Alas! I was not admitted as far as the parlour, she immediately called me a vile wretch, bade me begone, and pushing me violently from the door, shut it in my face', while a cousin drove her off 'with scorn and contempt, and he even threatened to beat me for having (as he said) the impudence to come to his house and scandalize it by my appearance'.[66]

None the less, there were plenty of 'Impures' happy to enjoy the same way of life as Mrs Leeson, there were clearly several brothels in Dublin besides her own, and at one time her clientele included the Lord Lieutenant. Among her acquaintances were various whores originally from Belfast and its environs. Some women may have resorted to prostitution as a temporary measure, until they had accumulated sufficient capital or found other methods of supporting themselves.[67] Numbers of prostitutes seem to have declined at the very end of the nineteenth century, but one estimate suggested that there might be as many as 4,000 prostitutes, including those who followed the profession as part-timers in the Monto area of Dublin in 1907.[68] Garrison towns also attracted prostitutes and their ranks may have been swollen by soldiers' common law wives as it was then the practice of the Army not to recognize soldiers' marriages unless they were living in married quarters.[69] None the less, prostitution was perceived as a social problem, and various methods of combating it, legal and charitable, were tried.

Statistics show that there were approximately 370 known prostitutes, a few under the age of sixteen, plying a trade in Belfast in 1868.[70] In the same year there were approximately ten times as many arrests for prostitution in Dublin.[71] Statistics concerning brothel-based prostitution in Edinburgh at about the same time suggest that 'each girl has twelve visitors per week'.[72] Today in the United States the girls are apparently rather busier, as the average street whore services 1500 clients annually.[73] To attempt a head count of whores themselves is problematical enough, let alone trying to estimate the extent of a potential clientele, but these figures do go some length towards challenging the usual perception of

Irish sexuality. Nineteenth-century prostitutes were reviled by respectable contemporary society; there was a charitable urge to help them to reform, and their profession was regarded as a social problem; but their existence in such numbers does not sit entirely comfortably with the generally held view of male and female chastity, often considered an absolute value of Irish society. Some nineteenth-century reformers acknowledged the existence of double standards in relation to sexuality and considered that 'it is men's unchastity and men's injustice which are mainly responsible for this crying wrong',[74] but the views of the moralists help to confirm that celibacy was not the inevitable order of the day.

On the domestic front, women may have been additionally motivated to favour the ideal of chastity and to promote the ideal of sexual abstinence as a means of preventing conception. Rates both of maternal and of infant mortality have historically been relatively high in Ireland,[75] and, for those who survived the experience, continual child-bearing and child-rearing could be debilitating and exhausting. In general, management of the process of childbirth was the domain of women, although advertisements in some contemporary newspapers show that by the eighteenth century some labours were attended by a 'man midwife'.[76] As the formal knowledge of obstetrics developed, those who could afford to might be attended by a recognized medical practitioner.

The Midwives Act, which made it illegal for a child to be born without the assistance of a qualified medical practitioner, was applied to Ireland in 1918, but even after this date many labours were assisted by the 'handywoman', the unofficial midwife, herself usually a mother, whose skills were gained and applied without the sanction of the authorities. By the early twentieth century, there is evidence that widows especially found midwifery a suitable profession which could readily be combined with single parenthood, and several widows gained a qualification entitling them to practice officially, even before 1918. It seems that, *c.*1900, handywomen without formal training could acquire official sanction by registering as midwives, without the need to undergo actual training. The skills of handywomen were, no doubt, uneven and must have differed greatly from individual to individual, but it seems that some qualified practitioners were glad to rely on their assistance, and they were held in high regard by the communities for whom they provided such important help.

As well as assisting at childbirth, the handywoman often took responsibility for laying out the dead. Special sets of white bedlinens were kept in many households for this purpose, and those who did not own some could borrow from a neighbour. Often the handywoman herself had a set which she would bring with her if required. The borrowers would be responsible for laundering the linens and returning them in due course. Sometimes these linens were received as wedding presents, or preparing a set might be among the first tasks awaiting a new bride.

The wearing of mourning dress after the death of a family member was required much more of women than of men. In the nineteenth century, when mourning was worn extensively among the middle classes, the associated regulations became very fixed. A man might marry for a second time before the end of the period of mourning for the first, and respectable society had the right to expect the new wife to appear dressed in mourning for her predecessor. Should her predecessor's parents die, she was also expected to wear mourning for them, a point which helps to establish the range of people an extended family might be expected to embrace. It is easy to view this in a negative way, but mourning wear had an important role to play in nineteenth-century fashion. The tones of mourning dominated the dress of the British court in the second half of the nineteenth century, and there seems to have been a tremendous vogue, for example for lilac dress prints in shades suggestive of secondary mourning. To dress in these tones was considered desirable.

On a less frivolous note, the wearing of mourning may have reflected the role of women as the domestic heads of their households. Dressed in mourning, these women physically symbolized the condition of the family and made a statement about their own situation. The wearing of mourning was concerned with legitimate relationships:

> It would have been improper for a mistress or an unrecognised illegitimate son to go into mourning, however great might be their sorrow. It seems probable that this was because conventionalised mourning operated like a public statement of relationship.[77]

The wearing of mourning could help to reinforce the domestic role from which wives and mothers derived power and authority.

Despite the high rate of maternal mortality in Ireland, many women survived into widowhood, and some would live longer as widows than as wives.[78] Especially in the late nineteenth century, many of these women followed the example of Queen Victoria, dressing in the colours of mourning, frequently in black, for the rest of their lives. Retailers were ready to cater for their requirements, and many large department stores had sections devoted to mourning dress. Some shops sold nothing else. Ogilvy's Mourning Warehouse of Grafton Street, Dublin, advertised its wares thus:

ALEXANDER OGILVY directs the Special attention of FAMILIES requiring Mourning, and LADIES WHO WEAR BLACK from choice, to the many advantages they will have in purchasing at this Establishment, where they will have one of the largest Stocks of Black Goods in the Kingdom to select from, in every variety of make and price, all of which are purchased direct from the Manufacturer for cash, warranted of the best materials, and at prices which cannot be equalled ... Owing to the many calls for sudden Mourning there is always a large Stock of the above ready for immediate wear, in correct taste and finish, thereby enabling Ladies to appear in full mourning in a few hours, all of which has been made by experienced workers of Black Goods on the Premises, and in the Latest Fashion. Where bereavement prevents Ladies leaving home, one of the experienced Saleswomen and Dressmakers (with a well-selected Stock of DRESSES, SKIRTS, BONNETS, MANTLES, JACKETS, GLOVES, STOCKINGS, TIES, JETS, &c.) will be sent to any part of Dublin or Ireland (on receipt of letter or telegram) free of any charge. [79]

Many other shops were ready to supply similar advice and requirements. For the middle-class widow, or for any with aspirations to respectability and social credibility, knowledge of mourning regulations and conventions was absolutely *de rigueur*. Recalling his boyhood in the Co. Antrim town of Portglenone during the 1890s, one man observed:

My mother was a widow, and I remember very well on Sundays and on special occasions such as a 'party' or an 'at home' [her] wearing the prescribed widow's bonnet. This was a bonnet made of black crepe, with a long train-like affair of black crepe flowing down at the back as far as the waist. This was the usual dress for widows, and was worn for a couple of years, when the black crepe was replaced by a similar headdress made of black lace or tulle or chiffon, with the long train-like affair flowing down the back. It was only after some years that I remember seeing my mother wearing a hat.[80]

The married status of women might be denoted through dress in various ways, especially by covering the head. Dr Hunter describes society in Portglenone late in the nineteenth century:

During the holidays ... it was usual for parties to be given. When one was given by my grandfather, the routine was as follows: dressed in my best clothes I was put on duty to open the hall door to the guests,

Young widow from near Dublin, carrying her baby in traditional fashion, folded in her shawl. Although she does not wear full mourning, a black crape band surrounds her bonnet. Her husband was drowned in a boating accident, and her baby born the same day. From Halls' *Ireland*, vol. 2, p. 350.

whilst my aunts hovered round to come forward to shake hands with them, and take them upstairs to a bed-room where the ladies (there were never any men at these parties) would take off their outdoor clothes, and married ladies would put on their lace caps. At that time it was the custom for all married ladies to wear lace caps, and they were never seen without them, except when wearing a bonnet for outdoor wear.[81]

Like their fashionable or society-conscious urbanized counterparts, married women in rural areas also kept their heads covered. A description from Connemara of '[o]ne of the best of our country women' suggests that there may have been a strong practical reason for this:

If unmarried, her glossy black or auburn hair will be turned in a very becoming madonna behind her ears and fastened with a large black pin, if married, you have but little chance of seeing it neatly kept, and, therefore, it is well that it should be concealed beneath a linen cap.[82]

(This remark, incidentally, highlights the fact that married women could expect to have little time to devote to themselves.) In the seventeenth century, married women in comfortable circumstances were distinguished by wearing large white kerchiefs on their heads.[83] Other aspects of the dress of rural women may have reflected marital status. There is a tradition that, in parts of the west of Ireland, this governed the number of bands or tucks which decorated a woman's skirt. The hooded cloak, still worn by some women in Co. Cork in the early twentieth century, may have been the prerogative of the married woman.[84]

Aspirations to respectability also helped to reinforce the idea that the woman's place was in the home. Only the most daring of middle-class women considered following a paid profession, although it was perfectly appropriate to engage in work of a charitable or benevolent nature. A woman who met her husband when both were training as pharmacists in the early years of the twentieth century found that she could not work alongside him when he established a business in the town of Lisburn, towards the end of the First World War. For her to have done so would have implied that her husband was incapable of keeping her. Domestic servants were not encouraged to marry,[85] and many professions operated a marriage bar which often applied to salaried women, compelling them to give up work if they married. In the Irish Republic, the ban on recruiting and employing married women in the Civil Service and in related types of work was not lifted until the passage of the Civil Service (Employment of Married Women) Act in 1973. Similar legislation was not passed in Northern Ireland until 1976. In practice, many organizations had ceased to operate marriage bars by this time. Late in 1968, married women were enabled to join the Royal Ulster Constabulary, and they had begun to do so by the middle of the following year.[86] It has to be admitted that some women were themselves in favour of the marriage bar. For example, it is claimed that the unmarried Head Constable Margaret MacMillan 'once said at a meeting that a woman could not be a policewoman and look after a husband, family and home at the same time'.[87]

During the nineteenth century, some employers had the power to enforce a marriage bar on male employees. For a time, male officers in the Royal Irish Constabulary found that this applied to them:

> Up to the 1860s, constables who were generally unmarried lived in groups of four or five in barracks under a system of strict discipline ... Constabulary Regulations reflecting both pressure on accommodation and an early policy of avoiding inconvenient local attachments, made marriage difficult to the extent of restricting married men to a maximum of 20 per cent of the force. Married men were ineligible for enlistment, and seven years' good service was required before permission to marry could be granted.[88]

Policemen's wives sometimes came in for special scrutiny. In 1896, a Royal Commission on Liquor Licensing Laws was appointed, and in the section of the report which relates to Ireland it is recommended 'that licenses should not be granted to the wives of Police Officers'.[89] Campaigners against prostitution considered that employment conditions could effectively debar a man from marriage even if no actual marriage bar was applied. Among the causes of prostitution cited by Thomas Haslam was 'the poor pay of some men which did not allow them to marry'.[90]

Some members of the working classes sought to emulate the standards of respectability according to which the middle classes ordered their lives. For some working-class families, it was a matter of pride to ensure that women remained in the home. One Belfast woman, employed in a linen mill, explained:

> When I got married, my mother-in-law said none of the Bells' wives ever worked, and she made me leave. When I told the boss I'd have to leave, he paid me off instead, so that I could get the dole.[91]

Two years after her marriage, Mrs Bell gave birth to a daughter who suffered from asthma:

> That was a crucifixion because we had no money but we had to get the doctor and you had to pay the doctor in those days. It was very tough. So I wasn't supposed to work out, but I used to do wee charring jobs. I'd have done anything just to get a few shillings.[92]

Members of the middle classes, too, might be placed under severe strain by the effort of maintaining a home on a single income: 'Full blown middle-class respectability was difficult to maintain on much below £250 a year', which, *c.*1910, was a salary level out of reach to many men under the age of thirty.[93]

In the nineteenth and early twentieth centuries, domestic help was essential to the running of the middle-class household. The actual nature of household chores, especially when coupled with child-rearing, meant that help was needed on a practical level,[94] and employment of domestic staff no doubt contributed to a household's perceived respectability. Relationships also had symbolic quality, and the housewife had to be careful to strike the right note with her staff.[95] Obviously there were great differences between the household with several servants, in which there could be degrees of specialization, and the household dependent upon a sole general maid; and there must have been many households in which engaging a servant was a very expensive luxury.

Whether they were shared with a servant, entirely delegated or entirely undertaken by herself, domestic duties were firmly under the control of the housewife. Women were expected to take total responsibility for work of this type. Some writers have stressed the interdependence of married couples, at least implying a sense of balance and of mutual cooperation in achieving the smooth running of the household.[96] Others have shown the domestic responsibilities of women in a different light, demonstrating that this could be exploited by males in the family.[97] Nevertheless, many women took great pride in domestic competence, and readily embraced the role of domestic head of the household, and this system was often perpetuated by mothers while rearing families. For some, this may have actually meant performance of all domestic work single handed, but others may have negotiated better supported methods of running their homes. A survey conducted in 'a low income estate in Belfast during the 1980s supported the view that male unemployment does not lead to a significant shift in the domestic division of labour',[98] although 'there was some evidence to indicate that spouses of formally employed women did slightly increase their participation in domestic work ... without departing significantly from traditionally established patterns'.[99]

Although the ideal of mutual co-operation in marriage in the past is often taken to imply that, while the woman worked in the home, the man acted as breadwinner and provider, women found various ways of contributing to the household income. Several writers have drawn attention to the Irish housewife's responsibility for the hens and for the dairy,[100] a responsibility shared by women in other, similarly organized societies.[101] Needlework and in earlier times spinning could also make an important contribution to the income of the family, especially in regions where employment was scarce. Statistics show that a family living in the Rosses area of Co. Donegal could expect needlework to be their second largest source of income, exceeded only by earnings for migratory labour to Scotland.[102] It has been pointed out that, in the mid nineteenth century, 'if a family could no longer live by independent labour, the wife regularly became the sole family breadwinner for the crisis period. In the economy of labouring families begging was women's work.'[103] It has been shown, too, that families could be entirely supported by begging, at least for a period of some months, giving the father time to work and save in an attempt to re-establish a more stable base for the household.[104]

In urban areas of the north of Ireland, working-class women often became the major breadwinners. In Londonderry and its environs, and in some other areas, shirt-making and closely related activities offered employment. In Belfast and in other centres, the linen industry provided opportunities for women to earn a wage. Recalling her childhood experiences in the Shankill area of Belfast in the 1920s, Winifred Campbell observed:

> Women competed for a few hours charring, washing, sewing, anything to help out. Some were lucky enough to get back into the mill but even there the work was scarce.
>
> On a limited scale there was a relief scheme whereby a man could be employed for a few weeks on the roads. This was eagerly sought after, but one had to be interviewed by various boards and sometimes a man could be robbed of all dignity. One man, between interviews, had an addition to his family. When he stated this change of circumstances he was asked by a woman interviewer, 'Why do you breed them when you can't feed them?' The payment of this couple of weeks' work was made in the form of a chit for groceries. A

Connemara knitter, mid nineteenth century, her head covered denoting her married status, her baby folded in her shawl. These women were often itinerant, staying for a while in the home of a farmer and thus earning their keep and perhaps a little surplus cash. From Halls's *Ireland*, vol. 3, p. 472.

woman producing one of these chits was often ignored and made to wait until the customers paying cash were served.[105]

Although so easily robbed, dignity was highly valued, as another of Campbell's comments illustrates: 'United by a common poverty we lived a sort of communal life. Help, such as it was, was given and received with simple dignity.'[106]

Not everyone viewed this communal spirit in the same way, and some found it irreconcilable with the concept of dignity which for them was expressed by remaining aloof. Winifred Campbell's contemporary, Mary Bell, recalled her childhood experiences gained in the same area of Belfast:

> My mother hadn't even a penny for the gas. And she couldn't borrow any for she never neighboured. In those days, people kept their doors lying open – my mother kept hers closed. She never asked nobody for nothing. Many a day we'd no dinner or anything, but she wouldn't ask anyone for anything.[107]

Among the working classes, children were often expected to contribute to the family income, and their earnings could be of great importance to the household economy, especially among poorer people. The daughters of wealthier families, on the other hand, might find they faced parental opposition if they wished to undertake paid employment. One young girl, who by 1910 was working as a fully qualified nurse in Belfast, was among those who went out to work against the wishes of her father. Her granddaughter explained:

> My grandmother ... trained at Belfast City Hospital, and 'lived in' whilst training. Her father did not approve, and she had to save up the £5 needed to enrol. (This was paid back to the students over the course of their training ...) Eventually, father had to accept the inevitable, but he was never very happy about it.[108]

Nursing, especially midwifery, was a popular profession to which widows often returned in order to support themselves and their children.

In addition to domestic chores, the household budget was often administered by the housewife. Winifred Campbell again explains:

> In working class circles, it was customary for the wife to manage. A man handed over a proportion of his wages, usually an agreed sum, and depending on how generous he was. It was considered only just

that he should retain a little for himself, and this was his sum to use as he wanted.[109]

Especially when times were difficult, many families resorted to the pawn shop, and credit must have seemed an attractive option to many women struggling to feed a family. Writing in the 1860s, one Mrs Balfour, strenuously warned her readers against this temptation, and advised:

> When a man is in work is the time for the wife to get a little before-hand. A woman of sense will have one morning in the week for marketing, she will buy with caution at a good shop, put her marketing nicely away in her store cupboard, use all with great care, and try what she can eke out of the consumption of one week to help another, and any savings she can make she will put away to buy a stock of coals in. And if she can use her pen, she will have a little book in which she will enter all she spends in housekeeping; so that she can tell exactly whether she is making both ends meet, and a little over ... and she will be able to compare one time with another, and keep a check on any falling into extravagance.[110]

Domestic account books were sometimes given as wedding presents. Several decades later, similar advice was offered by Flora Klickman, who recommended weekly saving from 'your housekeeping money' for emergencies and 'a regular day for paying the tradesmen's books (of which have as few as possible, as they are a great snare) never letting them run over a week. It is far better', she continues, 'if possible to go yourself and order in personally what you want, as you then see what is in best condition, most plentiful and cheapest.'[111]

Many women had a thorough understanding of the efficient management of domestic economy. May Holmes remembered the skills possessed by her widowed mother, and recalled her own childhood in early twentieth-century Belfast:

> My mother could have made a dinner out of nothing. She used to go to Sandy Row every Tuesday when it was pork day. If it wasn't a pig's knee she bought, it was an oxtail – if it wasn't an oxtail, it was ribs, and if it wasn't ribs it was griskins. And she baked twice a week.[112]

Of her own experience, Mary Bell remarked:

> I used to carry a stone of potatoes and a full week's vegetables from the Shankill Road for a shilling, and that did me all week. And I bought a roast for four shillings. I roasted it for Sunday, took it cold

on Monday, put it in a stew on Tuesday – I worked it till Thursday, till my husband was fed up looking at it, because he only had about two pounds a week, and the rent was fourteen shillings.[113]

For many poorer families, finding the rent was paramount, although available information on income and expenditure among working class families in Dublin *c.*1907 suggest that only 12% of the average income was spent on lodgings, 50% being spent on food.[114] The responsibility for making ends meet largely fell on women, who often exercised great ingenuity stretching resources to cover the gap,[115] and faced guilt and the prospect of being considered incompetent if they failed.

Winifred Campbell, who paints a vivid picture of the domestic economy of the Belfast unemployed in the 1920s, says that soup was a staple of even the better times in the Shankill Road area of Belfast:

Soup was practically the national dish ... everybody made it, and it was gorgeous stuff ... First, shin of beef and marrow bones were boiled until tender, with barley and peas, then removed. Leeks, celery, carrot and parsnip were added to the stock, and the whole allowed to simmer on the hob for a couple of hours. Sunday was usually soup day, as enough could be made for Monday, wash day.[116]

Many domestic skills were passed in the home from mother to daughter, but they were also fostered to an extent in school, and by the Department of Agriculture and Technical Institution for Ireland. For almost a decade in the early twentieth century, Florence Irwin was employed to teach cookery along with laundering and dressmaking to women and children throughout Ireland. She soon discovered the shortcomings of domestic equipment in some kitchens. On one occasion, she was asked at her lodgings to make a steak pie for the main meal of the day:

When I arrived in the kitchen there was no mixing bowl – only the basin the 'wee fellas' washed their faces in – it also did duty for the dirty dishes, no rolling pin, no bake board, no scales. She suggested if I returned in twenty minutes all would be ready for me. In the meantime the china flowerpot disappeared from the geranium in my window. On my returning to the kitchen there it was on the well-scrubbed table to serve as my mixing bowl. A length newly sawed off the window pole was my rolling-pin – and a pie-dish which would have required 6lbs. of meat to fill. Well, I went 'down the street' to my lecture hall and borrowed the necessary equipment from it, excusing myself by saying I liked working with my own utensils as I was used to them.[117]

Miss Irwin carried her equipment, which included a 'Mistress' American stove, from place to place. She helped to create a demand for improvements in many kitchens. Shopkeepers came to investigate the implements increasingly required by their customers and she regularly returned to work at the beginning of the week after a visit home 'laden with egg-beaters, wooden spoons and what-not',[118] as her ideas were enthusiastically adopted by her students. The slow modernization of the Irish kitchen has continued throughout the twentieth century, changes coming quickest in the larger towns, then spreading to rural areas. By the late 1970s there were few differences between urban dwellings and larger dwellings in terms of availability of domestic appliances, although those living on smaller farms were found to be slower than their neighbours to adapt to change.[119]

In general, personal accounts of the experience of married life suggest an impression of harmony, often in the face of adversity, poverty and other disadvantages. Mary Bell said:

> I went to my husband without one penny in the world. We used to have wee arguments and he would bring up that I had nothing, and I would say, 'I know I'd nothing – I hadn't even got happiness till I met you.'[120]

Other households were subject to greater disharmony, women and sometimes men experiencing domestic violence. In 1484, one William Osere was granted a separation from his wife on the grounds that she 'was attempting to murder him'.[121] In 1518, the court in Ardee learned that Margery Kelly's husband frequently struck her with an iron rake, a long knife and other weapons, and that her life would be endangered if she remained with him.[122] Such extreme cases might be viewed as grounds for separation, but there is evidence to suggest that a certain level of domestic violence was considered to be acceptable. The seventeenth-century Session Book of Templepatrick Presbyterian church records instances of men being censured for beating either their wives or their children 'On the Lord's Day', when presumably their energies should have been otherwise employed.[123]

It has been established that in Britain in the eighteenth and nineteenth centuries, perpetrators of domestic violence were increasingly subjected to 'rough music by means of which their neighbours could express disapproval of their behaviour'.[124] In contemporary Ireland there seems to have been no such reaction. When they report an encounter with a beaten wife, the Halls are less concerned to highlight the woman's predicament than to illustrate 'the fidelity of the poor Irish wife', who will endure labour, hunger and even ill usage to an almost incredible extent, rather than break the marriage vow. They quote her as saying: 'He beat me, and yet that don't hurt me half so much as he's saying that maybe little Ned wasn't his; that's breaking the heart in me entirely ... I don't mind a hasty stroke, for its hard on him to see us wanting a potato.'[125] Their account contributes to a picture of passive acceptance in the interests of apparent harmony and stability.

Later in the nineteenth century, it was found in London that Irish labourers were responsible for a great many cases of wife beating, but the idea prevailed that in Ireland the problem did not exist:

> Abused wives, unless they were murdered, found their stories buried amidst other petty crimes such as adulterating milk, watering pints, wrenching knockers off doors and breaking the licensing laws ... We can only surmise that there existed some kind of collective wish to ignore this social crime.[126]

When in April 1910 Isabella Cole sued for maintenance her husband of eight months, summoning him for assault before Holywood Petty Sessions, she was granted alimony of 15s. per week, although 'some of the magistrates were of the opinion that the defendant acted under some provocation'.[127] It is difficult to escape the conclusion that domestic violence was not itself considered to be unacceptable, and paradoxically, this may have helped reinforce the idea that it was not a problem to begin with. There is a substantial gap between the actual experience of domestic violence and the perception that in Ireland this was not a social concern. The widespread idea that 'Irishmen at home were in general kind and chivalrous to their wives' has recently been identified as a myth.[128] The popular and prevalent image of companionate Irish family life is further bolstered by the ideal of universal extra-marital chastity. While the image was steadily upheld, the actuality often fell far short of the ideal.

Since the late 1980s there has been a sharp rise in the number of divorces in Northern Ireland, and, with the recent liberalization of divorce laws, there are predictions that the increase will continue for some time.[129] In the Irish Republic, divorce is not available, although this situation is under review at the time of writing. Among the findings about causes of separation in Northern Ireland is the interesting discovery that marriages between couples of different religious faiths are less prone to failure,[130] although such courtships are still likely to meet with considerable parental opposition in many cases, so perhaps a large number of such potential partnerships never actually mature into marriage.

The infinite variability of experience of marriage is reflected in folktale and oral tradition, which help to highlight ambivalences and suggest the enormous range of possible responses. There is, for example, the story of the second wife who discovers the legend 'Be thou also ready' on the headstone of her predecessor, but perhaps the last word might be left to the young lady who pretended to be looking for work at a hiring fair:

'I just stood in the line of them wantin' places and an auld fella came along and seemed to fancy me, after giving me a good lookin' over. He asked me what I could do. I told him, and mebbe a bit more. Then I asked him what he would want me to do, an' I'll tell you, Ma'am, from five o'clock in the morning till any hour you like at night Theresa would be busy.' 'What did you say to him?' said her mistress. 'Say? I gave him a dunch and said: "Howl [hold] yer tongue, man, it's a wife you're lookin' for." '[131]

NOTES

Abbreviations

JRSAI = *Journal of the Royal Society of Antiquaries of Ireland*
PRONI = Public Record Office of Northern Ireland
UFTM = The Ulster Folk and Transport Museum

Introduction

1. See C. W. von Sydow, 'Geography and folktale oictotypes', *Selected Papers on Folklore* (Copenhagen, 1948), pp. 44–59; also L .M. Ballard, 'The formulation of the oictotype', *Fabula* 2 (1983).
2. See Art Cosgrove (ed.), *Marriage in Ireland* (Dublin, 1985).
3. R. Benchley, 'Do We Sleep Enough?', *My Ten Years in a Quandary and How They Grew* (London, 1951), p.99.
4. J. Barkley, 'Marriage and the Presbyterian tradition', *Ulster Folklife* 39 (1993), p. 29.
5. J. B. Cunningham, 'The struggle for the Belleek–Pettigo Salient, 1922', *Donegal Annual* 34 (1982), p. 39.
6. See the editorial to *Ullans* 2 (Spring 1994), p. 4.

Chapter One   Preparations for Marriage

1. See K. M. Connell, *The Population of Ireland* 1750– 1845 (Connecticut, 1975). See also D. Dickson, 'No Scythians here: women and marriage in seventeenth century Ireland', *Women in Early Modern Ireland*, ed. M. MacCurtain and M. O'Dowd (Edinburgh, 1991).
2. See C. Curtin, 'Marriage and family', *Ireland, a Sociological Profile*, ed. P. Clancy, S. Drudy, K. Lynch and L. O'Dowd (Dublin, 1986).
3. See Dickson, 'No Scythians here'.
4. Dickson, 'No Scythians here', p. 231.
5. Curtin, 'Marriage and family'. Damien Courtney has shown that men substantially outnumber women in the Irish Republic, and has commented on how this contributed to the 'depressing impact on marriage patterns, especially in rural areas'. See 'Demographic structure and change', *Ireland, a Sociological Profile*, ed. Clancy *et al*, p. 26.
6. S. J. Connolly, 'Marriage in pre-Famine Ireland', *Marriage in Ireland*, ed. A. Cosgrove (Dublin, 1985), p. 83.
7. See J. J. Lee 'Women and the Church since the Famine', *Women in Irish Society*, ed. M. MacCurtain and D. Ó Corrain (Dublin, 1978).
8. *The Manual of Needlework for the Use of National Schools*, which was first published in Dublin in 1853 and was subsequently reissued throughout the century, recommends in its introduction a knowledge of sewing as 'one of the most important acquirements for females' and suggests that daily needlework lessons with regular inspections of work should be available at National Schools.
9. See Florence Irwin's wonderful account in *The Cookin' Woman* (Edinburgh and London, 1949) of her experiences as an itinerant cookery instructress during the years 1905–1913, when she was employed by the Department of Agriculture and Technical Instruction for Ireland. She spent between six and eight weeks in each place she visited and on pp. 2–3 explains:

I carried round with me a 'Mistress' American stove and equipment for taking practical classes of 20–24 women, or children sometimes, for cookery, laundry work and dressmaking ... I learned a little of the scarcity of equipment in some houses and by my classes soon created a desire to remedy this, the county shopkeeper after coming to my kitchen to have a look at what his customers wanted him to order. On Mondays, arriving from the city after my weekends I was laden with egg-beaters, wooden spoons and what not from the 'Penny Bazaar' lately come to town.

10. See L. M. Ballard, 'Irish lace: tradition or commodity?', *Folklife* 31 (1992/3), pp. 43–56; also *Ulster Needlework, a Continuing Tradition* (Cultra, 1990), passim.
11. See H. Crawford, *Needlework Samplers of Northern Ireland* (Crawfordsburn, 1989), p.19.
12. Quoted by A. F. Bryson, *Ayrshire Needlework* (London, 1989), p.18.
13. The collection of the UFTM includes a winding sheet which was never used for its intended purpose but which was passed from mother to daughter as an essential part of a bottom drawer.
14. Alison Adburgham (intr.), *Victorian Shopping*. Facsimile of Harrod's Stores 1895 price list (Devon, 1972). Lists of household linens are given, pp. 1011-17. Belfast was among the cities to which delivery by rail was available, at a cost of £10 'and upwards'. A detailed table of postage illustrates the possibility of deliveries to the most exotic destinations.
15. *Irish Society* , 22 October 1898, p. 1454.
16. See, for example, Lee, 'Women and the Church since the Famine', p. 38.
17. The increasing demands of housework have been considered, for example by Lee, 'Women and the Church since the Famine', and by Caroline Davidson, *A Woman's Work is Never Done* (London, 1982), p. 184. See also Joanna Bourke, *Husbandry to Housewifery* (Oxford, 1993), esp. pt 3, 'Houseworkers', pp. 201–83; Tony Farmar, *Ordinary Lives: Three Generations of Irish Middle Class Experience 1902, 1932, 1963* (Dublin, 1991), pp. 35, 178; UFTM R.89.4.
18. UFTM R.93.75.
19. *Girls' Own Paper*, 2 March 1895, vol. 16, no.795, p. 407.
20. Jennifer Fitzgerald's lecture 'Marriage as prostitution' delivered at the Ulster Folk and Transport Museum, 22 April 1992 (Dept. of English, Queen's University, Belfast).
21. Report on the wedding of Miss Rock to Prince Raoul de Rohen of Bohemia, *Irish Society,* 20 October 1888, p. 549.
22. *Irish Society*, 20 October 1898, p. 1454.
23. See, for example, her foreword to *Irish Rural Life and Industry* (Dublin, 1907).
24. *Irish Society*, 3 August 1889, p. 483.
25. Connell, *Population of Ireland*, p. 53.
26. See Connolly, 'Marriage in pre-Famine Ireland', p. 83.
27. V. A. Dunn, *Cattle Raids and Courtships* (New York and London, 1989), p. 38. Dunn also comments in a footnote: ' ... the Pillow Talk scene [in the *Táin Bó Cuailnge*] emphasises the fact that when Alill married Medb, she came with insufficient cattle to make her Alill's equal. Her desire to raid may be seen as a desire to regain her status' (p. 67). A similar issue is taken up by the nineteenth-century writer George Egerton: ' ... no Zulu strikes a harder bargain for cows with his prospective father-in-law than the average Irishman for a girl's dowry. They are huckstered and traded for, and matches made for them, just the same as they bargain for heifers at a fair'. *Discords* (London, 1894), p. 55.
28. J. C. Walker, 'An historical essay on the dress of the ancient Irish' (1788), p. 21.
29. See A.T. Lucas, *Cattle in Ancient Ireland* (Kilkenny, 1989).
30. Quoted by J. P. Pendergast in his notes to 'Extracts from the journal of Thomas Dineley esq.', *Journal of the Kilkenny and South East of Ireland Archaeological Society*, NS, vol.1, 1856–7, p. 183.

31. 'Extracts from the journal of Thomas Dineley', pp. 183–4.
32. Connolly, 'Marriage in pre-Famine Ireland', p. 81.
33. P. W. Joyce, *A Social History of Ancient Ireland*, vol. 2 (Dublin, 1920), pp. 4–5.
34. E. O'Curry, Manners and Customs of the Ancient Irish, vol.1 (introduction) (Dublin and New York, 1873), p. clxxv.
35. Lucas, 'Marriage in pre-Famine Ireland', pp. 231–4.
36. D. Ó Córráin, 'Marriage in early Ireland', *Marriage in Ireland*, p. 17.
37. H. D. Inglis, *A Journey through Ireland*, vol. 2 (London, 1834), p. 28.
38. UFTM R.85.26.
39. C. Curtin, E. Devereux and D. Shields, 'Replaying the Match – Marriage Settlements in north Galway', *Irish Journal of Sociology* 2 (1992), p. 93. In some cases stipulations were made as to how the dowry could be used.
40. C. M. Arensberg and D. I. Kimball, *Family and Community in Ireland* (Harvard, repr. 1961), p. 118.
41. S. J. Connolly, *Priests and People in pre-Famine Ireland* (New York, 1982), p. 195.
42. D. Fitzpatrick, 'Marriage in post-Famine Ireland', *Marriage in Ireland*, p. 121.
43. Ibid, p. 127.

Chapter Two   Marriage Divination

1. This question has already been discussed above. See also K. H. Connell, *Irish Peasant Society* (Oxford, 1968), p 117:

> By, perhaps, the end of the [nineteenth] century peasant marriage was usually 'arranged'; and then more markedly than before, peasant children married little and late. They married late because a 'boy' not needing a wife until his mother could no more milk the cows, was not entitled to one until his father at last made over the land, and because the years had gone by before Lolita had the muscle and bone, the skill and dowry, sought in an old man's daughter-in-law. They married little because, though the normal family was large, only one of its boys and one of its girls married like their parents into peasant society: for the others (save in emigration) there was small chance of wife or husband.

2. Author's personal recollection of dormitory life. The custom may well have been more widespread, but it was an important feature of boarding school lore, to the extent that flattened crumbs of cake were salvaged and would do duty under many pillows before they disintegrated.
3. UFTM Notebook compiled by Izabel Archibald, Limavady.
4. N. Chambre and T. G. F. Paterson, 'Folktales from Cadian', *Ulster Journal of Archaeology*, ser. 3, vol. 3, p. 5.
5. R. Buchanan, 'Calendar Customs, Part 1, New Year's Day to Michaelmas', *Ulster Folklife* 8 (1962), p. 30. See also K. Danaher, *The Year in Ireland* (Cork, 1972). The custom involving yarrow was also known in Scotland. A similar custom was also known in parts of England, where it was apparently associated with St Valentine's Day, a festival little observed in rural Ireland. See A. R. Wright, *British Calendar Customs, England*, vol. 2 (London: Folklore Society, 1936), p. 153.
6. From John Keats, 'The Eve of St Agnes', *The Poetical Works of John Keats* (Oxford, 1927; repr. 1973), pp. 207–19.
7. See Danaher, *The Year in Ireland*.
8. Fitzpatrick, 'Marriage in post-Famine Ireland', p. 124. For a further discussion of seasonality and marriage, see the following chapter.
9. See Art Cosgrove, 'Marriage in medieval Ireland', *Marriage in Ireland*, ed. Cosgrove, pp. 37–8.

10. See P. W. Joyce, *A Social History of Ancient Ireland,* vol. 2 (Dublin, 1920).
11. *Poor Rabbin's Ollminick for the Town of Belfast,* 1861, by Billy McGart, p. 25.
12. R. H. Buchanan, 'Calendar Customs Part 2, Harvest to Christmas', *Ulster Folklife* 9 (1963), p. 67. Buchanan provides detailed information on many types of marriage divination popularly practised. See also Danaher, *The Year in Ireland* , pp. 218–27, and A. J. Pollock, 'Hallowe'en customs in Lecale, Co. Down, *Ulster Folklife* 6 (1960).
13. See Buchanan, 'Calendar Customs, Part 2'.
14. UFTM C.76.52. This method of divination was widely known throughout the country.
15. UFTM C.78.37.
16. J. Gamble, *A view of society and manners in the North of Ireland in the Summer and Autumn of 1812* (London, 1813), pp. 331, 332.
17. *Belfast Penny Journal,* 7 November 1846
18. See Wright, *British Calendar Customs,* vol. 2, pp. 110–18.

Chapter Three   Courtship and Made Marriages

1. D. Ó Corráin, 'Marriage in early Ireland', p. 18.
2. Ibid, p. 19.
3. Dunn, *Cattle Raids and Courtships*, p. 40.
4. Connolly, 'Marriage in pre-Famine Ireland', p. 86.
5. UFTM C.78.48.
6. E. Wakefield, *An Account of Ireland Statistical and Political,* vol. 2 (1812), p. 769.
7. A.T. Malcolmson, *The Pursuit of the Heiress, Aristocratic Marriage in Ireland, 1750–1820* (Belfast: Ulster Historical Foundation, 1982), p. 16.
8. Angélique Day (ed.), *Letters from Georgian Ireland* (Belfast, 1991), p. 43.
9. G. V. Sampson, *A Memoir explanatory of the Chart and Survey of the County of London-Derry* (London, 1814), p. 191.
10. *Saunder's Newsletter,* 19 July 1785.
11. UFTM C.76.36.
12. Ibid.
13. R. Leitch, *Ireland Picturesque and Romantic* (London, 1838), p. 149.
14. UFTM R.85.242.
15. Ibid.
16. UFTM R.81.67.
17. Arensberg and Kimball, *Family and Community in Ireland*, pp. 118–20.
18. Reports of his Majesty's Commissioners for inquiry into the condition of the Poorer Classes in Ireland, Appendix F, p. 41. Quoted by Connolly, 'Marriage in pre-Famine Ireland', pp. 85–6.
19. British Parliamentary Sessional Papers Poor Inquiry, (Ireland), appendix H, part 2 (London, 1836), p. 19.
20. See C. Ó Danachair, 'Marriage in Irish folk tradition', *Marriage in Ireland,* ed. Cosgrove, esp. pp. 104–7.
21. Fitzpatrick, 'Marriage in post-Famine Ireland'.
22. Malcolmson, *Pursuit of the Heiress,* p. 6.
23. Curtin, 'Marriage and family'.
24. P. Bourdieu, 'Marriage strategies as strategies of social reproduction, *Family and Society,* ed. R. Forster and O. Ranum (Baltimore and London, 1976), p. 130.
25. UFTM R.81.143.
26. P. Sayers, *An Old Woman's Reflections* (London, 1962), p. x.
27. See UFTM R.93.75.
28. UFTM R.81.143.

29. UFTM Notebooks, Mrs Brunt, Fivemiletown, Co. Tyrone.
30. Mr and Mrs S. C. Hall, *Ireland, it's Scenery, Character, etc.* (London 1845), vol 1. p. 169.
31. Day, *Letters from Georgian Ireland*, p. 95.
32. UFTM R.85.143.
33. UFTM Notebooks, Francilla Stevenson.
34. For a version of this story (in which the wealthy duped bride is a young English woman tricked by a cunning Tyrone lad), see M. J. Murphy, 'Old Lord Erin's Son, a Tyrone folk-tale', *Ulster Folklife* 4 (1958), pp. 50–5.
35. 'An Irish wedding, by one who has seen many', *Dublin University Magazine* (September 1862), p. 361.
36. Charles Sloan, 'Some of the stories of James McAllister of Fathom', *Ulster Folklife* 13 (1967), p. 10.
37. J. Gillis, *For Better, for Worse* (New York, 1985), p. 121.
38. Letter from George B. Thompson to the author. Gillis's description of similar attitudes gives some detail of the treatment an interloper could expect, and of the punishment to be meted out to the young woman involved, if the courtship persisted (see the above source, pp. 121–2). M. J. Murphy shows that the same attitude existed in rural Ireland, *Ulster Folk of Field and Fireside* (Dundalk, 1983), p. 2.
39. Hall, Ireland, vol. 3, p. 401.
40. A. Young, *A Tour in Ireland* (Dublin, 1780), pp. 250–1.
41. These and other related customs are described by Ó Danachair, 'Marriage in Irish folk tradition', pp. 101–2.
42. Séamus O'Duilearga (intr.), 'The Cake Dance', *Bealoideas* 11 (1945), pp. 137–8.
43. For further details of harvest knots, see T.G.F. Paterson, 'Harvest knots and Brigid's crosses', *Ulster Folklife* 1 (1955), pp.16–18; also Buchanan, 'Seasonal customs', *Ulster Folklife* 8 (1962).
44. Mentioned by member of audience after talk on wedding customs given by L. M. Ballard at St Patrick's Church, Jordanstown, 22/3/94, to members of the Mothers' Union.
45. The popularity of Valentine's Day in rural England is discussed by Wright, *British Calendar Customs*, vol. 1, pp. 136–56.
46. Archive of the Ulster Folk and Transport Museum.
47. Archive of the Ulster Folk and Transport Museum.
48. See M. Baker, *Wedding Customs and Folklore* (Newton Abbot, 1977), p. 21, which includes reference to a Scottish Ordnance of 1288 concerning Leap Year and marriage.
49. See L. Stone, *The Road to Divorce* (Oxford, 1990), p. 87. The right to take legal action for Breach of Promise is acknowledged by 32 and 33 Vict. C68 paragraph 2.
50. The Family Law (Miscellaneous Provisions) (Northern Ireland) Order, 1984, SI 1984/1989 (NI 14), which came into effect in February 1985, abolished the right to sue for Breach of Promise. I am indebted to Mrs Ruth Lavery for this reference.
51. I am indebted to the late Mr Ronnie Adams former librarian of the UFTM and author-ity on the *Belfast Newsletter* for this information.
52. And for this, to Mr Dan McGloughlan.
53. *Irish Law Times*, Reports, 1932, p. 32.
54. See Stone, *Road to Divorce*, p. 37
55. *Downpatrick Recorder*, 18 July 1846.
56. PRONI T2541/IAC/12/54.
57. See *Ulster Journal of Archaeology*, ser. 2, vol.7 (1901), p. 159.
58. PRONI Mic 160, Diary of Robert Gage.
59. UFTM C.78.36. Dancing also worried clergy in other denominations. George Cathcart OBE recalled that, in Co. Fermanagh, dances could not be held in the church hall in Bellanaleck, although socials, which might include rowdy games like Postman's Knock were acceptable to the rector, Canon Sirr, who considered dancing too intimate. To hold

dances it was necessary to have another building, and Bellanaleck Orange Lodge opened one in 1952, where jiving and other fashionable dances could be enjoyed. S. H. King and S. McMahon, *Hope and History* (Belfast 1996), p. 112.

60. 'Session book of Templepatrick Presbyterian church', *JRSAI* 25 (1895), p. 133.
61. R. Twiss, *A Tour in Ireland in 1755*, (London 1776), pp. 115–17.
62. Gillis, *For Better, for Worse*, p. 114.
63. UFTM C.78.48. Perhaps misguidedly, I stopped short of acquiring it.
64. Cosgrove, 'Marriage in medieval Ireland', pp. 29 and 42.
65. Gillis, *For Better, for Worse*, p. 279.

Chapter Four   The Wedding

1. Cosgrove, 'Marriage in medieval Ireland', p. 30.
2. *Belfast Newsletter*, 28 March 1845.
3. Malcolmson, *Pursuit of the Heiress*, p. 2.
4. S. Connolly, *Religion, Law and Power, The Making of Protestant Ireland 1660–1760* (Oxford, 1992), p. 156.
5. *Belfast Newsletter*, 1 April 1845.
6. 33 Henry VIII C6, 1542.
7. Margaret MacCurtain, 'Marriage in Tudor Ireland', *Marriage in Ireland*, ed. Cosgrove, p. 62.
8. See P. J. Corish, 'Catholic marriage under the Penal Code', *Marriage in Ireland*, ed. Cosgrove.
9. Ibid; also Cosgrove, 'Marriage in medieval Ireland' and Dickson, 'No Scythians here'.
10. Dickson, 'No Scythians here', p. 225.
11. Wentworth to Laud, 31 Jan. 1633/34, Letter Book 6, Strafford MSS, Sheffield Public Library, quoted by MacCurtain, 'Marriage in Tudor Ireland'.
12. Poor Inquiry – (Ireland) Appendix G. British Parliamentary Sessional Papers. Report on the State of the Irish Poor in Great Britain, p. 62. See also Gillis, *For Better, for Worse*, p. 205.
13. Poor Inquiry – (Ireland), Appendix 8, p. 62.
14. 'The revenue and endowments of the Church of Ireland were confiscated after 1649': T. C. Barnard, *Cromwellian Ireland* (London, 1975), p. 155.
15. Dickson, 'No Scythians here', pp. 226–7
16. Corish, 'Catholic Marriage under the Penal Code', p. 71.
17. Ibid; see also Dickson, 'No Scythians here'.
18. 19 George III C13.
19. W. T. Latimer, *A History of the Irish Presbyterians* (Belfast), 1902.
20. J. C. Beckett, *Protestant Dissent in Ireland 1687–1780* (London), 1948, p. 121.
21. Ibid, p. 117.
22. *JRSAI* 28 (1890), p. 346.
23. Day, *Letters from Georgian Ireland*, p. 111.
24. Latimer, *History of the Irish Presbyterians*, p. 343.
25. 'Presbyterian marriage register of Banbridge', *JRSAI* 39 (1909), p. 76.
26. Latimer, *History of the Irish Presbyterians*, p. 342.
27. Rev. W.S. Smith, 'Early register of the old Presbyterian congregation of Antrim', *Ulster Journal of Archaeology*, ser. 2, no.1 (1898), p. 185.
28. 'Presbyterian marriage register of Banbridge', (1904) p. 76.
29. Beckett, *Protestant Dissent in Ireland*, p. 122.
30. Latimer, *History of the Irish Presbyterians*, p. 472.
31. See Neville H. Newhouse, *A History of Friends' School, Lisburn* (Lurgan, 1974), pp. 23–7. Maurice J. Wigham, *The Irish Quakers* (Dublin, 1992) remarks that this wedding 'was followed by several others' (p. 69).

32. Cosgrove, 'Marriage in medieval Ireland', pp. 30–1.

33. Dickson, 'No Scythians here', p. 227.

34. Wigham, *Irish Quakers*, pp. 60, 83 and 96.

35. See P. J. Corish, *The Irish Catholic Experience* (Dublin, 1985), pp. 220–2. The relevant legislation of the early 1870s is 33 and 34 Vict C110 34 and 35 Vict C119. Murphy refers to this practice in rural Ireland, *Ulster Folk of Field and Fireside*, p. 82.

36. 'A special record was kept over a period of 25 years in the present century, and there were more mixed marriages in Northern Ireland than in the South. Nevertheless, as many were successful in converting the Roman Catholic partner to Methodism as — the official Roman Policy had its way.' F. Jeffery, *Irish Methodism* (Belfast, 1964), p. 94.

37. See, for example, A. D. Buckley and M. C. Kenney, *Negotiating Identity* (Washington DC, 1995), p. 6.

38. See, for example, Gillis, *For Better, for Worse*, p. 94.

39. See Cosgrove, 'Marriage in medieval Ireland', p. 39.

40. Connolly, *Priests and People in pre-Famine Ireland*, p. 200.

41. Ibid, p. 206.

42. Mary Lyons (ed.), *The Memoirs of Mrs Leeson, Madam* (Dublin, 1995), p. 168.

43. Ibid, p. 169.

44. Malcolmson, *Pursuit of the Heiress*, p. 38.

45. Memoir of J. Bleakly, Raloo Parish. *Ordnance Survey Memoirs of Ireland, vol. 32, Parishes of Co. Antrim XII, 1833–5*, (Belfast, 1995) p. 126.

46. Father Buckley, who describes himself as 'proud and happy to be the unofficial chaplain to Ireland's liberal or alienated Catholics', gives a clear insight into his perspective on the Catholic Church in his recently published book *A Thorn in the Side* (Dublin, 1994), pp.187–8, where he explains:

    The marriages I celebrate are regarded as legal Roman Catholic marriages in Scotland, Northern Ireland and the Republic of Ireland. When I began celebrating marriages ... after Bishop Daly had dismissed me in 1986, I approached the Registrar General in Belfast ... His legal team studied the matter and concluded that any episcopally ordained priest, whether or not in good standing with the church could, from the civil law point of view, validly solemnise marriages.

47. D. Stewart, *Seceders in Ireland* (Belfast, 1950), p. 412.

48. Latimer, *History of the Irish Presbyterians*, p. 343.

49. Memoir of James Boyle, Antrim Parish, 1838, *Ordnance Survey Memoirs of Ireland*, vol. 29 (1995), p.19.

50. UFTM Questionnaire, UFM/67/Q3, response 673121, Trillick, Co. Tyrone.

51. Memoir for Clonleigh Parish, *Ordnance Survey Memoirs of Ireland*, vol. 39 (1997), p.11.

52. Hall, *Ireland*, vol. 1, p.164.

53. A. Day and P. McWilliams (eds), *Ordnance Survey Memoirs of Ireland*, vol. 17 (1992), p. 17.

54. Corish, *Irish Catholic Experience*, p. 219.

55. Corish, 'Catholic marriage under the Penal Code', p. 72. See also Connolly, *Priests and People in pre-Famine Ireland*, who points out that severe penalties could be meted out to Catholic priests marrying Catholics to non-Catholics and who states (p.197) that one suspended priest was executed for this in 1726.

56. James O'Shea, *Priests, Politics and Society in Post-Famine Ireland* (Dublin, 1983).

57. 33 and 34 Vict. ch. 110.

58. 34 and 35 Vict. ch. 49.

59. This case, so notorious that contemporary pamphlets on the subject were published, is succinctly described, for example by R.L. Prager, *Official Guide to County Down and the Mourne Mountains* (Belfast, 1898), pp. 186–7.

60. James J. Donnelly Jnr, 'The Rightboy Movement, 1785–8', *Studia Hibernica* 17 and 18 (1977–8), esp. pp. 163–7.

61. Gillis, *For Better, for Worse*, p. 63.

62. M. J. F. McCarthy, *Priests and People in Ireland* (Dublin, 1902), p. 24. In the mid nineteenth century, Hariet Martineau remarked (*Letters from Ireland*, 1852, p. 206): 'The marriage fee is established at 10/=d. The priest now demands £1.0.0d. Even at this price his gains are much diminished, for the custom of handing round the plate used to yield him from ten-fold to a hundred-fold what is got by fees from the married. A priest used to get sometimes a hundred pounds from the plate – in the days when priests kept horses and carts.'

63. Connell, *Population of Ireland,* p. 80. Connell also includes the passage from Martineau's letters quoted above.

64. Hall, *Ireland,* vol. 1, p. 164.

65. See, for example, *Letters from the Irish Highlands* (London, 1825), pp. 96–7.

66. British Parliamentary Sessional Papers Appendix D (Poorer Classes in Ireland) 1836.

67. Connell, *Population of Ireland*, p. 80.

68. UFTM Tape archive, C78.36.

69. Murphy, *Ulster Folk of Field and Fireside*, p. 203. Fear of the jealousy of women, combined with suspicion of women with red hair, is echoed in this Co. Down tale told by Brigid Murphy:

> It was my grandfather, as a matter of fact, the story goes, and he was supposed to be very good looking, and this neighbour girl, as they used to say in them days, had a notion of him. And there was one Sunday morning he took out the horse to give him some exercise it was, being in the wintertime, or the beginning of the spring, and he took out the horse to give him some exercise and he went down, trotting down the road past her house, and he met the girl coming along to take a bucket of water in the well, along the road, and they bid other 'good morning' and he went down the road a bit further and the horse tripped and he went over the horse's head and fell on the road. And he was unconscious, and brought him back to his own house and the doctor was sent for, and I suppose he had a bit of concussion or something, but he lay there for about nine or ten days, and he wasn't getting any better. So they thought there might have been some kind of a spell cast over him and the horse or something like that. And there was a woman lived up at Ardee in the County Louth and she was supposed to be a charmer or a soothsayer or something like that they called them in them days, and she was able to remove any evil spells and all that. And they sat, they brought her down to his house and she went into the room and where he was lying on the bed, and he was unconscious, still unconscious after nine or ten days and she talked to him. She put the rest of the people up out of the room that had been there, and she prayed over him and put her hands on his head and prayed over him. And she came down after some time to the kitchen and she told his father and mother that he would be alright now. And they asked her what happened and she said, 'Well, he met a red haired girl on the road. And this girl wished with all her heart that she had him, and she had put some kind of a spell on him, and that was what, he fell off the horse and was still un——but,' she said 'he'll be alright now.' So in a matter of days or so he was alright and up and going about again. That's the way the yarn goes.' UFTM PR 8.

70. Letter from Anne Ward to her Aunt, Jane Mahon, 27 March 1845 (Percival-Price Papers, Saintfield).

71. *Belfast Telegraph*, 27 September 1990.

72. *Belfast Newsletter*, 27 June 1902.

73. Wedding, Killinchy, Co. Down, 1861, of Emily Ward to James Lyle, as described by the bride's mother (Percival-Price Papers).

74. Notebook of Francilla Stevenson, UFTM archive V.19.1. Mrs Stevenson was born in 1880. Drumclamph is in Ardstraw Parish in the barony of Strabane Lower.

75. UFTM Questionnaire 67/Q3 673085.

76. Day, *Letters from Georgian Ireland*, p. 84.

77. Jeanne Cooper Foster, *Ulster Folklore* (Belfast, 1951), p. 12.

78. C. Ó Danachair, 'Some marriage customs and their regional distribution', *Bealoideas* 42–4 (1974–76), pp. 136–7.

79. A. H. Wescott and A. M. Robinson, *The Ladies' Book* (London, c.1900), p. 67.

80. Archive note associated with UFTM specimen 526.1972.

81. P. Gallagher, *My Story* (Dungloe, n.d.), p. 77.

82. UFTM R81.79.

83. UFTM R81.140.

84. UFTM R85.32.

85. R. Fox, *The Tory Islanders* (Cambridge, 1978), p. 157.

86. *Belfast Newsletter*, 21 October 1902. This account of the wedding is summarized from lengthy reports carried by the newspaper in that and the next issue, supplemented by details from the Belfast Street Directory.

87. PRONI D1828/24. Letter to his father from Robert Smith, Philadelphia, 25 March 1844.

68. PRONI D1828/25. Letter to his parents from Robert Smith, Philadelphia, 14 August 1844.

89. PRONI D1828/26. Letter to his parents from Robert Smith, Philadelphia, 24 December 1844.

90. PRONI D1859/27. Letter to his parents from Robert Smith, Philadelphia, 1 May 1845.

91. Ibid.

92. PRONI D1828/28. I am indebted to Dr Joan Reedy for drawing my attention to these papers.

93. See, for example, Thomas H. Mason, *The Islands of Ireland* (London, 1938), p. 76.

94. Figures abstracted from Ernest Salisbury, 'The immigration of G. I. Brides', *Monthly Review* (apparently 1946), p. 306.

95. Annual Report of the Immigration and Naturalisation Service, United States Department of Justice, Washington DC, for the Fiscal Year Ended 30 June 1949.

96. Salisbury, 'Immigration of G. I. Brides'.

97. 'War Brides and their shipment to the United States', *Occupation Forces in Europe Series, 1945–46*, Office of the Chief Historian, European Command, Frankfurt-Am-Main, Germany, 1942.

98. Annual Report of the Immigration and Naturalisation Service, United States Department of Justice, Philadelphia, Pennsylvania, for the fiscal year ended 30 June, 1946; also Salisbury, 'Immigration of G.I. Brides'.

99. R. Hanna, *Pardon me Boy, the Americans in Ulster 1942–45* (Belfast, 1991), p. 3.

100. Mrs Sally Skilling recalled this incident from her childhood and told it to the writer, 28/1/1993.

101. Hanna, *Pardon me Boy*, pp. 67–8.

102. UFTM R.90.77.

103. *The Great War, 1914–1918, Ulster Greets her Brave and Faithful Sons and Remembers her Glorious Dead* (Belfast, 1919), pp. 11–12.

104. Ibid, p. 14.

105. 'Within four years, the number of Ulstermen and Irishmen who were to give their lives totalled 50,000.' M. Hall, *Sacrifice on the Somme* (Belfast, n.d.), p. 3.

106. UFTM DB 107.

107. UFTM DB 764.

108. UFTM DB 764.

109. *Carrickfergus Advertiser and East Antrim Gazette*, 3 June 1971.
110. Gillis, *For Better, for Worse*, p. 19.
111. UFTM Notebooks, V.13.5. See also Foster, *Ulster Folklore*, p. 12. 'Among noncon-formists, a wedding ring was not to be considered essential, and many people were married without it.'
112. William Tegy, *The Knot Tied* (London, 1877), p. 312. See also Shirley Bury, *An Introduction to Rings* (London, 1984), p. 15: ' ... ephemeral rings made from rushes were found convenient for temporary liaisons'.
113. John Denton, *Teague Land, or A Merry Ramble to the Wild Irish, Letters from Ireland, 1698*, ed. Edward MacLysaght (Dublin, 1982), pp. 45–6.
114. Bury, *Introduction to Rings*, p. 15.
115. Rosalin K. Marshall, 'The wearing of wedding rings in Scotland', *Review of Scottish Culture* 2 (1986), p. 1.
116. See Westcott and Robinson, *Ladies' Book*, p. 64; also Bury, *Introduction to Rings*, p.15, and Marshall, 'The wearing of wedding rings in Scotland', p. 8.
117. UFTM R85.33.
118. Tegy, *Knot Tied*, p. 314.
119. George F. Kunz, *Rings for the Fingers*, (Philadelphia, 1917; repr. New York, 1973), p. 226.
120. Michael J. Murphy, *Sayings and Stories from Slieve Gullion* (Dundalk, 1990), p. 65.
121. Tegy, *Knot Tied*, p. 313.
122. Bury, *Introduction to Rings*, p.16.
123. For an analysis of fede rings, see Marshall, 'Wearing of wedding rings in Scotland', pp. 1–7.
124. Examples are held by the Ulster Museum. See Linda Ballard, *Tying the Knot* (Cultra: Ulster Folk and Transport Museum, n.d. [1991]), p. 10.
125. Hall, *Ireland*, vol. 3, p. 458. See also Etienne Rynne, *Tourist Train of Old Galway* (Galway, 1989), pp. 29–31.
126. UFTM C76–5.
127. PRONI D2035/3/6. Will of Robert Ramsey of the City of Londonderry, Bookseller, who bequeaths to his 'sister-in-law Hannah Davison my dinner service of blue delf with the broach and wedding ring with its keeper which formerly belonged to my late wife ... '
128. Westcott and Robinson, *Ladies' Book*, p. 64.
129. Diary of Alice Ward, 5 January 1869. Percival-Price Papers.
130. The collection of the UFTM includes a mourning band believed to have been worn as a 'keeper'. See also Marshall, 'Wearing of wedding rings in Scotland', p. 5.
131. G. Monger, '"To marry in May": an investigation of a superstitition', *Folklore* 105 (1994), p. 104.
132. See, for example, the notebook of William Clarke, Ballinamallard, Co. Fermanagh, UFTM.
133. Archive note associated with UFTM specimen 210–1986.
134. Sharon Gmelch, *Nan: The Life of an Irish Travelling Woman* (New York, 1986), p. 236.
135. Sharon Gmelch, *Tinkers and Travellers* (Dublin, 1975), p. 68.
136. Ibid, p. 74.
137. Gmelch, *Nan*, p. 77.
138. Ó Danachair, 'Some marriage customs and their regional distribution', p.136.
139. *Modern Etiquette in Public and Private* (London, 1890), p. 98.

Chapter 5   Dressing for the Day

1. *Belfast Telegraph*, 4 March 1991.
2. Specially designed dresses may cost as much as this, and some retailers of exclusive label gowns may stock dresses in this price range.

3. Sally Skilling, whose career began in the mid/late 1950s, when she worked as a typist-book keeper, recalled this information, remarking that her first wage, £2.5s per week, was considered very good pay at the time.
4. Edmund Spencer, *Poetical Works*, ed. J. C. Smith and E. de Selincourt (Oxford, 1970), p.581 ('The Epithalamium', first publ.1595)
5. *A View of Society and Manners in the North of Ireland in the Summer and Autumn of 1812* (London, 1813), p. 94.
6. Day and McWilliams, *Ordnance Survey Memoirs*, vol. 2 (1991), p. 130.
7. Ibid, p. 54
8. Denton, *Teague Land*, p. 45.
9. For an authorative analysis of Irish dress, see Mairead Dunlevy, *Dress in Ireland* (London, 1989). For the points addressed here, see especially pp. 84–5, and colour pl. 7.
10. See, for example, Madeline Ginsburg, *Wedding Dress, 1740 –1970* (London: HMSO, 1981), p. 17.
11. For a brief illustrated introduction to the subject of Ulster wedding dresses, see Ballard, *Tying the Knot*.
12. Sarah Levitt, *Victorians Unbuttoned* (London, 1986), p. 73.
13. Lou Taylor, *Mourning Dress, a Costume and Social History* (London, 1983), p. 255.
14. *Irish Society*, 23 September 1893.
15. *Irish Society*, 26 January 1889.
16. Notebook of Francilla Stevenson, UFTM Archive.
17. See, for example, Avril Landsdell, *Wedding Fashions 1860–1980* (Princes Risborough, 1983), p. 69.
18. Northern Ireland came into being as a separate entity in 1920. In June 1921, its own parliament sat for the first time, and the Irish Free State came into existence the same year, with the signing of a treaty that December. The Free State became the Republic of Ireland in 1937. Many individual citizens of the Republic also fought as part of HM Forces during the Second World War.
19. UFTM R90.77.
20. Jill McKenna, *Divvies, Coke and Black Soap* (Belfast, 1991), pp. 7–8.
21. Mason, *Islands of Ireland*, p. 76.
22. Letter from Mrs Cummings (née Waite), 8 July 1990, UFTM Archive.
23. UFTM R92.25. The dress is now in the collection of the UFTM.
24. *Everywoman*, February 1957, p. 41.
25. UFTM R94.22.
26. R. H. Langbridge (comp.), *Edwardian Shopping, A Selection from the Army and Navy Stores Catalogues, 1898–1913* (Newton Abbott), 1975.
27. See Anne Monsarrat, *And the Bride Wore* (London, 1973), p. 113.
28. Hall, *Ireland*, vol.1, p. 88.
29. Letter from Anne Ward, 27 March 1845 (Percival-Price Papers).
30. Diary of Ann Ward, 5 January 1869 (Percival-Price Papers).
31. Ann Page, *The Complete Guide to Wedding Etiquette* (London, 1950), p.44.
32. Diary of Ann Ward (Percival-Price Papers).
33. Diary of Charlotte Ward, 5 January1869 (Percival-Price Papers).
34. See, for example, *Modern Etiquette*, p. 83: 'It is unnecessary to say that a bridal bouquet should be made entirely of white flowers ... '
35. Monsarrat, *And the Bride Wore*, pp. 115 –16.
36. Mentioned in discussion following lecture on marriage customs given by L. M. Ballard to the Bangor branch of the Family History Society of Northern Ireland. One member recalled that when a forebear, Fanny Morris, was married *c*.1890 in Belfast, she wore a brown gown and carried a bouquet of montbretia.
37. This photograph is preserved in the collection of Armagh Museum (neg. no. N239).

38. Monsarrat, *And the Bride Wore*, p. 209.
39. *Modern Etiquette*, p. 83.
40. *Irish Society*, 23 September 1893.
41. *Irish Society*, 2 December 1893.
42. *Irish Society*, 6 October 1888.
43. *Irish Society*, 28 January 1888.
44. *Irish Society*, 1 March 1890.
45. *Irish Society*, 14 June 1890.
46. *Belfast Newsletter*, Thursday, 27 June 1907.
47. Henry Best, quoted by Gillis, *For Better, for Worse*, p . 52.
48. Gillis, *For Better, for Worse*, p. 294.
49. Stella Blum, *Victorian Fashions and Costumes from Harper's Bazaar, 1867–1898* (New York, 1974), p. 120.
50. For further discussion of these and related matters, see L. M. Ballard, 'Some aspects of tradition ... ', *Ulster Folklife* 38 (1992), pp. 68–78.
51. Newhouse, *History of Friends' School, Lisburn*, p.23.
52. Baker, *Wedding Customs and Folklore*, p.131.
53. Description of wedding by bride's mother (Percival-Price Papers). Honiton is a style of English lace.
54. *Irish Society*, 14 June 1890.
55. Gillis, *For Better, for Worse*, p.120.
56. L. Stone, *The Family, Sex and Marriage in England, 1500–1800* (Harmondsworth,1982) p. 224.
57. Diary of Alice Ward, 5 January 1869 (Percival-Price Papers).
58. UFTM Questionnaire 76/Q3.
59. Information from a prospective bride, Ballyclare, 1992.
60. Diary of Alice Ward, 5 January 1869 (Percival-Price Papers). I have specified orange blossom to prevent any possible confusion with orange lilies.
61. Diary of Charlotte Ward, 5 January 1869 (Percival-Price Papers).
62. *Irish Society*, 14 June 1890.
63. Diary of Charlotte Ward, 5 January 1869 (Percival-Price Papers).
64. *Irish Society*, 14 June1890.
65. *Irish Society*, 29 December 1888.
66. The wedding was reported on by *Irish Society*, 6 May 1893.
67. See Monsarrat, *And the Bride Wore*, p. 120.
68. Letter from Anne Ward, March 1845 (Percival-Price Papers).
69. *Irish Society*, 23 September 1893.
70. Letter from Anne Ward, March 1845 (Percival-Price Papers).
71. *Irish Society*, 12 November 1898.
72. *Irish Society*, 26 January 1889.
73. *Irish Society,* 14 June 1890.
74. *Irish Society*, 20 October 1888.
75. A newspaper report of a Belfast wedding, 1931, describes both Miss June Ross and Master Bunny Ross as pages. Unidentified cutting, UFTM Archive.
76. Dunlevy, *Dress in Ireland*, p.100.
77. UFTM specimen 252. 1994.
78. UFTM Archive (unclassified letter sent to L. M. Ballard following lecture in Co.Tyrone, 1991).
79. Diary of Alice Ward, 5 January 1869 (Percival-Price Papers).
80. Blum, *Victorian Fashions,* p. 277.
81. *Irish Society*, 3 August 1889.
82. This photograph is part of the collection of Down County Museum.

83. *Irish Society*, 20 October 1888.
84. *Irish Society*, 23 September 1893.
85. Ann Page, *The Complete Guide to Wedding Etiquette*, p. 48.

Chapter Six   Celebration, Prank and Disruption

 1. See O'Córráin, 'Marriage in early Ireland'.
 2. Lageniensis, *Irish Folklore* (Glasgow and London, 1870), p. 235.
 3. See, for example, Ordnance Survey Memoir for Skerry Parish, Co. Antrim. 'At chris-
     tenings and weddings they indulge in drinking and carousing, and celebrate these
     events with great festivity.' Day and McWilliams, *Ordnance Survey Memoirs of Ireland*,
     vol.13 (1992), p.113.
 4. Day, *Letters from Georgian Ireland*, p. 167.
 5. Ibid, p.168. Favours like those mentioned here remained fashionable throughout the
     following century. An illustration of the bridal group of the then Duke of York and
     Princess Mary of Teck in July 1893 shows that all the female attendants wore floral
     favours on their shoulders. The bridegroom, who wore uniform, sported white ribbon
     favours on his epaulets. See F. G. H.Salusbury, *King Emperor's Jubilee 1910–1935.*
     (London, 1935), p. 15.
 6. Ibid, p. 84. It was for Thomas, a son of this couple, that Mrs Delany made an embroi-
     dered coverlet now preserved in the collection of the Ulster Museum.
 7. Original document preserved in the Historical Library of the Society of Friends,
     Dublin. I am indebted to Sheelah Peile for drawing this to my attention, and for shar-
     ing with me information which she in turn received from John Richardson. The house
     Topsyturvey is described in W.H. Crowe, *Village in Seven Hills* (Dundalk, 1972), p. 30.
     Describing a Kerry wedding, Mr and Mrs Hall remark that the priest sits at the head of
     the table with the young couple close by (*Ireland*, vol. 1, p. 165).
 8. Diary of Charlotte Ward, 7 June 1878 (Percival-Price Papers).
 9. Ibid, 5 January 1869.
10. Gamble, *A View of Society and Manners*, p. 94.
11. See, for example, *Modern Etiquette*, pp. 88–92.
12. *Lady's Pictorial*, 16 April 1892.
13. McCarthy, *Priests and People*, p. 23.
14. *Irish Society*, 14 June 1890.
15. Ibid.
16. See H. C. Davidson (ed.), *The Book of the Home*, vol. 7 (London, 1900), p. 335.
17. UFTM Questionnaire (Wedding Customs) (UFTM 67/Q3, response 673055).
18. UFTM Questionnaire 67/Q3, unnumbered response.
19. McKenna, *Divvies, Coke and Black Soap*, p. 7. This account was from a woman who
     married after a courtship lasting six weeks. The couple met on Boxing Night and mar-
     ried on 23 February. The bride remarked: 'My mother didn't say anything, I think she
     was glad to be rid of me. I wasn't working, I wasn't bringing in any money, so she didn't
     worry.'
20. UFTM R.90.77.
21. UFTM Questionnaire 67/Q3, 673992.
22. *Modern Etiquette*, p. 90.
23. A report of this wedding was carried by the *Belfast Newsletter*, 1 April 1944.
24. *Modern Etiquette*, p.89. This advice is echoed in Davidson, *Book of the Home*, vol. 8, p.
     335.
25. *Irish Society*, 22 April 1899.
26. Letter from Anne Ward to her aunt, Jane Mahon, March 1845 (Percival-Price Papers).
27. Diary of Alice Ward, 5 January 1869 (Percival-Price Papers).

28. Diary of Charlotte Ward, 5 January1869 (Percival-Price Papers).
29. Letter from Mary Delany to Mary Dewes, 6 October 1764. Day, *Letters from Georgian Ireland*, p. 84.
30. See *Cassell's Illustrated Exhibitor* (London and New York, 1862), pp. 85–6.
31. *Lady's Pictorial*, 16 April 1892.
32. Adburgham, *Victorian Shopping*, p. 161.
33. *Irish Society*, October 1898.
34. Illustrated in Baker, *Wedding Customs*, p. 112.
35. Day and McWilliams, *Ordnance Survey Memo*irs of Ireland, vol.11 (1991), p. 130.
36. Gillis, *For Better, for Worse*, p. 95. Gillis also refers to the breaking of cake over the heads of a bridal couple at a Gloucester wedding in 1712, p. 137.
37. See Baker, *Wedding Customs*, p. 122.
38. McCarthy, *Priests and People in Ireland*, p. 24.
39. See Mr and Mrs Hall, *Ireland*, vol.1, p. 164. The same source also describes how 'the bridecake is brought in and placed before the priest who, putting on his stole, blesses it and cuts it up into small slices ... Each guest takes a slice of the cake, and lays down in place of it a donation for the priest, consisting of pounds, crowns or shillings, according to the ability of the donor.'
40. McCarthy, *Priests and People in Ireland*, p. 24.
41. UFTM Questionnaire 63/Q3, response 673094. Collections might also be taken up in order to pay the musicians and to give to the poor.
42. UFTM R83-115. The public house referred to was a little way along the road from Church Bay to the Point.
43. *Irish Society*, 23 September 1893.
44. *Irish Society*, 2 December 1893.
45. Both lists are still in the possession of the women concerned, who were kind enough to show them to the author.
46. UFTM Archive, notebook of Mrs Brunt, V.19.7.
47. *Modern Etiquette*.
48. This is now in the collection of the Ulster Folk and Transport Museum.
49. *Belfast Newsletter*, 10 August 1883.
50. *Modern Etiquette*, p. 77.
51. Wescott and Robinson, *Ladies' Book,* p. 66.
52. These pre-wedding parties are among the issues discussed by Simon Charsley in *Rites of Marrying* (Manchester, 1991).
53. A similar custom is observed in other parts of the British Isles. See, for example, Gillis, *For Better, for Worse*, p. 291.
54. Reported by the *Belfast Telegraph*, 9 July 1994.
55. UFTM Questionnaire 67/Q3.
56. Ibid.
57. Ibid.
58. Ibid.
59. Ibid.
60. Ibid.
61. Ó Danachair, 'Some marriage customs', p. 147.
62. *Ordnance Survey Memoirs of Ireland,* vol. 11 (1991), p. 130.
63. UFTM Questionnaire 67/Q3.
64. UFTM C78.22.
65. Reported by the *Irish Independent*, 13 July 1992, and cited in *Archaeology Ireland*, vol. 6, no. 3 (Autumn 1992), p. 5. Ó Danachair has identified the custom of shooting after the couple as being typical of northern regions of Ireland ('Some marriage customs', p. 152).

66. G. V., *A Statistical Survey of the County of Londonderry* (Dublin, 1802), p. 457.
67. *Irish Society*, 5 May 1888.
68. *Belfast Newsletter*, 10 August 1883.
69. Diary of Alice Ward (Percival-Price Papers).
70. UFTM Questionnaire, 67/Q3.
71. Ibid.
72. Ibid.
73. Ibid.
74. A substantial selection of lines from this poem has been reprinted by Patrick Fagan in *A Georgian Celebration* (Dublin, 1989), pp. 61–6.
75. *Ordnance Survey Memoirs of Ireland*, vol. 11 (1991), p. 130.
76. Hall, *Ireland*, vol.1, p. 163.
77. UFTM 67/Q3.
78. Anna Sexton, 'Matchmaking and marriage in Co. Cavan in the late nineteenth century', *Heart of Breifne*, vol. 1 (1978), pp. 24–30.
79. Lageniensis, *Irish Folklore*, p. 236.
80. UFTM 67/Q3.
81. Ibid.
82. Jane Austen, *Pride and Prejudice* (London, 1975), p. 251.
83. *Modern Etiquette*, pp. 98–9.
84. Lageniensis, *Irish Folklore*, p. 235

Chapter Seven   Life in the Home

1. See Gillis, *For Better, for Worse*, p. 15; also chaps 4 and 6 above.
2. See for example 'Notes and explanation of sources' in Day, *Letters from Georgian Ireland*, p. 3; also Maria Luddy (ed.), *The Diary of Mary Matthew* (Tipperary, 1991), p.107.
3. D. McLoughlin, 'Workhouses and Irish female paupers, 1840–1870', *Women Surviving*, ed. M. Luddy and C. Murphy (Swords, 1989), p. 128.
4. Gillis, *For Better, for Worse*, p. 165.
5. McLoughlin, 'Workhouses and Irish female paupers', p. 128.
6. Ibid, p. 130.
7. Gillis, *For Better, for Worse*, p. 183.
8. *Dublin University Magazine*, May 1862, p. 542.
9. F. Lautman, 'Differences or changes in family organisation', *Family and Society*, ed. R. Forster and O. Ranum (Baltimore and London, 1976), p. 252.
10. O' Curry, *On the Manners and Customs of the Ancient Irish*, vol.1 , pp. 175–6.
11. For instance, Presbyterians in late seventeenth-century Ulster countenanced divorce 'where there is complete marriage breakdown'. Barkley, 'Marriage and the Presbyterian tradition', pp. 37–8.
12. Gillis, *For Better, for Worse*, p. 99.
13. Cosgrove, 'Marriage in medieval Ireland', p. 8.
14. See MacCurtain, 'Marriage in Tudor Ireland', p. 57.
15. Curtin, Devereux and Shields, 'Replaying the match'.
16. Ibid.
17. See, for example, Curtin, 'Marriage and family', p. 161.
18. S. J. Connolly, 'Family, love and marriage, some evidence from the early eighteenth century', *Women in Early Modern Ireland*, ed. MacCurtain and O'Dowd.
19. Curtin, 'Marriage and family', p. 161.
20. See L. M. Ballard, 'Some photographic evidence of the practice of dressing boys in skirts', *Ulster Folklife* 34 (1988).

21. E. Boyle, ' "Linen aprons": the rise of the textile industry', *Belfast, The Making of the City*, ed. J. C. Beckett *et al.* (Belfast, 1983), p. 51.

22. L. M. Ballard, ' "Just whatever they had handy": aspects of childbirth and early child care in Northern Ireland prior to 1948', *Ulster Folklife* 31 (1985), p. 70.

23. See, for example, James Kelly, 'Infanticide in eighteenth-century Ireland', *Irish Economic and Social History*, vol.19 (1992); A. O'Connor, 'Women in Irish folklore: the testimony regarding illegitimacy, abortion and infanticide', *Women in Early Modern Ireland*, ed. MacCurtain and O'Dowd.

24. See Mary Cullen, 'Breadwinners and providers. women in the household economy of labouring families, 1835-36', *Women Surviving*, ed. Luddy and Murphy.

25. Fitzpatrick, 'Marriage in post-Famine Ireland', p. 127.

26. Summarized from McLoughlin's account of the Hackett family's case in 'Workhouses and Irish Female Paupers', p. 131.

27. Ibid, pp. 135–6.

28. See above, p. 138.

29. Fitzpatrick, 'Marriage in post-Famine Ireland', p. 127.

30. UFTM R.90.89.

31. William Trevor's story, 'Kathleen's Field', pp. 230–1 of *Family Sins* (London, 1990), set in the rural Ireland of 1948, highlights the issues of inheritance and of sibling responsibility:

> He reflected as he drank that he hardly needed the bank agent's reminder about the times being bad. Seven of his ten children had emigrated, four to Canada and America, the three others to England. Kathleen, the youngest, now sixteen, was left, with Biddy, who wasn't herself, and Con, who would inherit the farm. But without the Lallys' field it wouldn't be easy for Con to keep going. Sooner or later he would want to marry the Kilfedder girl, and there'd always have to be a home for Biddy on the farm, and for a while at least an elderly mother and father would have to be accommodated also. Sometimes one or other of the exiled children sent back a cheque and Hagerty never objected to accepting it. But none of hem could afford the price of a field, and he wasn't going to ask them. Nor would Con accept these little presents when his time came to take over the farm entirely, for how could the oldest brother be beholden like that in the prime of his life?

32. R. A. Gailey, *Rural Houses of the North of Ireland* (Edinburgh, 1984), pp. 35–40. Gailey points out that, as the situation began to change, it often reflected subdivision of existing space for specialized use, rather than extension of the dwelling.

33. T. Reid, *Travels in Ireland* (London, 1823). On the subject of using garments as bedding, Mairead Dunlevy comments (*Dress in Ireland*, p.166):

> The cloak ... was disliked by the disciplinarians of the mid nineteenth century on the grounds that it was used ... like its predecessor the Irish mantle, both as a day cover and night blanket and that it was never washed, although made of wool, which retained both dampness and infection.

34. Wakefield, *An Account of Ireland* , vol. 2, p.772.

35. See Gillis, *For Better, for Worse*, pp. 74, 75, 118.

36. As recited by the late Matt Meharg.

37. Anna Sexton, 'Matchmaking and marriage'. See also Rosemary Harris, *Prejudice and Tolerance in Ulster* (Manchester, 1972), p. 114.

38. Paddy Gallagher describes a marriage of this sort in his autobiography, *My Story* (Dungloe, n.d.), although his account refers to his experience of working as a migratory farm labourer in Scotland.

39. UFTM Questionnaire 67/Q3. Another description is given by Nora Cooper of Warrenpoint: 'The bride's show was the Sunday after a couple got married. The young people would dance in a field, and the boys would catch a girl and race her down the field.'

40. Wescott and Robinson, *Ladies' Book*, p.68.
41. Ibid, p.67.
42. *Modern Etiquette*, p. 99.
43. Connolly, 'Marriage in pre-Famine Ireland', p. 93.
44. UFTM R.84.4 Belfast.
45. The First Book of Common Prayer of Edward VI and the Ordnance of 1549, together with the Order of Communion, 1548 (repr. London, 1876).
46. UFTM R.83.145.
47. UFTM R.83.139.
48. UFTM R.81.143. See also N. Belmont's, 'Levana, or how to raise up children', *Family and Society*, ed. Forster and Ranam.
49. UFTM R.83.151.
50. McLoughlin, 'Workhouses and Irish female paupers', p. 142.
51. See Maria Luddy, 'Prostitution and rescue work in nineteenth century Ireland', *Women Surviving*, ed. Luddy and Murphy, p. 64.
52. See Ballard, 'Just whatever they had handy'.
53. Curtin, 'Marriage and family', p. 159.
54. Connolly, *Priests and People in pre-Famine Ireland*, p. 190.
55. Farmar, *Ordinary Lives,* p. 191.
56. Reported in the *Sunday Tribune*, 31 March 1996.
57. Oral tradition helps to illustrate the arrangements which might be made in the countryside to help resolve delicate situations. One account tells of a young girl with an illegitimate child who was brought to an extensive Co. Tyrone farm as wet nurse for two babies, one belonging to an expert ploughman whose wife had died in childbirth, leaving him with four children, the other to the farmer's wife. After a time, the girl fell pregnant by the farmer, and, in order to avoid scandal, a deal was done with the ploughman, who married the girl in return for a farm of his own. UFTM R84.147.
58. See, for example, Connell, *Population of Ireland* ; also McLoughlin, 'Workhouses and Irish female paupers'.
59. McLoughlin, 'Workhouses and Irish female paupers', p. 128.
60. See Ballard, '"Just whatever they had handy"'.
61. *Belfast Newsletter*, 5 February 1740. Reprinted in J. R. R. Adams, 'Ulster Folklife 1738–40 from the pages of the Belfast Newsletter', *Ulster Folklife*, 31 (1989), pp41–58.
62. Farmar, *Ordinary Lives*, p. 191.
63. B. Messenger, *Picking up the Linen Threads* (Austin and London, 1975), p.174. Messenger makes it clear that ribaldry and teasing did not equate to lack of chastity.
64. *Belfast Newsletter,* 6 March 1739. Reprinted in Adams,' Ulster Folklife'. Adams remarks of this and similar reports that they 'even if not true give a very good flavour of some aspects of early eighteenth century life'.
65. Huddleson MSS, UFTM Archive.
66. Lyons, *Memoirs of Mrs Leeson*, p. 224.
67. Ibid, p. 26.
68. See Luddy, 'Prostitution and rescue work'.
69. Farmar, *Ordinary Lives*, p.15, citing J. V. O'Brien, *Dear Dirty Dublin* (California, 1982).
70. Luddy, 'Prostitution and rescue work', p. 60.
71. A. Jordan, *Who Cared? Charity in Victorian and Edwardian Belfast* (Belfast, 1992), p. 169.
72. Luddy, 'Prostitution and Rescue work', p. 54.
73. Jordan, *Who Cared?* , p. 170.
74. Nickie Roberts, *Whores in History* (London, 1992), p. 336.
75. Thomas Haslam's pamphlet on the Contagious Diseases Acts in Ireland, quoted by Maria Luddy in 'Women and the Contagious Diseases Acts, 1864–1886', *History Ireland,* vol.1, no. 1, (Spring 1993), p. 33.

76. K. H. Connell, 'The Population of Ireland from 1750 to 1846' (PhD thesis) n.d. [*c.* 1950]) illustrates that rates of fertility and of infant mortality were substantially higher in Ireland than in contemporary England and Wales.

77. See, for example, Day, *Letters from Georgian Ireland.* Some male midwives advertised their services in the *Belfast Newsletter* as early as the eighteenth century.

78. Sybil Woolfrom, *Inlaws and Outlaws, Kinship and Marriage in England* (London and Sydney, 1987), p. 59.

79. L. A Clarkson and E. M. Crawford, 'Life after death: widows in Carrick-on-Suir, 1799', *Women in Early Modern Ireland*, ed. MacCurtain and O'Dowd, p. 237.

80. This advertisement was widely reprinted, for example, in *London and North Western Railway, Tours in Ireland* for the 1896 season.

81. Notebook of Dr Richard Hunter, UFTM Archive.

82. Ibid.

83. *Letters from the Irish Highlands of Connemara* (written by Mrs Blake of Renvyle), (London, 1825), p. 67. See also A. Day, 'Habits of the people': traditional life in Ireland, 1830–1840', *Ulster Folklife* 30 (1984), p. 31.

84. E. McLysaght, *Irish Life in the Seventeenth Century* (Cork, 1950), p. 355.

85. Laura Jones, 'Dress in nineteenth century Ireland', *Folk Life* 16 (1978), p. 52.

86. Mona Hearn, 'Life for domestic servants in Dublin, 1880–1920', *Women Surviving*, ed. Luddy and Murphy, p. 156.

87. Margaret Cameron, *The Women in Green* (Belfast, 1993), pp. 69–70.

88. Ibid, 70.

89. W. J. Lowe and E.L. Malcolm, 'The domestication of the Royal Irish Constabulary', *Irish Economic and Social History* 19 (1992), pp. 38–9.

90. *The Brewers 'and Wine and Spirit Trade Annual* (1907), p. 342.

91. See Luddy, 'Women and the Contagious Diseases Acts', p. 33.

92. Jill McKenna (ed.), *Mary's Memories* (Belfast, 1990), p. 13.

93. Ibid.

94. Farmar, *Ordinary Lives*, p. 25.

95. Hearn, 'Life for domestic servants in Dublin'.

96. See for example, Christine Herrick, *The Expert Maid Servant* (New York and London, 1904).

97. See Gillis, *For Better, for Worse*, p.117; K. M. Connell, *The Population of Ireland, 1750–1845* (Connecticut, 1975), p. 80.

98. Farmar, *Ordinary Lives* (Dublin, 1991), p. 35.

99. Madeleine Leonard, 'Ourselves alone: household work strategies in a deprived community', *Irish Journal of Sociology* 2 (1992), p. 73.

100. Ibid, p. 75.

101. See, for example, J. Bell, *People and the Land* (Belfast, 1992), p. 82; J. Bourke, 'Women and poultry in Ireland 1891–1914', *Irish Historical Studies* 25 (1986–7).

102. Micheline Baulant, 'The scattered family, another aspect of seventeenth century demography', *Family and Society*, ed. Forster and Ranum, p. 106.

103. W. L. Micks, *An Account of the Constitution, Administration and Dissolution of the Congested Districts Board for Ireland from 1891 to 1923* (Dublin, 1925), p. 250.

104. Cullen, 'Breadwinners and providers', ed. Luddy and Murphy, p. 86.

105. Ibid, p. 107.

106. Winifred Campbell, 'Down the Shankill', *Ulster Folklife* 22 (1976), p. 15.

107. Ibid.

108. McKenna, *Mary's Memories*, p. 16.

109. Information from Mrs Deborah Bennett, part of this nurse's uniform is preserved in the collection of the UFTM.

110. Campbell, 'Down the Shankill', p. 11.

111. Mrs Clara Lucas Balfour, *Homely Hints in Household Management* (London, 1867), pp. 37, 40–1.
112. Flora Klickman (ed.), *The Mistress of the Little House* (London, n.d. [c. 1912]), p. 111.
113. Jill McKenna, *Cures, Linen and Laundries* (Belfast, 1990), p. 6.
114. McKenna, *Mary's Memories*, p. 13.
115. Farmar, *Ordinary Lives*, p. 26.
116. Ronnie Munck and Bill Rolston, *Belfast in the Thirties, an Oral History* (Belfast, 1987), pp. 63–79.
117. Campbell, 'Down the Shankill', p. 4.
118. Irwin, *Cookin' Woman*, pp. 2–3.
119. Ibid, p. 3.
120. Patrick Commins, 'Rural social change', *Ireland , a Sociological Profile*, ed. Clancy *et al.*, p. 60.
121. McKenna, *Mary's Memories*, p. 15.
122. Cosgrove, 'Marriage in medieval Ireland', p. 47.
123. Ibid, p. 46.
124. See 'Session book of Templepatrick Presbyterian church'.
125. Gillis, *For Better, for Worse*, p. 132.
126. E. Steiner Scott, 'To bounce a boot off her now and then: domestic violence in post Famine Ireland', *Women in Irish History*, ed. M.G. Valiulis, M. Giaianella and M. O'Dowd (Dublin, 1997), pp. 125–43.
127. *Belfast Newsletter*, 24 October 1910.
128. Steiner Scott, 'To bounce a boot off her'.
129. *Belfast Telegraph*, 17 June 1993.
130. Ibid.
131. Irwin, *Cookin' Woman*, pp. 11–12.

Select Bibliography

Adams, J. R. R. 'Ulster Folklife 1738 to 1840 from the pages of the Belfast Newsletter', *Ulster Folklife* 31 (1985)

Adburgham, A. *Victorian Shopping.* Devon, 1972

Arensberg, C. M. and Kimball, D. T. *Family and Community in Ireland.* Harvard, 1961

Austen, J. *Pride and Prejudice.* London, 1975

Baker, M. *Wedding Customs and Folklore.* Newton Abbot, 1977

Balfour, C. L. *Homely Hints in Household Management.* London, 1867

Ballard, L. M. ' "Just whatever they had handy" ': aspects of childbirth and early childcare in Northern Ireland prior to 1948', *Ulster Folklife* 31 (1992–3)

———— 'Some photographic evidence of the practice of dressing boys in skirts', *Ulster Folklife* 34 (1988)

———— 'Irish lace : tradition or commodity', *Folklife* 31 (1985)

———— Some aspects of tradition among female religious in Belfast', *Ulster Folklife* 38 (1992)

———— *Tying the Knot.* Cultra: Ulster Folk and Transport Museum, n.d. [1991]

Barkley, J. 'Marriage and the Presbyterian tradition', *Ulster Folklife* 39 (1993)

Barnard, T.C. *Cromwellian Ireland.* Oxford, 1975

Baulant, M. 'The scattered family, another aspect of seventeenth-century demography' in R. Forster and O. Ranum (eds), *Family and Society.* Baltimore and London, 1976

Bell, J. *People and the Land.* Belfast, 1992

Benchley, R. 'Do We Sleep Enough?' *My Ten Years in a Quandary, and How They Grew.* London, 1951

[Blake, Mrs, of Renvyle] *Letters from the Irish Highlands of Connemara.* London, 1825

Blum, S. *Victorian Fashions and Costumes from Harper's Bazaar, 1867–1898.* New York, 1974

Bourdieu, P. 'Marriage strategies as strategies of social reproduction' in R. Forster and O. Ranum (eds), *Family and Society.* Baltimore and London, 1976

Bourke, J. 'Women and poultry in Ireland, 1891–1914', *Irish Historical Studies* 25 (1986–7)

———— *Husbandry to Housewifery: Women, Economic Change and Housework in Ireland.* Oxford, 1993

Boyle, E. ' "Linen aprons": the rise of the textile industry' in J. C. Beckett *et al.*, *Belfast, the Making of the City.* Belfast, 1983

The Brewers 'and Wine and Spirit Trade Annual. London, 1907

Bryson, A. F. *Ayrshire Needlework.* London, 1989

Buchanan, R. H. 'Calendar Customs, Part 1, New Year's Day to Michaelmas', *Ulster Folklife* 8 (1962)

———— 'Calendar Customs, Part 2, Harvest to Christmas', *Ulster Folklife* 9 (1963)

Buckley, A. D., and Kenney, M.C. *Negotiating Identity.* Washington DC, 1995

Buckley, P. A. *A Thorn in the Side.* Dublin, 1994

Bury, S. *An Introduction to Rings.* London, 1984

Cameron, M. *The Women in Green*. Belfast, 1993

Campbell, W. 'Down the Shankill', *Ulster Folklife* 22 (1976)

Chambre, N., and Paterson, T. G. F. 'Folktales from Cadian', *Ulster Journal of Archaeology*, ser. 3, vol. 3 (1896)

Charsley, S. *Rites of Marrying*. Manchester, 1991

Clancy, P., Drudy, S., Lynch, K., and O'Dowd, L. *Ireland, a Sociological Profile*. Dublin, 1986

Clarkson, L. A. and Crawford, E. M. 'Life after death : widows in Carrick-on-Suir, 1799' in M. MacCurtain and M. O'Dowd (eds), *Women in Early Modern Ireland*. Edinburgh, 1991

Commins, P. 'Rural social change' in P. Clancy *et al.* (eds), *Ireland, a Sociological Profile*. Dublin, 1986

Connell, K. H. *Irish Peasant Society*. Oxford, 1968

———— *The Population of Ireland 1750–1845*. Connecticut, 1950

Connolly, S. *Religion, Law and Power. The Making of Protestant Ireland, 1660–1760*. Oxford, 1992

Connolly, S. J. *Priests and People in pre-Famine Ireland*. New York, 1982

———— 'Marriage in pre-Famine Ireland' in A. Cosgrove (ed.), *Marriage in Ireland*. Dublin, 1985

———— 'Family, love and marriage, some evidence from the early eighteenth century' in M. MacCurtain and M. O'Dowd (eds), *Women in Early Modern Ireland*. Edinburgh, 1991

Cooper Foster, J. *Ulster Folklore*. Belfast, 1951

Corish, P. J. 'Catholic marriage under the Penal Code' in A. Cosgrove (ed.), *Marriage in Ireland*. Dublin, 1985

Corish, P. J. *The Irish Catholic Experience*. Dublin, 1985

Cosgrove, A. *Marriage in Ireland*. Dublin, 1985

———— 'Marriage in medieval Ireland' in A. Cosgrove (ed.), *Marriage in Ireland*. Dublin, 1985

Courtney, D. 'Demographic structure and change' in P. Clancy *et al.* (eds), *Ireland, a Sociological Profile*. Dublin, 1986

Crawford, H. *Needlework Samplers of Northern Ireland*. Crawfordsburn, 1989

Cullen, M. 'Breadwinners and providers. Women in the household economy of labouring families, 1835–36' in M. Luddy and C. Murphy (eds), *Women Surviving*. Dublin, 1989

Cunningham, J. B. 'The struggle for the Belleek–Pettigo Salient, 1922', *Donegal Annual* 34 (1982)

Curtin, C. 'Marriage and family' in P. Clancy *et al.* (eds), *Ireland, a Sociological Profile*. Dublin, 1986

Curtin, C., Devereux, E., and Shields, D. 'Replaying the match – marriage settlements in North Galway', *Irish Journal of Sociology* 2

Danahar, K. *The Year in Ireland*. Cork, 1972

Davidson, C. *A Woman's Work is Never Done*. London, 1982

Davidson, H. C. *The Book of the Home*. London, 1900

Day, A. *Letters from Georgian Ireland*. Belfast, 1991

Day, A., and McWilliams, P. *Ordnance Survey Memoirs of Ireland*. 39 vols. Belfast, 1990–7

Day, A. 'Habits of the people: traditional life in Ireland, 1830–1840', *Ulster Folklife* 30 (1984)

Denton, J. *Teague Land, or A Merry Ramble to the Wild Irish, Letters from Ireland, 1698*, ed. E. MacLysaght. Dublin, 1982

Dickson, D. 'No Scythians here, women and marriage in seventeenth-century Ireland' in M. MacCurtain and M. O'Dowd, *Women in Early Modern Ireland*. Edinburgh, 1991

Donnelly, J. J. 'The Rightboy Movement, 1785–8', *Studia Hibernica* 17 and 18 (1977-8)

Dunlevy, M. *Dress in Ireland*. London, 1989

Dunn, V. A. *Cattle Raids and Courtships: Medieval Narrative Genres in a Traditional Context*. New York and London, 1989

Egerton, G. *Discords.* London, 1894

Farmar, T. *Ordinary Lives:Three Generations of Irish Middle Class Experience, 1902, 1932, 1963*. Dublin, 1991

Fitzpatrick, D. 'Marriage in post-Famine Ireland' in A. Cosgrove (ed.), *Marriage in Ireland*. Dublin, 1985

Fox, R. *The Tory Islanders*. Cambridge, 1978

Gailey, R. A. *Rural Houses of the North of Ireland*. Edinburgh, 1984

Gallagher, P. *My Story*. Dungloe, n.d.

Gamble, J. *A View of Society and Manners in the North of Ireland in the Summer and Autumn of 1812*. London, 1813

Gillis, J. *For Better, for Worse*. New York, 1985

Ginsburg, M. *Wedding Dress, 1740-1970*. London: HMSO, 1981

Gmelch, S. *Tinkers and Travellers*. Dublin, 1975

———— *Nan, The Life of an Irish Travelling Woman*. New York, 1986

Hall, M. *Sacrifice on the Somme*. Belfast, n.d.

Hall, Mr and Mrs S.C. *Ireland, its Scenery, Character etc.* 3 vols. London, 1845

Hanna, R. *Pardon Me, Boy, the Americans in Ulster, 1942–45*. Belfast, 1991

Harris, R. *Prejudice and Tolerance in Ulster*. Manchester, 1972

Hearn, M. 'Life for domestic servants in Dublin, 1880-1920' in M. Luddy and C. Murphy (eds), *Women Surviving*. Dublin, 1989

Herrick, C. *The Expert Maid Servant*. New York and London, 1904

Inglis, H. D. *A Journey through Ireland*, vol.11. London, 1834

Irwin, F. *The Cookin' Woman*. Edinburgh and London, 1949; repr. Belfast, 1986, 1988, 1992

Jeffery, F. *Irish Methodism*. Belfast, 1964

Jones, L. 'Dress in nineteenth century Ireland', *Folk Life* 16 (1978)

Jordan, A. *Who Cared? Charity in Victorian and Edwardian Belfast*. Belfast, 1992

King, S. H. and S. McMahon, *Hope and History: Eyewitness Accounts of Twentieth Century Ulster*. Belfast, 1996

Klickman, F. *The Mistress of the Little House*. London, n.d. [c. 1912]

Lageniensis. *Irish Folklore*. Glasgow and London, 1870

Langbridge, R. H. *Edwardian Shopping. A Selection from the Army and Navy Stores Catalogues, 1898–1913*. Newton Abbot, 1975

Lansdell, A. *Wedding Fashions, 1860–1980*. Aylesbury, 1977

Latimer, A. *A History of Irish Presbyterians.* Belfast, 1902

Lautman, F. 'Differences and changes in family organisation' in R. Foster and O. Ranum (eds), *Family and Society*. Baltimore and London, 1976

Lee, J. J. 'Women and the Church since the Famine' in M. MacCurtain and D. Ó Corráin (eds), *Women in Irish Society*. Dublin, 1973

Leonard, M. 'Ourselves alone: household work strategies in a deprived community', *Irish Journal of Sociology* 2 (1992).

Levitt, S. *Victorians Unbuttoned*. London, 1986

Lowe, W. J., and Malcolm, E.L. 'The domesticisation of the Royal Irish Constabulary', *Irish Economic and Social History* 19 (1992)

Lucas, A.T. *Cattle in Ancient Ireland*. Kilkenny, 1989

Luddy, M. 'Prostitution and rescue work in nineteenth-century Ireland' in M. Luddy and C. Murphy (eds), *Women Surviving*. Dublin, 1989

———— *The Diary of Mary Matthews*. Tipperary, 1991

———— 'Women and the Contagious Diseases Acts, 1864–1886', *History Ireland*, vol. 1, no.1 (Spring, 1993)

Lyons, M. *The Memoirs of Mrs Leeson, Madam*. Dublin, 1995

MacCurtain, M. 'Marriage in Tudor Ireland' in A. Cosgrove (ed.), *Marriage in Ireland*. Dublin, 1985

Malcolmson, A. T. *The Pursuit of the Heiress: Aristocratic Marriage in Ireland, 1750–1820*. Belfast: Ulster Historical Foundation, 1982

Marshall, R. K. 'The wearing of wedding rings in Scotland', *Review of Scottish Culture* 2 (1986)

Mason, T. H. *The Islands of Ireland*. London, 1936

McCarthy, M. J. F. *Priests and People in Ireland*. Dublin, 1902

McGart, B. *Poor Rabbin's Ollminick for the Town of Belfast, 1861*. Belfast, 1861.

McKenna, J. *Cures, Linen and Laundries*. Belfast, 1990

———— *Mary's Memories*. Belfast, 1991

———— *Divvies, Coke and Black Soap*. Belfast, 1991

McLoughlin, D. 'Workhouses and Irish female paupers, 1840–70' in M. Luddy and C. Murphy (eds), *Women Surviving*. Swords, 1989

McLysaght, E. *Irish Life in the Seventeenth Century*. Cork, 1950

Messenger, B. *Picking up the Linen Threads*. Austin and London, 1975

Micks, W. L. *An Account of the Constitution, Administration and Dissolution of the Congested Districts Board for Ireland from 1891 to 1923*. Dublin, 1925

Monger, G. '"To marry in May": an investigation of a superstition', *Folklore* 105 (1994)

Monsarrat, A. *And the Bride Wore*. London, 1973

Munck, R. and Rolston, B. *Belfast in the Thirties, an Oral History*. Belfast, 1987

Murphy, M. J. 'Old Lord Erin's Son, a Tyrone folktale', *Ulster Folklife* 4 (1958)

———— *Ulster Folk of Field and Fireside*. Dundalk, 1983

———— *Sayings and Stories from Slieve Gullion*. Dundalk, 1990

Newhouse, N. H. *A History of Friends' School, Lisburn*. Lurgan, 1974

Ó Corráin, D. 'Marriage in early Ireland' in A. Cosgrove (ed.), *Marriage in Ireland*. Dublin, 1985.

Ó Danachair, C. 'Some marriage customs and their regional distribution', *Bealoideas* 42–44 (1974–6)

———— 'Marriage in Irish folk tradition' in A. Cosgrove (ed.), *Marriage in Ireland*. Dublin, 1985

O'Curry, E. *On the Manners and Customs of the Ancient Irish.* Dublin, 1873

O'Duilearga, S. 'The Cake Dance', *Bealoideas* 11 (1945)

O'Shea, J. *Priests, Politics and Society in Post-Famine Ireland.* Dublin, 1983

Page, A. *The Complete Guide to Wedding Etiquette.* London, 1952

Paterson, T. G. F. 'Harvest knots and Brigid's crosses', *Ulster Folklife* 1 (1955)

Pendergast, J. P. 'Extracts from the journal of Thomas Dineley esq.', *Kilkenny and South East of Ireland Archaeological Society Journal.* Series 2, vols 1 and 2, 4–6 (1856–67)

Pollock, A. J. 'Hallowe'en customs in Lecale, Co. Down', *Ulster Folklife* 6 (1960)

Praegar, R. L. *The Official Guide to County Down and the Mourne Mountains.* Belfast, 1898

Reid, T. *Travels in Ireland.* London, 1823

Ritchie, L. *Ireland Picturesque and Romantic.* London, 1838

Roberts, N. *Whores in History.* London, 1992

Rynne, E. *Tourist Trail of Old Galway.* Galway, 1989

Sampson, G. V. *A Statistical Survey on the County of Londonderry.* Dublin, 1802

————— *A Memoir Explanatory of the Chart and Survey of the County of London-Derry.* London, 1814

Sayers, P. *An Old Woman's Reflections.* Oxford, 1962

Sexton, A. 'Matchmaking and marriage in Co. Cavan in the late nineteenth century'. *Heart of Breifne*, vol.1, no. 1 (1978)

Sloan, C. 'Some of the stories of James McAllister of Fathom', *Ulster Folklife* 13 (1967)

Spenser, E. *Poetical Works,* ed. J. C. Smith and E. de Selincourt. Oxford, 1970

Smith, W. S. 'Early register of the old Presbyterian congregation of Antrim', *Ulster Journal of Archaeology*, ser. 2, no.1 (1898)

Stewart, D. *Seceders in Ireland.* Belfast, 1950

Stone, L. *The Family, Sex and Marriage in England, 1500–1800.* Harmondsworth, 1982

————— *The Road to Divorce.* Oxford, 1990

Taylor, L. *Mourning Dress, a Costume and Social History.* London 1983

Tegy, W. *The Knot Tied.* London, 1877

Trevor, W. *Family Sins.* London, 1990

Wakefield, E. *An Account of Ireland Statistical and Political.* 2 vols. London, 1812

Walker, J. C. *An Historical Essay on the Dress of the Ancient Irish.* 1788

Wescott, A. H., and Robinson, A. M. *The Ladies' Book.* London, *c.* 1900

Wigham, M. J. *The Irish Quakers.* Dublin, 1992

Woolfrom, S. *Inlaws and Outlaws, Kinship and Marriage in England.* London and Sydney, 1987

Wright, A. R. *British Calendar Customs, England.* 2 vols. London, 1936

Young, A. *A Tour in Ireland.* Dublin, 1780

INDEX